THE FRENCH REVOLUTION

THE FRENCH REVOLUTION

10 Years of English Football after Cantona

Alex Hayes and Daniel Ortelli
with Xavier Rivoire

MAINSTREAM
PUBLISHING

EDINBURGH AND LONDON

First published in Great Britain in 2002 by
MAINSTREAM PUBLISHING COMPANY (EDINBURGH) LTD
7 Albany Street
Edinburgh EH1 3UG

ISBN 1 84018 650 X

A catalogue record for this book is available from the British Library

Typeset in Berkeley and Civet

Printed in Great Britain by
Creative Print and Design Wales

Contents

THANK YOU VERY MUCH! (Acknowledgements)

A big thank you, first and foremost, to an incredible cast:

The French players: Jérémie Aliadière, Pegguy Arphexad, Patrick Colleter, Olivier Dacourt, Marcel Desailly, Didier Deschamps, Bernard Diomède, Youri Djorkaeff, Rémi Garde, Alain Goma, Gilles Grimandi, David Ginola, Thierry Henry, Frédéric Kanouté, Christian Karembeu, Marc Keller, Frank Leboeuf, Steed Malbranque, Emmanuel Petit, Robert Pires, Laurent Robert, Bruno Rodriguez, Eric Roy, Louis Saha, Sébastien Schemmel, Mikaël Silvestre, Didier Six, Patrick Vieira, Grégory Vignal, who trusted us and took the time to tell us everything . . . or almost.

All their fellow professionals from another country, such as John Collins and Lee Clark, for taking the time to tell us how they like them . . . after all!

The managers, technicians and coaches, whatever you call them, on both sides of the Channel: Gérard Houllier, Patrice Bergues, Jean Tigana, Christian Damiano, Roger Propos, Philippe Patry, Arsène Wenger, Tiburce Darrou, Jean-Luc Ettori, Claude Dusseau, Graham Rix, Howard Wilkinson, for their thoughtful insights into a complex game.

The experts: Professor John Williams, Claude Boli, Patrick Mignon, for taking part in a challenging conference at the Institut Français, in London, on the day after the Champions League final.

The fans: Josie, Peggy, Steve, Benjamin Lambert, Ernest and Michael Moore, 'John Reeder' and all the others, for their passion.

The journalists: Martin Lipton, Richard Williams, Henry Winter, for sparing the time to talk to us in the middle of the World Cup, David Fairclough and Glenn Moore for their insight on a few French players and coaches. But also Jérôme Rasetti, Romain Bonte and Christine Salles, for helping us when we were in real trouble.

The statisticians: Rupert Webster, Matt Pomroy, Mark Willis, Rob Bateman and Spencer Field, at Opta, but also Justin Villelongue and Pierre Hiault.

The editors: Mat Snow and Hugh Sleight (*FourFourTwo*), Andy Lyons (*When Saturday Comes*), Gérard Ernault (*France Football*), Gilles Chappaz (*L'Equipe Magazine*), Richard Whitehead (*The Times Football Handbook*) Andy Mitten (*United We Stand*), Mike Francis (*The Gooner*), Arnold Aardvark (*Up the Arse*) for offering us so many great covers to illustrate the book.

The whole team at Mainstream, Bill, Peter, Graeme, Ailsa, Tina, etc. for helping us all the way . . .

Chelsea, Annabelle and Deborah, for their patience and shared love of football.

All of you that we forgot to thank on this page, but you might be able to find your name in the index!

AH, DO and XR
(London, 14 July 2002)

Before E.C.

Before each revolution comes the evolution. And so it was that the French Revolution in English football, which was triggered on 8 February 1992 by the arrival of a misunderstood Gallic genius, was the culmination of 88 years of football history between France and England – 88 years that can be broken down into three distinctive periods leading up to the phenomenon that was Eric Cantona.

First came the time when a Frenchman kept goal for Fulham before the First World War; then, a 1982 World Cup semi-finalist called Didier Six became the first-ever French outfield player in the top flight of English football; and, finally, five Englishmen returned the compliment by plying their trade in the French League in the late 1980s and early 1990s.

All three periods, though spanning almost nine decades and not apparently linked, helped pave the way for the incredible and unpredictable domination of French football in the last ten years.

THE PIONEER

Long before a young, swanky Scottish advertising executive called Adam became the first non-Englishman to take charge of the running of the Football Association, a Frenchman with the same surname had created his own bit of English football history. Georges Crozier kept goal for Fulham between 1904 and 1906, and is, for all intents and purposes, the founding father of the revolutionary movement.

Crozier's story had been rotting in the bins of history, but now the full episode can be told once more. Crozier was doing his military service in the early years of the twentieth century, when he decided to further his football career at the same time in London. Why he chose Fulham might never be known, but suffice it to say that he helped the Cottagers win the Southern League title and then climb up to what was called the National Second Division.

Crozier was also an international, representing *Les Bleus* when they were known as *Les Coqs*, and some of his journeys from London were priceless. One day, in May 1905, he had to make his own way to the France–Belgium border, where he would be met by the rest of the French team who were travelling by bus. They found him standing there, impeccably dressed, unmistakeable with his elegant moustache, and took him along to the stadium in Brussels for the match. By half-time, Crozier had let in three goals; by full-time, France had lost 7–0. But Crozier was not there to witness the last 25 minutes of the game. He had to catch the 1800 train back to his barracks, so missed the end of the embarrassing defeat.

It is difficult to imagine such a turn of events in the present day. Indeed, it is impossible to conceive that Belgium could knock seven goals past the French. But these were very different times, times when the thought of a cocky Frenchman ruling the English roost was but a distant dream.

SIX OF ONE

If the news that a Frenchman dared play in England before the great Cantona has upset anyone, please look away now. There is another revelation to come. Some eight years before the man they called 'Le King' started his English reign, another Gallic creator wove his magic for a season. Didier Six was, like Cantona when he arrived on these shores in the summer of 1984, a fully fledged international. He had, in fact, missed a penalty in the shoot-out against West Germany in the World Cup semifinal in Seville two years before he joined the then First Division with Aston Villa.

Six played 15 times for the Midlands club, scoring two goals. On the day of his arrival, one of the English papers ran the headline: 'Villa get Six for nothing' (an allusion to the fact that he came to Villa on a seasonlong loan from Mulhouse). The play on words still tickles the Frenchman today. Six dismisses the significance of his daring move, but another Frenchman, Marc Keller, who spent three years at West Ham in the late 1990s, insists the change in culture must have been tough. 'It would have been really difficult for Didier,' Keller says. 'Even when I arrived in England in 1998, the cultural and sporting shift was important enough. So just imagine how things would have been 20 years ago. All credit to him.'

Six prefers acknowledging others, like David Ginola, a fellow winger and traveller. 'The fact that David has been able to survive for so long in England is a credit to him,' Six says. 'It is not easy moving your whole life full-time, but he has obviously been accepted over there.' So far as Six is concerned, Ginola's longevity is impressive, but no Frenchman has had a similar impact to that of Cantona.

Ironically, Six's first match for the Villans was against Cantona's future club, Manchester United. Six is not about to forget the occasion. 'Man U were unbeaten when they turned up at Villa Park,' he recalls fondly, 'and yet we ended up beating them 3–0. I remember that first match was quite tough because I hadn't had much training, and, after 70 minutes, I was completely exhausted. I asked the coach to take me off, and, as I departed, 45,000 fans got up to clap me. Amazing.' Six's passage was brief but joyous. To this day, there are still pictures of the Frenchman adorning the Villa Park corridors. Most have forgotten now, but long before another Frenchman called Ginola wore the famous claret and blue shirt, Six, with his own long flowing locks and funky wing-play, had mesmerised a club.

Six's only two regrets are that he did not go to England younger and was not playing on these shores ten years later. An improbable combination if ever there was one. 'I came to England a little too old,' he admits. 'Had I been 25 or 26, I would have been able to blow people's minds.' Six is equally disappointed about the timing of his sojourn. A decade later, he believes, English football would have received the media attention it craved at the time. 'It's the one thing that still bothers me,' he says. 'I really wish I had played in England when the spotlight was on. Back in 1984, though, nobody really cared. English clubs, although they dominated European competitions, were very much left to their own devices.' Six, to this day, believes that he might have stayed in England a lot longer if the exposure had been greater. He will not talk in Cantonaesque terms, but Six is clearly thinking of what might have been. Ironically, Six might never have come to England at all. He had signed a pre-contract with Atalanta in the wake of France's triumph in the 1984 European Championship, and was due in Italy when he suddenly changed his mind. 'I fancied the English challenge,' he says. And the English immediately took him under their wing. 'Everyone was so friendly,' he says. 'I think it might have had something to do with the fact that I was a foreigner. All my teammates looked out for me. They would always be inviting me out for a beer. The only thing that sometimes annoyed me was the way English people made assumptions all the time. I think it's because they ruled the world for so long; they often think they have all the answers.'

The other first in Six's move to England was the man who made the deal, Graham Turner. Alex Ferguson was still in Scotland at the time, while Howard Wilkinson was cutting his managerial teeth in Yorkshire, when Turner spotted the potential of a French footballer. 'I made Didier realise how lucky he was to have the chance to become the first-ever outfield Frenchman to play in our League,' Turner says. 'I also felt, from a personal point of view, that it was a golden opportunity to show people why French football was so highly regarded by so many people in England at the time. And still is.'

Six settled in a house in Sutton Coldfield, on the outskirts of Birmingham. He enjoyed the town, while his wife liked the country. Their friends, meanwhile, loved having an excuse to pop over to do some shopping. 'People would come over to London to go to the shops,' Six recalls, 'and then they would hop in a car and come down to watch me play in Birmingham. I can't tell you how many Frenchmen and women came to see me at Villa.' And yet, despite his unquestionable success, Six refuses to be called a pioneer. 'That would give me too much importance,' he says. 'I went to England, and I had a good time, but I am not sure I opened that many doors. All I did, really, was show that a Frenchman could travel well.'

Six, who now runs football academies in France, still keeps in touch with the club chairman, Doug Ellis, as well as a number of ex-players. It tells you everything about the place that Villa still occupies in his heart that the Frenchman represents only one of his five former foreign clubs in veterans' competitions around the world. 'Just last year [in the spring of 2001],' he says, 'I went with my team to Hong Kong.' He pauses. 'When I say my team, I mean Aston Villa.'

REVERSE CYCLE

The ultimate irony of this Eric Cantona-led French Revolution is that its roots lie firmly in England. Indeed, had it not been for the foresight and courage of five English footballers, who leaped into the unknown by signing for French clubs long before Cantona had even so much as thought of joining the English League, there is doubt about whether the recent Gallic invasion could ever have taken place. In many ways, Glenn Hoddle, Mark Hateley, Chris Waddle, Trevor Steven and Graham Rix opened the eyes and minds of both the English and French football communities. The members of this quintet were both talented and young enough when they joined Monaco, Marseille and Caen respectively, to make people sit up and take note on both sides of the Channel. It was as if, quite suddenly, English players were worth buying, and French football worth playing.

Rix, who played a pivotal role in the signing of Frank Leboeuf when he was no. 2 to Ruud Gullit at Chelsea in the mid-1990s, has nothing but fond memories of his passage at Caen. 'By the late '80s,' he says, 'I think that English players were prepared to turn at least part of their attention away from their own little world, while the French were ready to accept that *Les Rosbifs* could be skilful athletes. I had just finished my career at Arsenal and fancied a change. When I got the chance of going to France, I leaped at it.'

Rix remembers how he signed for a club he had never heard of, nor, for the record, identified on a map. 'I'm sure it's the same for young French guys coming to England these days,' Rix says. 'I know, for example, that Frank Leboeuf didn't know where Chelsea was when he signed for us. And we were a big club, so you can imagine what some of the other guys are thinking when they join little, provincial places.'

Rix recalls how the deal came about. 'I got a call from my agent, and he said that this French club called Caen were interested. I asked him how much I could get; he told me; I signed immediately. Like the French kids in England today, we went to France ten years ago to get more money as much as anything.'

And what about the difference in culture? 'Well, that was fine,' Rix says, 'particularly for me in the north of France. I'm not sure Caen is all that different from parts of southern England, both in terms of the weather and lifestyle. No, the big difference was the style of play. I arrived in the French League in 1990, when the pace of the game there was still really slow. I remember sitting down with my new teammates and telling them that we should play more like an English team. They were confused at first, but, after we tried a few long balls and some rough tactics during a few games, they saw the positives a change could have. God, I had some fun teaching the French lads how to get stuck in.'

The English might not have taken over French football in the way their French counterparts have since managed on these shores, but those five Englishmen were the ones who broke the ice. 'We didn't think of it like that at the time,' Rix admits, 'but I guess we did play our part in changing attitudes. To a certain extent, it opened people's eyes to the possibilities a foreign signing could provide. If nothing else, it cemented the bond between England and France, and facilitated the arrival of some of their players.'

No one should underestimate the importance of the five English players' decision to entertain the French in their own back garden; and this, remember, was before Eric Cantona had transformed English football culture. Many of these men also influenced their French teammates. Cantona, for one, was always amazed to hear Waddle say that he was never more loved or worshipped than during his time at Marseille. The thought of being a hero in a foreign land came to Cantona there and then. Waddle in Marseille pushed Cantona to Manchester. If nothing else, it is comforting to know that an Englishman played some part in Cantona's eventual 'consecration' on these shores.

Say it quietly, but this French Revolution has clearly had several pioneering English influences.

Alex Hayes

CHAPTER 1

Cantona: The Magnificent 7

The guys on Planet Mars love their football, they have giant screens and everything, but sometimes they get bored with the beautiful game, so they ask a special envoy to spice it all up, and decide to help him out with all their extraordinary powers: Pelé in the '60s, Cruyff in the '70s, Maradona in the '80s. Once Diego had completed his mission, they had to find a guy with a European profile again, in order to follow the universal guidelines of the twentieth century, applied by FIFA for the designation of World Cup hosts: America, Europe, America, Europe, and nothing for the other continents until Korea/Japan 2002. One guy had the ideal profile for the '90s, the best skills and the right temper to make it all happen, in the era of football superpowers and image rights: Eric Cantona.

Ten years before the euro started ruling Euroland, Cantona was already the essential European with a Spanish maternal grandfather who fought against Franco, and an Italian paternal grandfather, from Sardinia, who decided to emigrate to France. The point of convergence was obvious: Marseille, midway between the two peninsulas. The young Eric Cantona was born there, in 1966. It's the year England won the World Cup (you must remember the Nike ad, at least), and this was the obvious sign that the baby was destined to greatness across the Channel. The guys from Mars really love it when they can have a good laugh at our expense. They plan it all, in detail, and we are left here, saying: 'What a coincidence! What a good story!' Now they have decided to change their plans, in order to make us even more confused at the beginning of the twenty-first century: three authentic world stars at the same time: Zidane, Beckham and Ronaldo, and a few injuries on top! But that's another story, let's go back to our point, the life and times of 'Monsieur' Cantona on this planet, and his immense legacy.

Flashback. The real story began in the winter of 1991, after E.C. turned 25. Everything before that was just a long dress-rehearsal, with lots of costume changes, from one club to another: Auxerre, Martigues, Marseille, Montpellier, Nîmes. There were lots of stages and scenes, where the main actor shouted, threw down his shirt, or called France coach Henri Michel a 'shit bag'. The guy was packed with talent, full of energy, but he was still a young actor, having to learn the tricks of his trade. In the winter of 1991, he was ready for the biggest stage of his life, but he did not know it . . . yet.

The reign of King Eric over English football has already been well documented, and this is not an attempt to rewrite the story. However, there are some bits and pieces which are worth mentioning, at the beginning of a book with such a pompous title: *The French Revolution*. And before we go any further, we should make sure that you are not mistaken by the title: it was a revolution, but it just happened to be French, just like Cantona happened to be born in France. By the same token, Eric just happened to be in the French Alps, that winter of 1991, when a series of phone calls, in an anonymous Val d'Isère phone booth, started to change the face of English football.

IN A PHONE BOOTH: THE DECISION OF A LIFETIME

Cantona was in Val d'Isère, the famous ski resort, with his friend Stéphane Paille, a fellow professional footballer and a good mate since the happy times of the great Under-21 French team of 1988, which fell at the last hurdle of the Euro Under-21 Championship because Cantona was suspended for the second leg. There was also Didier Fèvre, a staff photographer at *L'Equipe*, the French national sports daily, who had eventually become a friend of the big man, after taking dozens of pictures of the young player. The wives were also there, and Isabelle Cantona was somewhat concerned, because Eric had just decided to end his footballing career. The situation was serious, but not bad enough to cancel a family holiday.

'The plan was simple: we were going to start with a nice holiday week, pure Christmas style, and then, the second week, corner him and bring him back to football.' Fèvre remembers the whole set-up, and the strategy he had defined with Paille. 'Eric had literally quit, nobody knew where he was. At that time, I also covered World Cup skiing for *L'Equipe*, so I was able to filter the news, and make sure there was no leak about Eric being at Val d'Isère. Still, there was one leak: one day, [Jean-Jacques] Bertrand [Cantona's lawyer, as well as Jean Cacharel's, the Nîmes chairman] got here, we let him talk to Eric, and tell him how much it would cost him to end his contract with Nîmes. It was a tough reality-check, and it was not the first big story: Marseille, then Montpellier, now Nîmes, and a lot of money on the top of that. Eric was in a shitty situation, and it was likely to cost him a lot.'

Cacharel was also the founder and president of the eponymous clothing company. 'Eric respected Cacharel, but Bertrand's visit worried him quite a bit. The news was not good, Nîmes wanted a whole lot of money, and he had to find a solution. It was a big mess, and Eric was aware of it. In fact, that visit was a chance, because we realised that we had to get going with our plan, even more so.' Fèvre remembers everything: 'Besides that, everything was brilliant: good snow, great skiing, and we even got the chairlift to break down, in order to spend 20 minutes in mid-air, and talk about football. It is the chairlift over Bellevarde; it often stops because of the wind. I don't remember whether Steph was ahead or behind us, but we started telling him that we had to find a solution.'

Up there, hanging by an iron thread between two pylons, and looking down on the 'Face de Bellevarde' where the Olympic downhill would take place two months later in the Winter Games of Albertville 1992 (Albertville, as in Albert Cantona, Eric's father, just for the sake of mentioning it), Cantona started reflecting on his career, his future, his life. 'After a while, he told us: "OK, I don't mind playing football again, but I'm fed up with France and all this crap." He was at war with everybody, and gutted by the football milieu. His agent at that time was Alain Migliaccio, Paille's brother-in-law. I was good friends with Dominique Rocheteau [the former 'Green Angel' of AS St Etienne, unhappy finalists of the European Cup in Glasgow, against Bayern, in 1976]. At that time, Rocheteau started as an agent, there was like a new deal and he represented something, had some kind of aura. Eric asked me whether anything was possible in Japan. I asked Dominique, with Eric next to me in the phone booth. There was no mobile phone at that time.'

Can you imagine? A Christmas holiday in Val d'Isère, there were lots of fans of Manchester United, Liverpool and Arsenal in the trendy

French resort, very popular with English skiers, and E.C. was there, completely anonymous, on 27 or 28 December 1991, locked in a phone booth. 'I told Dominique that he was ready to play again, but as far as possible away from France, the media, the whole system; if possible in Japan. The next day, we went back to the phone booth, and Dominique confirmed that it was impossible, because their league ends in March. And then he told me: "Ask him if he would be OK for England." I will always remember this, because of everything that happened afterwards. I put my hand in front of the phone, and asked Eric: "Would you be OK for England?" He looked at me, thought for a few seconds, and answered: "Why not?" That was it. Dominique told me: "We'll see." We went back to the chalet, but we did not talk about England, because there was nothing to talk about, no specific club in sight. Three days later, the holidays were over, I left Eric at the Lyon-Satolas airport.'

Rocheteau talked to Michel Platini, who had almost joined Arsenal, a few years back, and was then the France coach. Gérard Houllier also helped. He was already a Liverpool fan at heart, and was then directeur technique national (DTN) at the French Football Federation (FFF), before succeeding Platini six months later.

Fèvre continues: 'It all happened very quickly. The next Tuesday, I was at Wengen for World Cup skiing and I got a message at the hotel: "Cantona going to Sheffield for a trial." At L'Equipe, any coverage of Eric was my assignment; it was weird sometimes. I phoned him, and I felt that he was very distant. He was very upset that he had to go through a trial. This was confirmed when I saw him in England a few days later: he did not want to know me any more. Our relationship had changed, in less than a week. This was the end of our friendship. From that moment, it was another story. But when I think of this phone booth, and of the exceptional career that he made for himself after that . . .'

Ten years later, Fèvre still remembers how 'disappointed' he was, how 'difficult' it was to accept that he was no longer a friend of Eric, and explains that 'it was so unpleasant that I disconnected completely'. He also says that 'Eric could have helped Steph [Paille] to come to England,' and tries to find some sort of explanation: 'When you move abroad, you sometimes develop other facets of yourself. Eric lives a lot on his feelings, he believes in himself a lot, and if he feels the thing, he goes for it. At that time, he was often with people who had nothing to do with football, but also English-type fans who have a beer and respect you – humble guys, tough guys, who don't have an easy life. He was something of a magician, and at the same time he discovered a new world; it was the first time for him. When I met him again, he had this empty and transparent look . . .'

IN THE CROWD: CLAUDE BOLI ON CANTONA

Exit Didier Fèvre, brother of Bertrand, aspiring director and assistant to Luc Besson on *The Big Blue*. Enter Claude Boli, brother of Basile and Roger, who played with Cantona at Marseille and Auxerre. Claude was studying in Manchester when Eric arrived after one week at Sheffield Wednesday and six months at Leeds United. A researcher in history and sociology, Claude quickly understood that Eric was worth following closely, in and out of Old Trafford, and that his research would be all the more valuable with such a case to study. Again, this is just a coincidence, Claude first meeting Eric in Auxerre, and then teaming up with him in Manchester. It really is a small world! And the guys on Mars have a laugh, again.

Ten years later, Claude can speak for hours about the passage of a shooting star named 'Canto' in the beautiful sky of English football: 'Eric's case is interesting because he managed to go beyond this notion of a foreign football player, to be loved by Man U fans, but also respected by fans of the other clubs. For one thing, he was humble. From Day 1, he said to himself: "I am going to learn. I cannot abandon something I love. I can live again, in a foreign country. It's a new context; I have everything to prove." He knows exactly what he is worth, so he believed that he could succeed here, but he needed a little time, for him to adapt, and for the others to adapt to him. And thanks to the feedback of the fans, little by little, he thought: "This is a place for me."

'In everything that was written about Eric, all the stereotypes used by the press, you will always find this image of the nonchalant Frenchman, creative, skilful, but likely to lose his temper. At Man U, it was a moment when, after Bryan Robson, the typical English player, they were in search of a leader, someone with charisma. Ferguson also looked for someone creative, to channel the force of this club. They were often the "Raymond Poulidor" [the famous French cyclist, always second . . . behind Eddy

Merckx], finishing second or third in the league. With Eric, he found that. He had experience of elite football, and he had adapted very fast at Leeds. Eric said to himself: "I can give a little bit more." He likes to learn, he is very humble. Eric was not here to change United's style, but to bring something extra. There was a mutual recognition between the player and the coach, and they gave each other some time to succeed.

'Eric succeeded even more against the clubs most hated by United fans, such as Liverpool. He had his best games against City, Arsenal, Leeds. The fans thought: "He is close to us, he understands us, he knows that it is much more important to win at Anfield than in Europe, against Liverpool than against Barcelona" – a very English thing. In Scotland, it's the same, you cannot miss Celtic–Rangers. He could feel this, and the club helped him to understand this. So the fans realised: he is the one we needed – not only did we wait 26 years for the title, but against clubs such as Liverpool, which have been dominating for a while, on the pitch and in the media, we win. The TV pundits are former Liverpool players, it is the big club. With Eric, United manages to tear that apart, to move the whole system.

'Had Eric not succeeded in bringing back trophies, his aura would not have been as powerful. There were very few years when he did not manage to win something. But the trophy cabinet does not tell the whole story. At Old Trafford, fans keep on singing "Cantona", even if he did not win the European Cup in 1999. If you compare the generations of great United players, he only stayed for five years, whereas Bobby Charlton spent all his career here, George Best and Bryan Robson ten years or so. Eric is the player of the century, but not only because of the trophies. It is a moment in the history of the club, and it is the way United won, against Liverpool in the FA Cup, against Leeds, Arsenal, the clubs with a very strong link to their supporters. Winning the European Cup is not enough.'

ON THE PITCH: THE BOYS ON CANTONA

Cantona won the FA Cup twice, but he never won the European Cup, because he retired from football in 1997, after his fifth title in six seasons. The only season when Man U did not win anything was 1995, because of the kung-fu kick on Matthew Simmons at Crystal Palace. And the season after Eric retired, in 1998, Beckham and Co. did not win anything again without their older brother. Even worse, Arsenal won the Double. In that Arsenal team was Emmanuel Petit. Just like many French players, he used to watch Eric on TV, on Sunday nights, before moving to England. And just like many others, Eric made him think that he could succeed as well, on the other side of the Channel.

Petit recalls: 'I have some memories of Eric, when he won the title with Leeds, and an FA Cup final against Liverpool. And a lob, during a game in Manchester: a sumptuous goal. I used to follow his feats on TV, and despite everything I could think of English football, one thing was obvious: they did not judge the player with regards to his personality, but what he could do on the pitch. The English don't give a damn whether the guy has personality, or is somewhat crazy. What they are interested in is his performance on the pitch. Canto was not welcome in France any more, so he started all over in England. I told myself: with the nature he has, the fact that he was almost like plague-stricken in France, and that I sometimes feel that people don't understand me, I might have an opportunity to flourish over there.'

Alongside Petit, Patrick Vieira constructed that 1998 Arsenal Double. 'Pat' is just as able as 'Manu' to recognise Cantona's influence on his decision to leave Milan for London: 'Before signing for England, I had seen games with Ginola or Cantona on TV, and Cantona really seemed to have a ball here. He has so much personality, he's a real character. Cantona–Vieira, it's a different story. I don't have the same personality, but one thing is certain: his success at Manchester helped me, Patrick Vieira, when I arrived in England. Thanks to him, to what he has achieved, the Frenchies are better accepted here. To see a Frenchman at the top of the Premiership has prepared English fans to accept us better. His success made my choice easier. But we don't have the same nature. I used to admire his big mouth, the man and his explosive nature, but I am much more reserved, so I don't think one can compare the two of us. Canto, some would like to copy him, but it is impossible.'

Before Petit and Vieira, two other French players were the first to follow Cantona's example, pack their bags, take their wives with them, and start an amazing journey in English football. Both were born in the south of France: David Ginola in Gassin, near St Tropez, and Frank Leboeuf in Marseille, just like Cantona. Both are good talkers, and their vision of Cantona, from a Mediterranean perspective, is all the more interesting.

In his autobiography, *Le Magnifique*, Ginola talks extensively about Cantona, and one extract from this is worth quoting:

> Remember my fellow Frenchman Eric Cantona's famous quote about the trawlers and the seagulls? I don't think there are many football fans in this country who could forget Eric's colourful career in the Premiership. Personally, I think mental pressure was something which Eric found difficult to handle. I'm convinced he resented me coming to play in England. Until I arrived at Newcastle in 1995 he had been the only French star in the English game. But I stole his limelight. Football came between our friendship. Football drove us apart. Eric was idolised at Manchester United and always wanted to be the king in England, but I wanted the same, so there was an inevitable clash.

Claude Boli is ready to use his analytic skills to compare Ginola with Cantona: 'These are two very gifted players, and Ginola is even more gifted, he is one of the best in the world. Eric arrives before Ginola, at Sheffield, but his success is, all in all, accidental. Had he not been sanctioned by a referee when at Nîmes, he might have never come here. And then Platini, Houllier and others told him: you are not going to stop. There was no choice, no career strategy, just particular circumstances. After one week at Sheffield, he goes to Leeds, wins the title, the fans discover someone who is different. He leaves Leeds in tense circumstances with regards to some of Leeds' bosses, and is recruited by United. And something happens.

'One of the main differences is the relationship with the club and being a professional footballer. Eric is more humble, he is more into constructing, although the English tend to use many more superlatives. They always say: he is the greatest, etc. So you'd better keep a cool head, not get carried away. Eric only talks at the last game.

'There is a big difference with Ginola: in 1995–96, when Newcastle is leading the League, 12 points ahead of United, Ginola says: "This year, we'll be champions." Here in England, you don't do that. And there is also the luck factor; David was less lucky than Eric. Keegan tried to create a style, to achieve some sort of jigsaw, but it's not that easy. At Newcastle, they also had rugby union. If he had played for Barcelona, if Newcastle had won the title, if . . .'

Nobody can stop Claude when he talks football: 'Eric tried not to enter into the media system too much, in order to preserve his footballer's life, as much as his private life. It's also a question of character, of experience. Ginola did lots of clubs, Toulon, Brest, Matra Racing, PSG. He had a choice between Real Madrid, Barcelona and Newcastle, and maybe he was unlucky, because he is a great player.'

'Gino' is a great player, but he is not exactly modest, everybody knows that. However, he has a definite admiration for Canto, and he is honest enought to recognise that in his autobiography:

> Eric was quite simply one of, if not the best player ever to play in English football, and he helped turn Manchester United into the world power they are today. But he didn't get the recognition he deserved in France, because people were scared of his character and he is sometimes difficult to understand. I think people love him or are scared of him. But we are similar in many ways. He, like me, is from the south of France and both of us are proud of our roots. We share similar views on life, and on things such as nature. Eric is a simple person who has different values. He once told me that when he looked to the future, he saw himself living in a cabin somewhere deep in the forest with a gun for hunting. He would certainly be clever enough to live like that. He described to me how he could see himself living near a stream and going fishing or shooting birds to get food for his family. He is a very expressive person, though he has a tendency to exaggerate things.

Ginola even wishes that one day, 'when our football lives are finished, we will have a *pastis* together and talk about everything'. At that little bistro on the seaside they could be joined by Leboeuf, and this would make for an interesting reunion, with one possible topic, fashion, and another one, the French squad.

Leboeuf: 'I used to play with the collar up in Strasbourg and the French team. When I got here, I stopped doing it, as a mark of respect for Eric, but also because I wanted to make sure that people would not say: "He's doing just like Cantona." I was the fourth Frenchman to play here [fifth, in fact. Leboeuf remembers Six, Cantona and Ginola, but has never heard about Georges Crozier, the French Fulham keeper in 1905], but the second one to win trophies. First, there was Canto, everybody said: what he has done is magnificent. It's still huge. Then I come, I meet Canto after two weeks, he says: "How are you, Mr Leboeuf?" I say: "I'm all right, Mr Cantona," but we lived on two different planets, him on the "star" planet, and me on the "little guy who gets there" planet. I will never achieve what he has achieved in England, but I made up for that with the French team. It's a different story. And in England, I did my share, winning the Cup twice, just like him. It was great.'

As a professional researcher, Boli is good at summarising things: 'When Eric succeeded, it gave ideas to other players. Ferguson had thought of Zidane, when Zidane was still in Bordeaux, but he was not sure that he could succeed in England. Eric's arrival allowed other borders to open, because a foreigner had succeeded, even if he still remained, above all, a French player. Other foreigners started dreaming to play at Man U, and some club bosses started thinking: "Why not?" Just like Eric in that Val d'Isère phone booth at the end of December 1991.

'I don't think they were inspired so much by Eric's advice. Most of them had learnt a lot from their previous experience, such as Vieira and Henry in Italy. Henry had a terrible time in Italy, and then someone helped him to bounce back: Wenger, just like Ferguson for Cantona. Guys like Vieira and Henry are very clever, so they understand quickly that they can succeed in England, because they are given all the good tools, and they have some experience of winning. On the contrary, some may have thought: if Eric has succeeded, it must be easy over there. They had seen 15 minutes of Premier League on Canal Plus [the French equivalent to Sky TV]: Eric scoring, the fans. They were in for a shock.'

This is exactly what happened to Bruno Rodriguez, a proud Corsican who only managed to play twice for Bradford during the 1999–2000 season: 'One of my idols was Eric Cantona. When he scored a goal, he remained stoic. I liked his nature, his frank talk, and his game. I think I have the same nature, I don't let people walk all over me, and some people don't like that. I left Paris St Germain because the club bosses had not kept their promises, but also because I loved English football. I had a couple of other offers, but I did not want to wait, and this proposal

[Bradford] arrived. In the spur of the moment, I decided to go, and I really thought that I had the right skills to succeed over there.'

On those dark Sunday nights in France, there were lots of aspiring players watching Canal Plus, the famous *L'Equipe du Dimanche* programme, with Premiership highlights, and Cantona's exploits. One of them was Thierry Henry, long before he joined Arsenal: 'I have two images left of Canto: when he throws his shirt to the face of Guy Roux; and when he scores one particular goal with Manchester – he turns to the crowd, shows his torso around and watches the crowd. It's a game that Man U had won 4–0 or 5–0, he had scored with a flick, it's an image that I still remember.'

Strangely enough, Mikaël Silvestre (Man U) remembers exactly the same goal: 'When he comes back from his suspension, one day he scores a goal, with a flick, he has his collar up, he puffs out his chest, and then he watches all around the stadium, he looks at every one, just like that. He must have made a mark on Manchester players, they talk about him sometimes. Personally, I was not that hooked on the Premiership. We all followed Cantona, because he was quite an attraction, he was the skipper, he scored goals.'

Christian Karembeu, who spent one season at Middlesbrough, takes a more global approach and just adds that 'You always need a reference, an example. Kopa had done it in Spain, Platini in Italy, and then there was a crazy migration of footballers. Canto did it here, and now it's England.'

Another passionate TV viewer was young Olivier Dacourt, a few years before signing for Everton and then Leeds United: 'The first who showed the way was Cantona. I remember him, because I really loved watching him on TV. On Sunday nights, I would watch *L'Equipe du Dimanche* only to see Canto, and then I would switch off the TV, without even watching the Italian league. Then there was Gino, he showed the way as well, and then Leboeuf and Pat [Vieira]. We can thank Canal Plus. It was so good. I remember a game between Newcastle and Manchester United, they scored five, and [Philippe] Albert scored a good one to Schmeichel. I have super memories. My best memory is of the Cup: it's Canto against Liverpool. He was my idol, he was class.'

The tribute to Canal Plus continues with Marc Keller, who played for West Ham and Blackburn before moving back to France and becoming the Strasbourg manager (see Chapter 9): 'Cantona showed the way and

Canal Plus did a lot for his fame in France. When Platini scored lots of goals in Italy, we could not see them. Suddenly, we saw all the big European leagues, and Cantona was successful. Thanks to Canal, we know English football. It's the conjunction of this and his success. He had technical ease, a good vision of the game, he was in a young team, all the young lads would run around him, he used that a lot. There was a communion with the crowd because he had something extra: talent. It is something rare.'

Eventually, some players managed to see Cantona live, and even talk to him, such as Robert Pires: 'When I met him after the Cup semi-final against Tottenham at Old Trafford [2–1 for Arsenal, spring 2001], I was a little bit like a youngster meeting a star. After a win like this one, to see such a man, Cantona, can only be impressive. He was happy with the rhythm of the match, the show, impressed by the speed. I asked him how he was, I told him I had seen him on TV, losing against Portugal at the beach-soccer world championships. He was happy to know that French players were following what he was doing. He was a player that I appreciated very much, and when I met him, I was like a kid asking for an autograph. Canto, for all the French players here, was the trigger. We could see that he could win, and that he made young people dream. The crowd at Old Trafford is not easy, but even today they still sing *La Marseillaise* in his honour. This shows that he made a mark. If I'm here today, it is because I want to do the same thing as him.'

Pires is definitely someone you can trust, because he very often does what he says. A few months after saying these words, he did exactly the same as Cantona: won a Player of the Year award, and then a Double with Arsenal, with the same number at the back of his shirt: 7 . . . and the same sort of consensus among all actors and spectators of the beautiful Premiership. If one player deserves to carry the flame that was lit by Cantona, just like an Olympic torch, it is definitely 'Robby' Pires. He is a match winner, he is an inspiration for the team, the crowd, and France missed him cruelly at World Cup 2002, much as France missed Cantona at Euro '96.

CANTONA, FRANCE, AND THE JACQUET-DESCHAMPS VETO

I will always remember that FA Cup final at Wembley in 1996. It was my very first time at Wembley, and it is also the reason why I moved to England two years later, and why I am writing this book now, but that's beside the point. The topic is Wembley '96, a few weeks before Euro '96, and a stadium filled with thousands of *tricolore* flags, with Cantona's face in the middle. Having read *L'Equipe* for years, starting with the English football news, Cantona's highs and lows, I had never suspected such a thing, so much passion, so much fervour.

It all started on the M25, when I saw that red Renault Clio with a *tricolore* at the back, Cantona's face, and English plates. The driver saw my French plates, so he started blowing his horn like a maniac, and this was several hours before kick-off. Then I saw the Liverpool players with their immaculate cream suits, their flashy shades and their red carnations. And then I saw this goal by Eric, five minutes from the end, on that corner. And then I saw him lift the trophy, and heard the crowd. Amazing. Beautiful.

When Cantona won that FA Cup final in 1996, he was objectively one of the best players in the world, due to his ability to win crucial games single-handedly, his capacity to lead a team by example, on the pitch and at the training ground, thanks to the mental power he had developed after the Selhurst Park incident, and his technical ability as a striker and provider, on all fronts for his team. For all these reasons, he deserved to be in the French Euro '96 team on sheer merit and skills, and there would have been another bonus: the English crowd would have been cheering for France . . . in all the other games than England's, of course. The Man U fans had the *tricolores*, with Eric's face on them, the semi-final was scheduled for Old Trafford, and everything was in place for Eric to conclude, with a French cherry on the Euro cake, the best season of his career.

This was not to be, however, because Eric was not a French international any more. The perfect pretext for kicking out Cantona from the French set-up was his Selhurst Park kung-fu kick, in January 1995. The French Federation, shocked by the images on TV, took the decision right away, and there was no way back. Even winning the European Cup would not have changed Aimé Jacquet's resolve to create a team with no big mouth in it, just his. Jacquet stuck to it, and he found a strong ally in the team: Didier Deschamps who had been called a 'water carrier' a few years earlier by Cantona, just like previous coach Henri Michel had been called a 'shit bag'. Deschamps was essential to the French system, and Jacquet probably thought that he did not need Cantona up front, with such a strong team at the back and in the midfield. He was proved wrong at Euro '96, as a sterile French team failed in the semis against the Czech Republic because of its inability to score goals. Eventually, he was proved right at World Cup 1998, when the same system, and a couple of young strikers on the bench, proved good enough to become world champions.

Nobody will ever know if the French domination would have started two years earlier, with Cantona in the squad. I think so, and I am not the only one. In his autobiography, Ginola writes that

> the fact that he [Cantona] was overlooked for the French national team competing in Euro '96 in England was, in my opinion, not fair. I am sure he would have been a great asset to France, playing on the grounds where he plied his trade week in, week out. Maybe that snub is what pushed him into making the decision to retire from the game altogether; he'd had enough and was fed up with football's mentality.

This, and a couple of other factors: that he was not as sharp any more in 1997, contrary to what was written on his shirt (the name of the main sponsor, Sharp); and that Man U were still making millions on his back, selling those shirts, without him making as much money as he could have expected. 'They treated me like a pair of socks,' Eric regretted in 2002, in an interview with Michael Carrick, for an astonishing BBC documentary about Sir Alex Ferguson. He would not go any further, because he still respects the club, he is the best player of its history, according to the fans, and he does not like to talk about the past anyway.

However, he does not mind celebrating the past, by participating in Johan Cruyff's jubilee in Barcelona, Diego Maradona's farewell party in Buenos Aires, or the ten-year anniversary match of Ryan Giggs's career, against Celtic. On that day in Manchester, Old Trafford was full, but nobody, not even the Welsh Wizard, expected to see Cantona, collar up, on the pitch. It was a well-kept secret, Eric got changed on his own, in a small locker-room, and when the speaker, 15 minutes from the end, announced 'Substitution for Manchester United: number seven . . . Eric Cantona', the crowd went crazy again for King Eric. Claude Boli was there, and he remembers the feeling, the shivering: 'It was just as when he came back after his suspension, just as strong.'

Only artists can move crowds like that. Cantona is an artist, some even say he is from another planet, but he is very human, and he still bears a grudge against Deschamps, the ultimate non-artist of French football, a few years down the line. I understood this when, after six months of literally harassing his brothers Joël and Jean-Marie for an exclusive interview with Eric for this book, Joël eventually gave me the reason for 'The King' refusing to take part in 'the same book as a couple of other people that he does not respect'. At that time I had already interviewed Deschamps. Joël had passed the book proposal to Eric who could see Deschamps' name in it, alongside his own, and, although Joël never gave me any name, I am 99 per cent sure that Deschamps is one of these two. For the other one, your guess is as good as mine: Ginola?

BEACH SOCCER: CANTONA'S FRENCH TEAM OF HIS OWN

Cantona may have been barred from the French team by Jacquet and Deschamps, but he found a way round his frustration by creating a French team of his own out of nowhere. It is the 'Equipe de France de beach-soccer', a bunch of great friends playing great football, all of them former pros and international players, on great beaches around the world. I had the chance to follow them for three days, in Hyde Park, for the London leg of the world 'pro beach-soccer' tour, in June 2001.

'Come on, don't play like oldies, don't try tricks. Play in the spirit, until the end, and play for the crowd.' There was only a handful of spectators in the stands, but Eric insisted, during the break: 'You have to make them happy.' And he led by example, scoring half of the French squad's goals, among them a couple of missiles sent from the halfway line. 'Shit!' he shouted, when a pass went AWOL, and nobody talked when he gave his orders, at half-time: 'There has to be someone staying at the back. We have to let them come, there is no point in running after them. Our organisation is better, it's great. We are going to win this game.' Forgetting about the stands, the advertising hoardings and the Sky Sport cameras, it is a scene directly taken from any six-a-side tournament in the Marseille region.

'We can bring the sun anywhere,' Cantona boasted afterwards, completely relaxed, in his orange T-shirt, army trousers and beach flappers. He had just been photographed between two beautiful babes in bikinis, and you could see that he enjoyed his new life. 'It's a wonderful life. When it's cold here, we go to Brazil to play. But the most important thing is that we fight, it's real competition. The pitch is small, so every mistake is paid for in cash.'

Cantona is really keen on promoting beach soccer, and there was a press conference to promote the event, so Eric, as professional as ever, gave the press what they wanted: lots of great quotes, his views on almost everything, from Maradona to drugs, from Cruyff to Vieira. It was just as good as any interview I could have done, and it was much more exciting. Rewind:

On beach soccer and the French team:

'I had enough about soccer and I needed to play another sport, because I need the adrenalin that goes with it. It's a different sport. Two years ago we were not very good, now we are one of the best teams in the world. I am a player, I work on the pitch. I play for France, I organise the team, that's it.'

On Vieira:

'I saw Vieira against Tottenham at Old Trafford. Vieira is wonderful, he has everything, he is one of the best midfielders France has ever had, and one of the best in the world. If he does not want to stay because he does not win, he's right. He does not have to stay because the fans, the manager, the players love him, no? Great players want to win, until the last day of their life, they want to win. Deschamps is nobody compared to him.'

On drugs in sport:

'You speak too quickly, are you coming from Mars? Do you like cocaine? I prefer a guy like Maradona who takes cocaine on Wednesday, but does not take drugs to win on the weekend, to win, and he can see himself in the mirror, he is proud of himself, and the team. Some people use drugs to win, how can they look at themselves in the mirror? I respect someone who does not take drugs, but I respect more someone like Maradona, than someone who takes drugs to win, to play with people, with the dream of the people. They are sellers of illusion.'

On 60,000 people idolising him at Old Trafford:

'I was prepared for that. I think the dangerous thing is to believe that all the women, and all the people, will love you all your life. They love you because you represent something at the moment, but from the day I start football, to the day I quit, I knew why the people love me, and I knew that when I will leave . . . so I don't need it, because I was prepared. In life, when you are prepared, you are not surprised by things, and you are happy. It's important not to dream too much, not to believe that you are a playboy, that you are a god. You are nobody, we are too small, the story of a life is like this.'

On returning to Manchester United:

'I'm not excited about returning to Old Trafford. They speak too much about that. Every time I come here you ask me the same question. I'm fed up. I enjoy my life, I don't need anything, I don't ask for anything, I don't need to meet people, to be recognised in the street, I just need to find things in life which make me happy. I don't know what tomorrow will be. Today, I can tell you what I feel today, tomorrow we'll see. There is no arrangement, not at all. I don't want to, I see, I read things, nobody say something to me, maybe it is summertime, and they need to say something, you can sell papers, and people can speak about Manchester more, but I am not a businessman and I don't want to be used by businessmen.'

On succeeding Sir Alex Ferguson:

'People need to speak, to read things, and sometimes people use me, but I enjoy beach soccer. I'm not sure I like it [to be a manager], so maybe I try, one or two weeks, and if I like it, maybe I come back. It's a bit like when you want to seduce a woman, yes, no, come to my room, but nobody needs to seduce me. I'm not a woman. If I want to come to your bed, I come to your bed. I've told you the truth before. I come to Manchester and I speak to Alex Ferguson. He says do you want to become a manager? No. Do you want to try with the youngsters, for a week or two? I say yes, and I see if I like it. It's not impossible to replace Sir Alex Ferguson, and win, but they need someone with a strong personality, who represents something for the players, otherwise they will not respect him. Somebody like Johan Cruyff. He was my idol when I was young, when he was a manager at Barcelona. They can only respect him, there are only two or three in the world.'

On becoming a manager:

'To take players who are 15, try to teach them how you see the football, how you want them to play, and when they will be 20–25, they play in your team, they play the football you started teaching them ten years ago. I think it is a dream for all the managers. If I come back in football, I don't want to play like the other ones, I have my proper vision of football, and I want to do something new, I want to see a team playing a football that has never been played before. Like United, or Barcelona before with Johan Cruyff, this kind of people. It's exciting to see a thing that you have never seen before. Would I play the same system, the same football as someone before? It would not be interesting for anybody. If I do it, what I want to do, or teach, is things that I never knew, and that I always wanted to do, or know, about football. I think it's like an artist with a new movement, in painting, the pop art, things like that, a new thing, like a revolution, a wonderful revolution.'

A 'wonderful revolution', by Eric Cantona, as if starting the French Revolution was not good enough. I can't wait to take part in this one, and maybe I'm not the only one. Cantona for president!

Daniel Ortelli

CHAPTER 2

Manchester United: *Merci Eric!*

It's 6 October 2001. We are in the 93rd minute of England's all-important World Cup qualifying match against Greece. Because Wembley Stadium is under construction, the England football team has been doing a tour of the country for the past 18 months. Today, the team is at Old Trafford, Manchester United's Theatre of Dreams. Today, the team is in deep trouble. What had been billed by the media as a celebratory party – a send-off for the lads before they fly to Japan and South Korea for the World Cup – is turning out to be a complete disaster. England is at sixes and sevens, struggling to string more than a few passes together and never putting any sustained pressure on the Greeks. Cue Goldenballs . . .

As the match enters the final minute of added-on time at the end of the 90, Teddy Sheringham wins a fortuitous free-kick 30 yards out. Only seconds remain and the players know that, as things stand with their group rivals Germany drawing 0–0 with Finland, England will have to enter the lottery of the play-offs. As the ball is placed onto the turf, two men quickly emerge as the likely candidates for the last kick of the match. Sheringham, who has been on as a substitute for 30 minutes and fancies his chances, is arguing his case with the other wannabe taker. No chance. David Beckham, the England captain, has been the best player on the pitch by a considerable distance and wants the responsibility. No matter that he has missed half a dozen free-kicks during the match, he knows that this is his territory. He knows, too, that he is at home here, that Old Trafford is his stage.

Not surprisingly, the arguments do not last long. Captain Beckham will take the free-kick. He has a feeling he will score. He knows this is well within his range. Less than 15 seconds later, the ball has travelled over the wall and into the top corner of the net. England have the draw they require to go through as group winners. The fans clap Beckham and thank the Lord for his incredible dead-ball skills.

In truth, they may as well just thank the King. Indeed, had Eric Cantona not played at Manchester United, David Beckham might never have scored that now famous free-kick.

For years, as he was a young lad learning his trade at the Manchester United academy, Beckham sat and watched his Gallic hero practising free-kicks and penalties. The boy-wonder dreamed of one day imitating his idol, but surely not even he could have imagined that he would make his mark at Old Trafford wearing an England shirt. 'Eric was my role model,' the England captain has said. 'He's the best I've ever played with. A great guy.'

And so the history books will show how the arrival of a talented but misunderstood Frenchman transformed the world's biggest football club into an all-conquering machine, as well as helped form the most exciting generation of English players for more than 40 years. Sir Alex Ferguson must still wonder how he managed to get this god of football for less than one million pounds.

The only regret about the Cantona story is that he jumped ship a little early. Having done so much to establish Manchester United as a force to be reckoned with, both at home and in Europe, it is sad that the King did not stay around to witness the ultimate coronation at the Nou Camp in May 1999. That night, as United produced the sort of escapology that even Harry Houdini would have been proud of to defeat Bayern Munich 2–1 and lift the European Cup for the first time in 31 years, you could not help but think of Cantona. In fact, as the team paraded around the streets of Manchester displaying the three trophies they acquired during the incredible 1998–99 Treble season, you kept thinking Cantona would appear. In so many ways, these were his trophies, his rewards for spending hours with a group of English teenagers and teaching them the wonders of the game.

Cantona would never admit it, but part of him must have wished he had played on just two more years and won the medal he always coveted. He had departed Old Trafford so suddenly two summers before, after yet another disappointment in the semi-finals of the Champions League (Man U lost 2–0 on aggregate to Borussia Dortmund of Germany), that he never had time to consider his options properly. The Frenchman has since said that he was forced out of the door because of an argument over image rights, but the real truth may never be known.

And perhaps it is best that way. For the fans, who still worship him and wave flags with 'King Eric lives on' written on them; for the manager, who staked so much on the maverick and found a soulmate; and, in particular, for the players, who remember to this day the impact Mr Eric Cantona has had on their lives.

THE CANTONA LEGACY

One of Beckham's proudest moments remains the day he scored that now famous goal from his own half against Wimbledon at Selhurst Park in August 1996. Afterwards, Cantona trotted up to him: 'Boutifull goelle,' he told the man who would later take over his number 7 shirt. Those words from Le King were all it took to convince Beckham he had at last made it big. 'I remember thinking: "One day I'd like to be as charismatic as him,"' Beckham recalls. Praise indeed when you consider the players that the 27-year-old has rubbed shoulders with.

More than any other player, Cantona inspired an entire generation of young and talented English players. Most significantly, though, the Frenchman proved to Sir Alex and the football community that a foreign star and his professional dedication could do wonders for a club. Just ask Beckham: 'That was the work ethic we have had pumped into us since we were apprentices,' the England captain says. 'Me, Gary [Neville], Scholesy [Paul Scholes] and Butty [Nicky Butt], we were brought up to work hard at our game and we knew the rewards in front of us if we did. We had to go back in the afternoons and some of us went back in the evenings to work when we were apprentices.' Now in the afternoons, Beckham will sometimes go back and practise free-kicks with bare feet, to improve his feel for the ball. 'It's something I have always done,' he says, and no, it doesn't bruise or damage his feet – not even the infamous left one.

The youth team coach, Eric Harrison, would always tell his protégés that they should play the game and not the occasion. 'Yeah,' Beckham says, 'it was the best thing to say to us really. Because when you are at a team like Man United you can step on to the pitch and look around and think, "Oh my God, what am I doing here?"' Sound familiar? That is because it echoes what Sir Alex, who often speaks of what makes a Manchester United player, once said of Eric Cantona; that he walked into Old Trafford and stuck out his chest as if to ask if the club was big enough for him. 'You have got to have a certain amount of arrogance to play at Man United, whether people like it or not,' Beckham explains. 'It is such a big club with so many expectations of you as a player. If you look through the United teams over the last ten years, they have had players who have got the arrogance and the determination to win. That's pumped into us even at a young age. We have all got the aggression. It's been proved a number of times. We all stick together and that's the important thing.'

Over the years, Beckham has drawn inspiration for his play and style of leadership from Cantona. Even Sir Alex recognises aspects of the Frenchman in the England superstar. 'For me, Beckham comes into the Eric Cantona category of captain,' the Scot says. 'He's a player who leads by example on the field. Cantona had a great presence on the field and was a scorer of important goals. Similarly, David impresses by his example on the field. He never stops running, he plays with supreme confidence, he always tries his hardest and he scores important goals.'

Other England players, too, have sought to follow the leadership of the unique Frenchman. The likes of Paul Scholes and Nicky Butt have both freely admitted that they would not be where they are today, were it not for the lessons they learned watching Cantona at United for five years. 'He's the greatest player I've ever shared a pitch with,' Scholes has said, 'and he did things with a football I did not even know could be done.'

DEFENDING THE EMPIRE

Whether out of respect or force of circumstance, Sir Alex Ferguson has never bought another Gallic forward or midfielder since Cantona's departure in the summer of 1997. The United manager is not known for his over-sensitivity, but with this exceptional player, he has always been prepared to make emotional exceptions. Cantona touched Sir Alex with his skill and passion, so, while the Scot has shied away from buying attacking Frenchmen, it is interesting to note that he has surrounded himself with *Les Bleus*' defenders. It is as if Ferguson's thinking is that

Cantona helped create an empire, so the club should now buy more players of his ilk to defend it.

Ferguson quickly realised that Cantona had served as the perfect prototype for the young and aspiring midfield trainees to copy. Beckham, Scholes and Butt had watched and learned almost everything from the French maestro. Defending, though, was never Cantona's forte. And nor, immediately after the Frenchman left, was it United's.

When Ferguson employed Cantona in 1992, he already had a solid defence in place. Peter Schmeichel guarded the net, while Steve Bruce (now the Birmingham City manager) and Gary Pallister provided the necessary shield in central defence. Bryan Robson, Paul Ince, Roy Keane and Nicky Butt have also added an extra layer of protection both for the defence and the sometimes cavalier attackers over the years. Times, however, have changed.

After Cantona retired, the defence often looked vulnerable and seemed to lack the leadership qualities the Frenchman once offered up front. True, United won the Treble in 1999 without the strongest rear-guard of all time, but that was an exceptional year – a freak of football nature. That season, United's motto was: 'No matter how many you score against us, we'll score one more.' And so it proved, as they managed to sneak past Arsenal in the FA Cup semi-final, and then Inter Milan, Juventus and Bayern Munich in the Champions League. It made for great viewing, but not even the blindest of United fans would disagree that the success was based on shaky defensive foundations.

The proof has come in the three years since that memorable triumph in Barcelona. Though United won the Premiership title at a canter twice more after the Treble season, results in Europe's elite tournament have been patchy. For some time now, Ferguson has known that his side's free-scoring ability will not get them out of jail forever.

And so he has placed his faith in French defenders and keepers to turn things around. In the post-Cantona years, the Scot has purchased Fabien Barthez, Mikaël Silvestre and Laurent Blanc. He also tried to buy Lilian Thuram and Julien Escudé. So far as Ferguson is concerned, French players will be the defenders of the empire Eric Cantona helped build.

THE THREE DEFENSIVE MUSKETEERS

Mister Barthez

Take one of your hands. Now open it. There you are, in front of you is the total number of French goalkeepers to have played in the top flight of English football. Five lonely Frenchmen to protect their English nets. Who on earth would be a keeper?

Naming the last four is not too tricky. There is, of course, the most recognisable keeper in the world, Manchester United's Fabien Barthez. But, while he is unquestionably the most titled and lauded of the *portiers*, he was actually last to cross the Channel. We will return to the man the United faithful call 'Ab Fab' shortly, but it is worth taking a moment to point out his four predecessors.

The first, as has already been mentioned in Chapter Zero, was the former Fulham great, one Georges Crozier, who spent two years on the banks of the Thames. Then, some 90 years later, came Lionel Perez at Sunderland, Newcastle, Scunthorpe and lately Cambridge. His most telling contribution to English football was to venture too far off his line and thus allow Eric Cantona to score one of the most memorable goals of his career. Remember the wonderful chip from the edge of the area in December 1996? Then you will also remember the puffed-out chest and look of utter contempt on Cantona's face.

Bernard Lama did not stay long, spending less than four months before the 1998 World Cup with West Ham and playing just 12 times for Harry Redknapp's team before returning to France. His time in east London was brief, but successful, as he managed to secure his berth in the World Cup squad, and helped the Hammers finish eighth in the Premiership. The fourth Frenchman to wear the gloves in England is Pegguy Arphexad, the unsung hero of the keepers. He has played second fiddle to the main keepers at Leicester and Liverpool, yet he has two League Cup medals and has never complained. Not bad for the man fans like to call Peggy Sue.

There is, however, only one French goalkeeper who stands out from the crowd. It tells you everything that Ferguson chose a French World Cup-winning goalkeeper to recapture the spirit of Cantona. When acquiring Barthez, the Scot was recognising two important factors: firstly, that Barthez had the potential to be the new leader and, secondly, that United were in desperate need of a magnetic figure at the back. Barthez may have his critics, but how many Premiership managers would secretly love to employ his services? Most, you suspect, because Barthez gives you something different, something extra.

Ever the diplomat, Barthez insists that it is Manchester United and the club's incredible 67,500-seater arena which gives players the sensation they are playing for a special club. 'When I first came here, for my medical,' he says, 'I remember thinking, "God, I've landed in the biggest club in the world." I was like an excited kid just before a great football match.' Significantly, the one thing that most impressed Barthez on his arrival was the quality of the facilities at United's new Carrington training ground. 'It was such a change from what I'd known before,' he says. 'Quite honestly, when you see the complex here you understand why Manchester United have achieved such incredible results. It is little wonder the trophy cabinet is packed.'

During his time in England, Barthez has given as many interviews as he has hairs on the top of his head. Even the chief football reporter of the *Manchester Evening News*, Stuart Mathieson, who is allowed to go to Carrington every day, has never sat down to speak to *Les Bleus*' keeper. He has bumped into him just twice for five minutes in two years. The second time, Barthez told him that he planned to finish his career at Manchester United. The news, predictably, toured the globe faster than you can say 'Oh la la'. The only time I managed to talk to him for any length of time was when the all-conquering French team were in Marseille for a friendly match against an All-Star World XI in the summer of 2000. And even then he was far from chatty.

Barthez is a nice guy, someone whom his teammates respect and his friends and family adore. He is, by the same token, someone who is deeply suspicious of, and therefore often misunderstood by, the press. Remind you of another Frenchman? It should come as no surprise that Barthez and Cantona are good friends. Sir Alex clearly sees similarities in the two Gallic players. Both are showmen, entertainers in an often dull game, and men who will always – in the words sung by Frank Sinatra – do things their way. Both, too, are great leaders on the pitch and yet withdrawn characters off it. They like to let their performances do the talking, and, mostly, they have succeeded.

Most significantly of all, however, both these men from the south of France have been selected by Sir Alex Ferguson, at different times in the recent history of Manchester United, to act as talismans. But, then, Ferguson has always liked a good vintage. 'Ferguson likes his wine, and he wants to speak French all the time,' says the French defender, Mikaël Silvestre. 'He would not want to speak French if he was not interested by France. When we played in Belgium, everything was written in French, and he kept saying: "This means that"; he always wanted us to correct him. The other day, we have a game, Fabien scores three goals, and Alex is trying to find the French word for hat-trick: "La chapelle, le chapeau?" During training, he often gets on the pitch and asks me: "What does this mean?" He does the same with Fabien. He wants to invest in France; he asks me for tips, but I tell him to go and see Fabien, who spends more time than me in the south of France. I don't know much about wine, but he tells me he keeps in touch with Guy Roux in Auxerre. The Scots are very close to the French, Jim Ryan told me. He likes France too.'

The Barthez deal was done in the summer of 2000. The former French keeper and one-time personal coach to Barthez at Monaco, Jean-Luc Ettori, remembers that period well. 'Fabien left during the holidays, so we never really had a chance to speak about things,' Ettori says. 'We had chatted about Italy before, but, to be honest, I think England is perfect. English football fits Fabien like a glove. What interests him is the game itself, matches. Everything that goes on around is not his cup of tea. The English are a little like that, too. It does not mean that they are not serious, but they have an approach to the job of footballer which is very different. They won't worry about a match three days before; instead, they'll just have a quick chat a few hours before the game and then get on with things. That is exactly the sort of football Fabien needed.' Barthez made an immediate impact. After arriving in Manchester on the back of a lucrative seven-year deal, much was expected of the player. He did not disappoint in his first season, helping United win the Premiership title with ease. Was Ettori surprised that Barthez was a success in England? 'No, not at all,' he says. 'Fabien could only ever make it there. He has never doubted his ability and has, to his credit, introduced a novel way of keeping to the English.' The heart-in-mouth style, one assumes? 'No, no,' Ettori sighs, 'what Fabien has done is teach kids that you don't have to be 1m 90cm tall, or on your line all the time trying to block shots. The longer he stays in the Premiership, the more keepers you will see being prepared to play the ball. He is so comfortable with his feet.'

It was ever thus. Just ask one of Barthez's coaches at Toulouse. 'When I first saw Fabien, he was just 17,' he says. 'I had never seen such a young keeper do the things he could. He was never afraid, always willing to dive around and try new things.' Being the centre of attention or playing the clown have long been part of Barthez's repertoire. From an early age, he would charge out of his area or execute a dramatic dive. He is not the tallest of keepers, but do not be completely fooled by appearances. 'You don't have to be the tallest to be a good keeper,' Barthez says. 'A lot of the players I looked up to, guys like Pascal Olmeta and Robin Huc, were not enormous but they were very agile.'

Barthez, though, has pushed his luck a bit too far at times. During the 2001–02 Champions League group match at Old Trafford against Deportivo La Coruna of Spain, Ab Fab was more like Bad Fab. Twice, he ventured so far out of his penalty box that he needed his passport to get back in goal. And, twice, he let goals in as Manchester United lost 3–2. Then, in the all-important Premiership match against Arsenal at Highbury in the same season, the France keeper made two more glaring errors to allow the Gunners to turn a one-goal deficit into a win. That is when the criticism was at its highest since he signed. That, too, is when Sir Alex and the rest of the squad rallied around him more vigorously than ever before. Like Cantona before him, Barthez is accepted with the sometimes rough as well as the often smooth.

'Here, respect and tradition are really important things,' Barthez says. 'It's not about whether you are a star, it's just about whether you play for the club. Eric [Cantona, who advised Barthez to sign for the Premiership champions] told me, "If you lose, fans won't spit in your face." That's important to me. They understand you can have a bad day and they always show respect to their present and former players. That affected my choice.'

The generous signing-on fee and ample weekly wages no doubt helped Barthez finalise his decision, too, but there is an unmistakable frankness about his discourse. 'I always knew this was going to be a huge challenge. This was always going to be a big task, particularly following in the footsteps of Eric [Cantona], but I'm getting there.'

Barthez, who, like the former France captain, Didier Deschamps, comes from a rugby family, always knew he wanted to play the beautiful game. Never fully able to detach himself from his oval-ball background, he chose the one position which enables him to show off both his handling and shooting skills. 'I love the freedom that the goalkeeper position allows you,' he says. 'But I also love the responsibility that goes with the job. That's why I love playing for a big club like Man U. In England, all the matches are important and that's what I like.'

By his impossibly high standards (Barthez has won every major honour in club and international football, including the European Cup with Marseille, and the World Cup and European Championship with France), he had a thoroughly disappointing second term. It is yet to be seen whether Barthez ever replaces, or even joins, the Great Dane, Peter Schmeichel, in the pantheon of memorable United keepers, but one thing is for sure: the bald Frenchman has been bold.

Mister Silvestre

The same could be said of the second defensive musketeer, Mikaël Silvestre. He has been bold, not only in the way he has played his football at Manchester United, but also in the way he has taken on his notoriously strict manager. One day, Mikaël Silvestre might decide to share a few memories with his grandson. Photo albums will come out, medals paraded and tales of glory with Manchester United and France recounted. But it is one particular story that may have to be told and retold. 'That's right, son,' Silvestre will boast, 'I took on Sir Alex Ferguson – and won.'

Not many – or is that none? – can make such a claim. A number of players have tried to get their way over the years, most notably Lee Sharpe, Andrei Kanchelskis and Paul Ince, but all suffered resounding defeats at the hands of the Scot. Ferguson's motto has always been: mention you are unhappy and you are out. So when Silvestre boldly went where few had dared go before and openly criticised his manager in November 2001, many felt the young Frenchman had shown himself the exit door.

Silvestre maintains that the exact comments he made while with France for a friendly in Australia were taken out of context, although he does not deny that he was unhappy at the time. 'There was never a rift between me and the manager,' he says, 'and anything that happened is all forgotten. Of course, I did not enjoy sitting on the bench at the beginning of the [2001–02] season, but I am playing all the time now and hold no grudges whatsoever.'

No matter that Silvestre might or might not have stated his views in a moderate tone, the fact remained that the 24-year-old had crossed swords with his manager and therefore looked to have played his last game for the club. Far from it. What happened next is something that will probably never be seen again while Ferguson completes what one assumes to be the last three years of his Old Trafford reign. Not only was Silvestre allowed to stay at the club, he was elevated to the first team as well.

The disagreement surrounded the continuing selection of Denis Irwin at left-back. Silvestre felt that, as the younger and quicker player, he was more suited to dealing with the weekly rigours of the Premiership and the Champions League. His views might have appeared conceited, but he has since been proved right. As soon as the ageing Irwin was removed from the starting XI, United looked far more secure defensively. But it was not until United's home defeat by Chelsea, their sixth in the League at the time, that Ferguson decided to ring the changes. Gary Neville moved from right-back to partner the other French defender, Laurent Blanc, in central defence; Phil Neville was promoted to right-back; and Silvestre was handed the left-back berth on a full-time basis. 'It did make us more solid,' Silvestre says.

Six months later, Silvestre had signed a new deal to keep him at Old Trafford with his manager. 'It's good that I'll continue to work with Sir Alex,' the Frenchman says. 'We all expected someone new to be announced for the end of the 2001–02 season, but instead the manager told us he was staying. I'm glad he's going to carry on because I have improved a lot under his guidance. He was strong with me and did his job. That helped me a lot. My aim when I joined the club [from Inter Milan in late 1999] was to play for the French national side and go to the World Cup. I've done that, so the manager must be doing something right.'

While Ferguson has undoubtedly played a part in Silvestre's development, the Frenchman must take much of the credit for his own transformation into an international defender. Much criticised when he first arrived in England, mainly because people felt he was all speed and no defensive nous, Silvestre has greatly improved. Not that the Frenchman will care much what his doubters think. Indeed, he has won two Premiership titles in his first three years in England. He has also won his first international cap whilst a Premiership player. Not bad, eh?

Silvestre is part of the new generation of French defenders, who marry attacking potential with good defending ability. These players have also, in the image of their predecessors Frank Leboeuf and Marcel Desailly, developed a taste for travelling and winning. Oh, and parenthood, too, as little Evy was born in the spring of 2001. Silvestre has clearly had a busy time since he arrived in England, joining Manchester United from Inter Milan to complete his second move abroad by the age of 22.

'The hardest thing,' Silvestre says, 'is your first move away from home. Particularly going from a small-town French club called Rennes to a world-renowned conglomerate like Inter Milan. To start off with, you have everything to discover at a new club. Meeting your new teammates – that's the toughest bit. It's crazy. But once you've crossed the barrier, it's OK. I'd say that when you have tasted life abroad, you want more.'

As soon as Silvestre arrived in the Serie A, he gained a place in the team, playing 18 matches in Serie A, six in the Champions League, and a handful in the Italian Cup. But the following season, things quickly turned sour. He realised, when Marcello Lippi took charge, that he was going to be used as back-up for the Greek defender, Grigoris Georgatos. 'I thought to myself that I was now a substitute and, worse still, when I did play I was on the flank almost as a midfielder as full-back. That's when I knew I was going to leave Inter.'

Bologna showed interest, but only two options seemed viable: Liverpool or Manchester United. Silvestre met representatives from the clubs, and then had to decide where he was more likely to be able to play in his favoured central-defender role. Gérard Houllier already had plenty of options to fill that position, so Silvestre went for Ferguson's Reds. 'I was desperate to play again,' Silvestre explains. 'Ferguson told me that he needed a defender. He never specified where he wanted me to play, but I knew that, with all the matches the club need to play, I would get my chance to shine.'

Silvestre can recall the time when Ferguson contacted him. 'I was on a trip to the Ukraine and Armenia with the French Under-21s when he called me. He said he was really keen for me to sign. He even tried to speak to me in pidgin French. So I flew to Paris and then Manchester, and he picked me up at the airport. We spoke for an hour and a half, during which time he told me that he had been tracking me for years and even planned to buy me from Rennes, only to see Inter pinch me. He said he needed me on the left flank to start with and that he would then try me out in the centre. "You will get your chance," he promised.'

Silvestre continues: 'It all happened very quickly from there. I arrived on Thursday, signed and then trained on the Friday. The next day, we went to Liverpool of all places. I remember it well and, to be fair, I got a good reception from the Liverpool fans who had read that morning in the paper that I had almost joined them. We won 4–3.'

Silvestre played at left-back for three matches, until Henning Berg got injured and opened the door for the young Frenchman in central defence. Ferguson, true to his word, moved his new recruit inside. Silvestre finished the season as the second most-used player in the United squad, with a total of 31 appearances. 'We won the Premiership title that year,' he says, 'and I was so happy. It was my first-ever bit of silverware and I was just so excited. It was a great feeling.'

Silvestre insists he knew very early on that he had made the right move. 'To be honest, I can look back now and say that I always knew I was going to enjoy England. Right from my first match, I thought: "Yeah, what fun." There are more spaces to run into. Defences are usually made up of four players as opposed to the five they use in Italy. Here in England, it is a lot less rigid. Everything about the game in the Premiership is mad and fun. Tactics are less important and the game is less regimented. Ultimately, there is more room to play with because the players are more likely to make mistakes, but I don't think that is a bad thing. It actually makes the Premiership more interesting. If there weren't any goals, like in Italy, people would be bored.'

Silvestre offers an interesting insight into the very specific way English fans behave towards their star players. 'They demand that you prove yourself,' he explains. 'The first year, I think they were unsure about me because I didn't have the same style as Jaap [Stam, the central defender who was sold to Lazio in August 2001]. I played a lot of matches, but I could sense that the fans were not convinced. Slowly but surely, they started telling me that they preferred seeing me on the left flank, from where I could launch runs and do a lot of attacking. They were less keen on my defending. I received quite a lot of mail. It wasn't nasty or critical, and people weren't aggressive or anything, it's just that they would address me as an attacking midfielder. They quickly forgot I was a defender by trade.'

By the same token, Manchester United quickly forgot that they were duty-bound to defend the FA Cup title they had won against Newcastle in May 1999. Instead, Silvestre's club went to Brazil to play in the World Club Championship. The fans were up in arms, the television companies were unhappy, and even the players were disappointed. A year later, when he finally discovered what all the fuss was about, Silvestre was amazed. 'La Cup,' as the Frenchman refers to the competition, 'is very special. If anything, the players go for it even more. In the Premiership, you are expected to play at 100 per cent, but in the Cup, it is 110 per cent. In France, La Cup is a chance for the small clubs to make a name for themselves. In England, it is a must for the big guns.'

Silvestre continues: 'In a sense, La Cup is the place where you can really tell the men from the boys. I remember us playing against Fulham in a tie in January 2001, when it was freezing cold, and their pitch was in a terrible state. We scored early, but they then equalised, and it took a great effort by Teddy Sheringham to win it. Then, we played West Ham at Old Trafford, and, having dominated the whole match, we got caught out right at the end, as Paolo Di Canio ran through. Fabien [Barthez] tried to put him off by putting his arm up and stopping, but Paolo knows these tricks and he scored. What a day. That sort of thing could only happen here.'

Having plied his trade in three different countries, Silvestre is better placed than most to compare the football styles. 'The main thing that makes English football stand out,' he says, 'is the fact that even when a team is winning 4–0 or 5–0, the coach will get up from his seat and yell: "Keep going". That's incredible. If you can score another, you try, whereas in Italy, if you are so much as a goal to the good, you look to close up shop, pass the ball around and start thinking about the next match. The styles are different and the risks are different. You are allowed to lose a match in England, even against a weaker team. That is not the case in Italy or France. But, then, that is also why I am here and not there. I love it.'

Mister Le President

It seems historically appropriate that the reign of a French king should eventually be followed by the arrival of a president. Unlike a certain Louis XVI, though, the king in question left his Manchester United kingdom with his head held high (and still on his shoulders). Four years after Eric Cantona brought an abrupt end to his influential Old Trafford career, another Frenchman, Laurent Blanc, was elected to run the club.

Not that anyone should be fooled. Despite their respective nicknames, 'King' Eric and 'President' Laurent cannot be the real rulers in the red half of Manchester. As his swift banishment of the apparently disloyal Jaap Stam demonstrated in July 2001, Sir Alex Ferguson is the force to be reckoned with. On the pitch, however, United had lacked leadership, particularly in defence, which, for all Stam's undoubted class, had rarely looked as solid since the departure of the experienced and vocal trio of Peter Schmeichel, Steve Bruce and Gary Pallister.

It took him a while in his first season, but it is now hoped that Blanc, who has signed a one-year extension to his contract, will have a similar talismanic effect on the team as his great friend Eric Cantona once did. 'He has great experience,' says Ferguson of the World and European champion, 'and he can organise players, which is something we needed with our young defenders. His presence alongside Silvestre, the Nevilles and Wes Brown has been vital to them and the team. I've no doubt he's improved us.'

Blanc has indeed put in a string of excellent (if strangely criticised in some quarters of the press) performances. 'I have no doubt that the most important factor in us turning around our 2001–02 season, when United finished third despite losing six League matches before Christmas, was Laurent's leadership,' Silvestre explains. 'His placement, his vision, his serenity: everything he does is perfect. We may not be the same type of defenders, but that does not mean that he cannot help me. I am always looking to learn from him; he's the boss.'

Apart from a mutual admiration for each other, Blanc and Ferguson also share one cherished dream. As both enter the twilight of their respective careers, they are desperate to get their hands on the most coveted club trophy of all. Three times Blanc was a member of teams who qualified for the Champions League (Auxerre, Barcelona and Marseille), but on each occasion he left during the summer and missed out on Europe's premier event. Now he has had a taste of it, he wants more. As for Ferguson, recapturing the prize which he last won in 1999 remains the priority.

Sir Alex has made no secret of the fact that the Champions League is the main target. Nor has he ever hidden his respect for Blanc. 'I'd tried to sign him on three or four different occasions over the last ten years,' Ferguson says. 'He's a player I've always admired.' Similarly, Blanc has always been attracted by English football, although even he admits moving to England was the biggest culture shock of his 20-year career. 'English football is very particular,' Blanc says. 'Not all the teams play the old-fashioned kick-and-rush any more, and yet the style remains unique. I knew I would be a little taken aback in my first match [against Everton's Duncan Ferguson] and that it would take me a while to get used to the more physical side of the English game. But I was not afraid of the challenge. I felt it was my responsibility to settle in and immerse myself in the English way. And I believe I did that.'

Blanc needs no reminding that he turns 37 on 19 November 2002, but, like another United old boy, Teddy Sheringham, he compensates for his lack of leg speed with a lightning-quick mental agility. 'I'd never been the type to dash around,' he says, 'so I was not worried when I signed. I've always learned to compensate in other ways. I believe that anticipation and good judgement are just as, if not more, important than speed and brute force. Timing,' adds Blanc, who just happens to be an avid collector of watches from the 1950s and 1960s, 'is everything.'

Blanc can laugh now, after proving his early detractors wrong, but there was a time when the President was in grave danger of being impeached. When Manchester United suffered their fifth Premiership defeat of the 2001–02 campaign in November, several newspapers gleefully pointed out that the initial letters of the teams that had beaten them spelled 'Blanc' (Bolton, Liverpool, Arsenal, Newcastle and Chelsea). If Ferguson had been superstitious, the Frenchman would have been banished there and then. But the defence, and not Blanc's nerves, tightened up when it mattered. 'Laurent was aware of a lot of the criticism, unfair of course, that was being directed at him,' Ferguson says. 'Some people had been looking for a scapegoat but they picked the wrong one because he has been marvellous for us.'

With that sort of support, it is perhaps no surprise that Blanc performed a U-turn and decided to shelve his retirement plans for one more year. 'It was always going to be his decision,' Ferguson says, 'but he is carrying no more weight than he did 10 or 15 years ago and I felt there was no need for him to pack it in. You've seen Teddy Sheringham play as a forward for Tottenham at 35 alongside Les Ferdinand and that makes you realise that Laurent Blanc could play for another year or two because the qualities he has don't require running.' Ferguson argues that Blanc's steadiness under fire, his sound positional sense and his experience of winning big games are more useful than half a yard of pace. 'He is not quick but he is quicker with his eyes than anybody,' says his fellow French defender, Silvestre.

Having made his mark in France, Italy and Spain, Blanc always felt that he was versatile enough to adapt to the demands of the Premiership. So, too, did his friends Eric and Fabien – Cantona and Barthez – who encouraged him to join the growing French contingent at Old Trafford. Cantona, who played with Blanc for Montpellier, Nîmes and France, has long advocated that 'Lolo' is the perfect United player. Barthez, one of Blanc's best friends from their time with *Les Bleus*, also helped smooth the original deal.

'The fact that Fabien was here influenced my decision,' Blanc now admits. 'We have a special relationship and I like playing in front of him.' To the chagrin of the United faithful, the defensive partnership with the keeper was resumed, but Blanc stopped planting the obligatory kiss on the Barthez cranium before every match.

Never mind. It would seem that even the club's notoriously demanding fans could be ready for a new French leader. The king may well be dead, but long live the president.

Alex Hayes

CHAPTER 3

Arsenal: Wenger, the Ambition and the Patience

'We did not come over here to start a revolution, but to give a little extra. When we can achieve that, we are very pleased.' Arsène Wenger was already a master of the understatement when he said this, a few months before completing his second Double in the space of four years. In May 2002, at the end of the most hard-fought Premiership campaign ever, the one with the greatest number of leaders, the most suspense, Arsène was again proved right on the pitch. This, added to his perfect mix of English composure and cold humour, probably won him the last of his detractors: Sir Alex Ferguson recognised that he was beaten fair and square, and treated his great rival to a drink, to put things right. He had regretted a few months earlier that Arsène did not always respect the tradition of going for a drink with the other manager after the game. So he opened one of his best bottles of red wine and shared it with Arsène, after Arsenal beat Man U at Old Trafford (1–0) to seal the 2002 title.

This game will remain one of the best memories of Lee Dixon's long and distinguished career, according to his words in the official Arsenal magazine, a few weeks later: 'Securing the Double had a dream-like quality about it. I don't believe in gloating, but it meant so much to take the title away from one of the best teams in Europe, on their home soil. It was an outstanding defensive performance, from the strikers as well as the back four. As Arsène Wenger consistently repeats, the best form of defence starts from the front. It was a perfect night and our game plan worked to perfection. It had shades of Liverpool 1989. Then, George Graham had wanted us to keep a clean sheet until half-time, and steal two goals. Wenger's policy was the same, with a view to a single goal early in the second half. Nullify United's early onslaught, keep the crowd quiet, and hit them on the break. They did not seem to have any answers, which showed how well we played. It was a killer blow once we'd scored. Mind you, if they had scored first, it would have been a completely different scenario. Two minutes before we went out for the second half, Arsène just had a short piece of advice: "Work-rate; defend from the front; and play a little more." It paid off.'

Strangely enough, the crucial goal was scored by Sylvain Wiltord, who, for a long time after his arrival in the summer of 2000, had worn the costume of Arsène's most disappointing French recruit in ages. Eventually, thanks to a lot of hard work in a less gratifying position, on the right of midfield, following the injuries of Fredrik Ljungberg and then Robert Pires, Wiltord became an all-important player in the quest for another Double. And he got a highly symbolic reward for that: the only goal at Old Trafford, more than one year after the Gunners were slaughtered (6–1) by the Red Devils on their way to a third consecutive crown (1999, 2000, 2001). It was 25 February 2001.

Pires still remembers the pain, and the comforting words of the fans the week after. 'I will always remember the week after we lost 6–1 at Manchester,' recalls Pires. 'That week, I met Arsenal supporters and they told me: "Right, what happened in Manchester is no big deal, you have to forget it, the important thing is to beat West Ham this coming Saturday." There is only one country where supporters can say that. And they are fully right, because the next week you win 3–0 and everybody forgets what happened the week before. When I hear things like that, I really want to give the maximum.' The passion of the fans is only one reason why the French players are so happy at Arsenal. There are many others.

Of course, Wenger agrees with Pires on this particular point: 'I recall the first time I came to England, I said to myself: "Without a doubt, football was created here!" There is a deeper connection between the public and the players. One never ceases to feel that, and would always fail to find the same elsewhere. Those who leave, wherever they go, will certainly be disappointed by the atmosphere elsewhere, because they will never find the same passion again. We can feel that the supporters suffer with the team, but silently. And they support with fervour. It is a dream because in other countries, it is just the contrary: the fans support in silence and criticise vehemently. The supporters, and the passion on the pitch, always push the players further.'

The fans are not the only ones to push the players further, and this is the second reason for French players' happiness at Arsenal: Arsène himself, the tall man from Alsace, who could have been a headmaster in another life, comforting the bullied, talking to the parents, motivating the teachers. Always kind, always polite, and knowing his job inside out. Wenger, a model of patience and confidence, with his sense of purpose and reassuring words for his players, whatever the result. Some may think his press conferences are reminiscent of the 'boring, boring Arsenal' of the 1970s, because Arsène never shouts and rarely criticises anybody in public. The main thing is that he always protects his team, and keeps his focus set on the main objective: improving, progressing, whatever you call it, preparing the next game; and when everything goes his way, such as in the springs of 1998 and 2002, winning a couple of trophies.

ARSÈNE WHO?

'Arsène Who?': the headline of the London *Evening Standard* said it all. When Wenger arrived, he had to face enormous scepticism. Very few people knew his name, but Wenger knew the history of the club he was going to manage. The basic rule was that he had to become almost English in order to succeed. By the same token, he had become Japanese when he coached Nagoya Grampus Eight, in the J-League, after being sacked by Monaco. He loved Japan, the calm of the people, the organisation of the country, so it took some convincing from his friend David Dein, the Arsenal vice-president, to leave Japan behind and land in north London, end of September 1996. 'I had promised myself to only come back to a big club. It was like coming back home,' Wenger says, a few years later.

For Wenger, home is everywhere, because he is a good example of how to integrate in a country. He has travelled a lot, he does not really feel French, he says he is a citizen of the world, just like the majority of coaches in the global football world these days. Ruud Gullit used to say the same when he coached Chelsea and Newcastle. But Wenger had a much different method in mind when he arrived at Arsenal, and his idea was certainly not to create another twentieth-century equivalent to the Tower of Babel. To start with, he wanted to keep the team as British as possible, so he kept the spine of it: a few true Brit players, who knew what football in this country is about, from David Seaman to Tony Adams and Ian Wright.

The first stage of the French evolution, Wenger-style, was to protect the best defence in England, but an ageing one, with a few outstanding midfielders that he knew: so young Patrick Vieira soon left the AC Milan bench, followed closely by Rémi Garde, but also Emmanuel Petit and Gilles Grimandi, who had both been managed by Wenger at AS Monaco. Vieira and Petit were to become the best defensive midfield pair in England and probably Europe, by a length. Garde and Grimandi were there to provide cover, in an area of the squad that needed improvement, as much as some extra workforce, just in case.

Petit remembers this transformation of Arsenal from the inside: 'The first six months were tough, because English football is very different, but I knew that I could succeed here. People trusted me, and 1998 was an enchantment.' The idea of a joint venture between Vieira and Petit 'came from both sides. We talked a lot with Arsène, several times. It was my first year at Arsenal and I remember that the whole team was concerned, because we let in lots of goals, and the defence was complaining that we did not protect them enough, Patrick and myself. I had just spent one year in midfield, at Monaco, on the left, but I was not exactly a defensive midfielder. I started my career as a centre-back, with [Patrick] Battiston, and then I succeeded [Manuel] Amoros at left-back. This experience helped me to create this position of a *relais*, because tactically I could feel what was going to happen, and I could be useful in every part of the pitch.

'There were some problems at the beginning, because Patrick and myself, we like to touch the ball, play it on the ground, send long passes. However, the English players were used to jumping over the line, so we had to work a lot on the training ground, to talk a lot, to convince them that it was better to use the midfield, to rely on the midfield players. With Patrick, right from the beginning, we knew that we could be an extraordinary pair, because physically we were above the rest, and we complemented each other perfectly. It was so perfect that, tactically, we were under the impression that we could play blindfolded. He knew that he could count on me, whatever happened, and it was the same for me. It was very clear, very honest.'

Peggy is in her 60s. She is in charge of the Arsenal supporters' club, and she remembers the pair with emotion: 'Petit and Vieira looked so much like friends. They had this small ritual at each and every game, I was fascinated just watching them. Before the game, Petit would go to the box, say a prayer for his [dead] brother, touch the grass and sign himself [doing the cross]. Then he would go to see Vieira, do the 'high five' and the 'big hug'. No matter how many times I saw them doing this ritual, I loved it. It never changed, and at every game I would wait for that moment. There was such a mutual comprehension between them in midfield. If anything happened to Vieira during a game, Petit was there, on the pitch, next to him, to protect him. I may sound sentimental, but it was superb to see their friendship.'

With still the best back four in the business, and now the best defensive midfield in the land, as well as a very promising Nicolas Anelka up front, Arsenal could do no wrong. Grimandi was not always in the team that season, but he remembers those last months of the 1997–98 campaign, from his privileged position on the bench: 'We played all the games and never lost. We got 11 or 12 points back from Manchester, stayed three months without losing, and we could feel that we were getting closer to the target. There was a spirit, we had the feeling that nothing could happen to us, the atmosphere was better and better. It was my first season in England, everything was beautiful. I did not realise how difficult it would be to win it again.'

Journalist Richard Williams was already impressed by Wenger: 'He is a very impressive man. You can tell, when you listen to him, that he knows what he is talking about. He is very self-contained, not emotional, not when he talks; though he is very emotional on the bench. He is just somebody who commands respect, and the results came so quickly that people realised he was doing good work.' The players were also impressed by the results, according to English midfielder Ray Parlour: 'The players all gave him a chance, and as results followed, it helped. By the end of the season, we had won the League, the FA Cup, and had qualified for the Champions League. He could have asked us anything. Respect came from the results that we got.'

IN THE GYM: TIBURCE, THE GIANT GYPSY

Enter Tiburce Darrou, a blond 50-year-old giant, sun-tanned by too many years spent on the tennis courts with Jimmy Connors, John McEnroe, Boris Becker and the Italian Davis Cup team. He also helped RC Lens and AS Monaco, star sailors Philippe Monnet and Catherine Chabaud, several motocross pilots and rally drivers, mountain-bike champions, basketball players. He is very close to Emmanuel Petit and spends a lot of time with Arsène Wenger when the Arsenal manager enjoys a little holiday near Antibes. He also spent some time with him in Japan when Arsène coached Nagoya Grampus Eight.

He also has an important role in the Arsenal set-up, as well as a tracksuit with 'TD' on it. When a player is badly injured, such as Tony Adams in the winter of 1998, Emmanuel Petit in 2000, or Robert Pires in the spring of 2002, Tiburce supervises the whole rehabilitation process, on the French Riviera, in an environment which is rather contradictory to the idea of working hard. However, it works, and many players can testify to Tiburce's skills and experience. He refuses to be called a fitness coach. He says he is not a guru, but a 'gypsy who tries to understand things'. He never talks to journalists, he does not like them, he thinks that they write too much nonsense. He has a big mouth, but very rarely opens it in front of a tape recorder. So when it happened, in his favourite restaurant, on a beach in Juan-les-Pins, some time in 2001, it was worth listening to . . . and recording:

'I am the only person outside of Arsenal who really knows Arsenal. I spend ten days here, ten days there. I cannot be in one club, there is too much routine. During three or four years, I used to take Arsène's players with me, because he did not have the facilities he has now [at Colney]. The best way to recover was here. There was nothing I could do at the hotel [Sopwell House], because there was nothing to work with. Ian Wright and Tony Adams are my most satisfying achievements. At that time, they were 12 points behind Manchester; Tony could not play any more. When he returned to England, they won the Double and it changed a lot of things. I also worked a lot with Manu [Petit], when he was badly injured. It was mostly because of the lack of facilities at Arsenal. Now, there is everything, the medical staff has improved, he has [Philippe] Boixel coming, an extraordinary gym. It's fine.'

Being very close to Arsène, Tiburce calls him on a regular basis, and sometimes gives him some advice: 'I was the one who told him, privately, to leave Japan. I convinced him to come back to Europe. It took some time for him to decide, because he liked it over there. And he went to Arsenal because David Dein was his friend. We have a very professional complicity, but I am not like him, I am a gypsy. Arsène will always go to the end of his contract, he has his own house. The day Arsène stops managing Arsenal, he stops managing for good. What he lives here is a dream. He did not need to invest one penny, but he manages the money of the club, he is the boss. What else could he dream of?

'Arsène, just like Ferguson, brought a great internationalisation of football. Had he gone directly from Monaco to Arsenal, he would not have done that. I know him so well. It's his life experience, his thinking, the fact that he is a clever man, but also that he was sacked once, went to Japan, etc. It's also the mix between a great president, David Dein, who is very open, and a club with a big name. Before Arsène went to Arsenal, it was already a big club. And in order to attract French players, the plus for Arsène is London, no doubt about it.'

You only have to listen to Wenger's present or former players to verify Tiburce's claim, and understand how much they love London in general, Hampstead in particular. For Pires, 'London has everything. We can do exactly what we like. Everything is open, seven days a week, there's always something to do. If I want to live here after football? I don't know, but I immensely appreciate living here.' Henry agrees, and brings in other reasons: 'People don't bother you here, when you go shopping or have a meal. They just have a look at you, maybe they say: "Well played yesterday," but they wait until you're finished, to ask you for an autograph. They don't go any further, they respect your life.'

Petit is not an Arsenal player any more, but he is back in London, plays for Chelsea, and lives in the same area: 'I like London for its diversity. From one neighbourhood to another, it's like going from one village to another. It's a little bit like Paris, but more electric and more concentrated, although it is an immense city. You know that in each area, you'll find everything. I love this city, because once you've been through the settling down period, everyday life is made easy. I have my landmarks, I know the people. I don't go out in the streets that much, because paparazzi are after me, but I feel that I live in a village, and I like it.'

FIRST LECTURES IN DIETETICS AND TRAINING

Easy transition, Manu, thank you: in a village, you tend to eat vegetables. This was one of the first lessons taught to Martin Keown, the tough centre-back, by Arsène Wenger, the incoming manager with brand new ideas on dietetics. One day, at Sopwell House, Martin Keown was eating fries over lunch, something you don't really do if you are a top athlete. Wenger sat in front of him, with his plate of broccoli and spinach, and he started eating. He did not say anything; Wenger does not say much. He kept on eating this sort of greenery stuff he had on his plate. Keown said later that something clicked in his mind: maybe that's the right thing to do. And Wenger now eats exactly the same thing as his players, in the beautiful cafeteria of the Colney training ground. Some even say that Wenger designed the forks and knives . . .

Another member of the Old Guard, David Seaman, was shocked by one of Wenger's new ideas. The following anecdote struck Professor John Williams, a renowned sociologist and a proud Liverpool fan, because it shows 'the contrast between the constant focus of English players on competition, and this new scientific approach of training by Wenger'. Williams also tells a funny story that he read in Seaman's autobiography, *Safe Hands*, about Wenger's approach:

> In his book, Seaman writes that one day, the Arsenal players were playing a four-a-side game, and it was fantastic, really intense. Both teams really wanted to win, it was 2–2, and Wenger said: right, the time is up, because that was the amount of time we had to devote to this particular amount of coaching. He had a schedule that he would stick to, no matter what, and the players complained bitterly: we can't stop the game now, there has to be a winner in this game, this is what training is about. Wenger said no, this is not what coaching is about, it's about a prepared, organised, structured, sequence of actions, to make you better able to play a game on a Saturday. He stopped, and no one questioned it.

Prof. Williams heads the Sir Norman Chester Centre of Research on Football, at the University of Leicester. He stresses that Wenger's influence, among others, 'is steeped in the new science of football, which is about diet and a much more holistic approach to preparing players. It is less about the mind–body dichotomy that we had in England, and more about understanding the mental aspect of the game. The players have to be good decision-makers, and it is important that they know a little bit more about the world than just football. But the kind of Anglophile approach to the game that they have is interesting ['they' stands for Wenger and Gérard Houllier at Liverpool], in this Anglo-French connection.

'It is also reflected in the type of players they bring over, because the key players for Wenger at Arsenal are really very strong defensive midfielders; Petit and Vieira are very British in their approach to playing the game. Vieira is a terrific player, but he is not a poet, he is not a Platini, he was built to play in the English league. Both Wenger and Houllier recognise that the English tradition is a very physical one. It's part of the reason why they like it, part of what attracts them, because of the intensity of the combat, because of the commitment of the players, and they choose to bring players to do this. It's a combination of pace, power, and also skill, as well as a new scientific preparation that Houllier and Wenger bring, to open the English up to new ways of coaching and organising the game.'

End of the demonstration, and back to Tiburce, his views on Arsène, his long-time friend: 'Arsène is not an innovator, except for one thing: the midfield player protecting his defence, Vieira. With Petit, it was the best recuperator midfield pairing in the world, there was nothing better. Because football is, first and foremost, about recuperating the ball. Arsène brought world champions to Arsenal, but he also brought players with a huge potential. Petit was not at the beginning of his career; Vieira was a great hope, even if they did not realise that in Milan, and Anelka, at Arsenal, had his two best seasons ever in professional football.'

When you start Tiburce on Arsenal players, you cannot stop him: 'Arsène brought a more important scope to English football, as well as a new idea of management in football: not throwing money through the windows; being patient, such as with Kanu [who had a major heart problem and was said to be lost for football]. He could only do that in a great and intelligent club; it would have been impossible in France. Kanu could not have recovered in Monaco, because after a month they would have asked him to be the best. Arsène's intelligence is that he has an idea about players, and often gets it right. He has a network, he listens to the guys, he sometimes gets it wrong, such as with Suker [Davor, the Croatian striker], but if you look at what he paid for Suker, he did not take a dive.

'Some players were lucky to have Arsène, otherwise they would have been sacked a long time ago, such as Wiltord. There are moments when his tactical choices are rubbish, but it's only rubbish because there is logic in his mind, whether you accept it or not. To put Henry and Wiltord together up front, it's rubbish. Stepanovs and Grimandi together as centre-backs, it's rubbish, and they took six goals in [against Man U, 25 February 2001]. Unfortunately, at that time, he had no choice: Adams was out, Keown was worn out, and he got it wrong with Luzhny. Luzhny is a good player, but he cannot play in England. Ashley Cole is better than Silvinho, but against Manchester he was just like the others.'

WENGER'S MISTAKES

Wenger is only human, so he makes mistakes. Petit's departure for Barcelona, along with Marc Overmars, in a sort of package deal, was Wenger's first big mistake at Arsenal, at the end of the 1999–2000 season. Petit remembers: 'I had problems, just like anybody in any given season. The way it happened, I felt that maybe Arsène thought I was not motivated enough to start another season with Arsenal, and I had the impression that Arsenal did not show a lot of motivation to keep me, so the story ended. It was a terrible heartbreak for me. I remember when we played a pre-season tournament in Holland [with Barcelona] the first game was against Arsenal. I went to see the players in the locker-room after the game, and the emotion was terrible, even for the other players.'

The season after the Double had been very good, Petit and Vieira provided Anelka with an abundance of ammunition, and 'Nico' the young Gunner scored 17 times, plus his own double at Wembley (a treble, in fact, as one perfectly valid goal was disallowed), against England (2–0). At the end of the season, Man U completed an historic Treble, but Wenger had no reason to worry, because Arsenal had finished second in the league, one point behind Man U, and lost an epic FA Cup semi-final to the Red Devils, after Dennis Bergkamp missed a penalty and Ryan Giggs scored an incredible goal. It was a very good season altogether, and much better than the one to come.

The 1999–2000 season was then littered with bookings and injuries; Vieira and Petit had more than their share of them, because there was more pressure on their shoulders. The defence was really ageing now, and, up front, Anelka had gone prematurely, replaced by his friend Thierry Henry. It took a few months for 'Titi' to get settled. There were more bookings, more injuries, more money in the bank, thanks to Anelka, but bad luck in the recruitment. All this combined to create a huge gap in the league – Man U won it again. There could have been a consolation prize though, but Arsenal lost a penalty shoot-out to Galatasaray at the end of the UEFA Cup final. There were serious incidents in the streets of Copenhagen, and Arsenal fans were injured. To top it all, Petit left.

'Arsène should not have sold Manu,' Tiburce stresses. 'Did he want to leave? Yes and no. He could have kept him. I took it on me, during those last six months, I was the buffer between the two of them. Arsène thought he was not happy any more in England. I told him, be patient. It was very quick, but Manu was sure about it, he is a mature man. Arsène made a mistake with Manu. And he cannot get him back, it would be too costly. I often talk to Arsène, but I don't believe in a player coming back.'

For the greatest part of the next season, Vieira was going to wander on the pitch, deprived of his twin brother. Wenger tried every solution he could think of, but neither Parlour, nor Lauren or Grimandi, could do the job as well as Manu. To make it worse, the referees were now on Vieira's back exclusively, as there was no Petit any more to alternate the bookings. Vieira recalls: 'My mind was split [over English refs] when I was their target. On the spot, I'd say to myself: "Again! But what do they have against me? Why do they punish me, when the same foul made by an English [player] a few minutes before is not a foul?" It was not me being paranoid, it was just me feeling the injustice of the whole situation.'

As a footnote to the 'Arsenal v. Refs' saga, which would deserve a whole chapter, if not a book, it's worth mentioning the anecdote of Petit's first two encounters with the men in black, recalled by the man with the blond ponytail himself: 'My first game was at Southampton. Carlton Palmer was in defence. He almost cut off my knee, but only got a yellow card. It was a scandal for me, but I had to get used to it, this sort of commitment, and the *laissez-faire* by the referees. The next game, at Highbury, there should have been a penalty for us, and the ref was running, but backwards. Suddenly, he turned to me and I put out my hands, so that we don't hit each other and injure ourselves. He got scared, because the crowd was shouting, as he did not give us the penalty, and he thought I was going to push him, so he took a red card out. It was [Paul] Durkin, my first sending-off.'

Back to the season 2000–01, the one after Petit's departure, and Wenger's second major mistake in a row: not rotating his squad enough, and eventually asking too much of Henry. He had recruited Pires and Wiltord, two European champions with a decisive input in the late stages of this new French triumph (Wiltord scored in injury time to make it 1–1 in the final against Italy, and then Pires offered the golden goal to Trezeguet, on a silver plate). He still had Ljungberg, Parlour, Bergkamp and Kanu. He had a luxury of talent to create chances up front, but he wasted it badly, for reasons known only to himself, such as sticking to his intangible 4-4-2. From the press box, it was obvious that Arsenal, game after game, were doing all the work, dominating games, but something was missing at the end.

The Champions League quarter-final against Valencia epitomised the whole season: Arsenal were the better team but only won 2–1 at Highbury, and then lost 1–0 in Spain. Henry missed a penalty and a couple of chances which would have probably sealed the qualification for a semi-final against . . . Leeds! There was more to come, in the form of that disappointing FA Cup final at Cardiff's Millennium Stadium, won by Liverpool (2–1) in the last seven minutes, thanks to a Michael Owen double. Owen had fresh legs, because Houllier's rotation at Liverpool worked perfectly, especially for the strikers. Time-sharing between Owen, Robbie Fowler and Emile Heskey, one of them always coming on for the last half-hour, with enough time to do something, eventually allowed Liverpool to complete an amazing Treble of cups. On the other side, Henry had already been exhausted for three months, producing miracles with two defenders on his back, while Bergkamp to a certain extent, but especially Kanu and Wiltord, were disappointed by the lack of playing time. They would come on, but only for the last ten minutes. Too little, too late. No balance in the team. Great potential in midfield, but not enough workforce up front. And visible, in the huge gap at the top of the league, although Man U freewheeled to the close of the season. Arsenal remained the vice-champions, but the title had been sealed early, even before this crushing 6–1 defeat at Old Trafford: game, set and match.

WENGER'S VIEWS

After so much criticism, it's about time for Wenger to express his views, as he does every Friday at Colney, and as he did in the January 2002 issue of the *Observer Sport Monthly*: 'There is always a balance to strike, given the basic principles. For me, football is first and foremost a game. It has a framework, yet it should leave a part for freedom of expression. What drove me towards the game was the very fact that the player could express himself. It requires a certain freedom, so the framework is not too rigid. In France, nowadays, we seem to have found the right balance between the organisation and the freedom given to the player. Here, we have witnessed games between English teams but with a strong foreign element who delivered a true Brit game in the rhythm they played. When you are in a foreign country, it is always hard to find the balance between the required openness to adjust to the local culture, and teaching your own ideas in order to survive yourself and to bring more. On the other hand, if you behave exactly like local people, you don't bring anything new.'

The man who brought 'something new' to Arsenal studied economics at the University of Strasbourg, and came to Cambridge University for a summer session. This must be the main reason why he is so good at speaking English, and so well-versed in the economics of modern football. In his early years, he also played professional football for Racing Club de Strasbourg, which allowed him to get rid of people trying to bother him: 'When I was young, I had one simple trick to get rid of someone who was too much on my back: I'd tell him or her that I was a footballer. The person would instantly leave my table. Football players were considered to have such a small pea turning around in their empty head. On the contrary, if I wanted this person to stick by me, I would say I was a student. As I can see with my Arsenal players, it's quite the reverse nowadays, isn't it?'

Thirty years down the line, Wenger is still a football freak, totally committed to his job, and able to spend a whole weekend watching football games on TV and video. 'I am still obsessed with football, but I am more cool now. I only spend 90 per cent of the time in which I am awake thinking about football.' When Wenger dreams about the English game, he dreams of 'a human tide: you follow the flow or else you die. Football is a remarkable thing here. It is because of this passion that so many incredible incidents happen during games. It is also why all French players have improved over here. The English players have a certain innocence vis-à-vis the scoreline and I admire that. It is what we call the British composure [*flegm* in French], and at the same time it shows they consider the game [of football] in itself as being more important than the result. There are some remnants of this behaviour; for instance, after the match, we go and have a drink with the opposing coach. Those remnants are the proof that in the past it was like a brotherhood contest. People wanted to win, of course, but it was not a matter of life or death. Everyone accepted the result as being a component of the problem. Things are changing.'

Things are changing, and some are changing thanks to the French input: 'The symbolic shift of power happened after the England–France match at Wembley [10 February 1999] that *Les Bleus* had dominated. To come to their home and to beat them was a shock [to the English]. They suddenly understood France had overcome them.' Although Anelka, bought by Wenger, scored the two French goals that day, Wenger remains modest about his achievements in English football: 'The influence has been more noticeable thanks to the players than to the coaches. When you look at the players, it is obvious: Cantona, Ginola, now Vieira, Henry, Desailly. There has surely been a stamp of French football on English football over the last ten years.' However, Wenger is not ready to decide who is the greatest French footballer ever to play in England: 'It is very hard to tell. It would be like asking, among the musicians of today, which name will be remembered in the next century. Maybe Cantona started it all, and the rest followed. Players like Vieira and Henry are now worshipped at Arsenal.'

VIEIRA LOVES ENGLAND . . .

Vieira is worshipped, because of his dominant role in Wenger's midfield for years, and for all the right reasons. Josie is in her 70s. She is an Arsenal fan, she still runs the Arsenal Fish Bar, and she is madly in love with Patrick: 'I wrote to Arsène Wenger six times, to tell him how extraordinary Vieira is. He always answered, saying that Patrick "will be very happy to hear what you think of him". I wrote to the FA to tell them how I felt about the treatment of Patrick by the referees, although it is slightly better now. I wrote to David Dein from the US, in the summer of 2001, to tell him that he should move earth and sky to keep him aboard. He answered our prayers, as we had no midfielder since [Liam] Brady! Give him whatever he wants, he deserves every penny he gets. If he wants 100,000 pounds a week, give it to him. It would be the end if he left, lots of fans would not renew their season ticket. I am surprised that he stayed that long. With him, I feel like a mum; he is not arrogant, he is fantastic. I am going to kidnap him.'

Opponents, referees, fans, Spanish and Italian clubs, everybody is after Vieira, including the tabloid press. He calls them the 'garbage hunters', and is more than happy to elaborate on that theme: 'You don't exactly expect that when you arrive in England. In Italy, I had been under scrutiny, feeling the heat of the "mediatic pressure" because the *tifosi* badly want their team to win. Journalists are ten times more numerous than in France, but there is no comparison with England. Over here, the "garbage media" don't give a damn about the sportsman, they probably don't know much [about football] anyway, but they track you down to publish something about your private life. Gossip is their only interest. When I was suspended [in August 2000], they bribed a chap from British Telecom so they could get my number since I'm not in the directory. They also sent someone to go through my garbage, so they could see what we ate and what we threw away! Some have even offered money to my girlfriend's ex-boyfriend to know more about my life with her: was it because of me that she had left him? And there are so many examples like that. They really dig for shit!'

Still, Patrick loves it in England, he did not leave for Spain in the summer of 2001, contrary to all the reports in the press claiming that it was a done deal with Real Madrid. He is still around when I write these lines, in the summer of 2002, and he is even going to take the skipper's armband for good, due to Tony Adams's retirement, and aim for the grail of European footballers, the Champions League. Since his arrival in 1996, Vieira has been leading by example, and even Marcel Desailly himself has to admit that he asked Patrick for advice before deciding to move to England: 'Vieira was already in England [in 1998, when Desailly was holding talks with Chelsea] and he had hinted that I would very much enjoy London and the English. Patrick particularly told me about life in England, and the general behaviour of the English. If he now feels so good here, there must be a reason. There are always rumours [surrounding Vieira] but from a more personal point of view, I can tell you how much he likes England. This is a country made for him. People might say he is on his way to Italy, I know he won't go back there because he saw for himself what the country, its championship, and the everyday life are made of. Okay, there might be a bit of passion but all stadia are not full, only when it's a big game. There is a constant hassle [for the players] and a lack of respect from a certain category of supporters. Patrick has gone from one extreme to the other. He has perfectly adjusted to English culture made of openness, respect and passion.'

HENRY, THE CHIEF GUNNER . . .

Another good example is Henry, the leader of a generation of strikers that the whole world still envies France for, in spite of them not being able to score one single goal in the first round of the 2002 World Cup. When he arrived in England, in the October of 1999, Titi was following in the footsteps of his good friend Nico Anelka, gone to Real Madrid after blaming his departure on the English press and the rest of the world. What a contrast with Henry, who was seduced right away by English football and the London way of life, after six difficult months in Italy. He made it clear, right away, that he wished to stay at least 'five years in England', and started working on his game. It was like starting again from his time as a 17-year-old striker at Monaco, under the benevolent supervision of Arsène Wenger himself. Since then, the results have been well documented, Titi has scored an average of 25 goals a season in England, and added Euro 2000 to his trophy cabinet, alongside World Cup 1998. He was the best striker in the Premiership for 2001–02, the season of his first Double, after three years in the waiting room. He is considered one of the best strikers in the world, but this is not enough. He wants to keep on improving, with one image in his mind: Marco Van Basten, the Dutch legend, and the only player that he accepts as a role model.

'People often talk about Van Basten, but they only see the scorer. Van Basten is all: class, assists, he could do anything – pass with a header, play in deep, go on the flank and cross the ball; he was everything. He would often end the season as the best scorer, but you should not forget that he also gave a number of assists. The only number that I have chosen in my career is 12 in the French team, because it was Van Basten's number at Euro 88; he was a sub. It is the only number that I chose with regards to someone else, when I started with the French team.' At Arsenal, Titi plays with number 14: 'It happened like that. I was the last in the locker-room and they gave me the 14. It went well, so I kept it.'

Titi laughs and looks at his mates. It is the beginning of August 2001, in Hampstead, the London suburb where the striker lives, just like Patrick Vieira and many other French players. Thierry is at The House on the Hill, one of his favourite restaurants and, as usual, he is with his cousin Franck Nema ('Amen in reverse,' Franck quips) as well as other Parisian friends who have come to visit him and spend a few days in London. This week, the guests are French rapper Pit Baccardi and two players who were with Titi at Clairefontaine and Monaco academies: Robert Camara, who just had a trial with an English club, and Ernst Atis-Clotaire. This will not prevent Titi, between two spoonfuls of crab salad or seafood risotto, talking extensively, and quietly, about his job, while his friends take care of serious business: eating and joking.

When Thierry was younger, he used to play funny tricks, such as a nutmeg when training with Monaco. He did it once on Marseille-born Eric Di Meco, a very proud international defender: 'It's my game. If I see a guy with open legs, I do it, I can't help it, I feel obliged to do it. Sometimes the lads don't like it, it is not a question of country. If you do this to them, they have to strike back. Di Meco then gave me a serious tackle.' Di Meco did not like it, so he struck back, but Thierry did not give up on funny tricks, and he kept doing them at Juventus: 'With Edgar [Davids], we had little competitions!' Game, pleasure, fun, these words come back endlessly in Titi's sentences: 'I have more fun playing against Manchester or Liverpool, or even Leeds, than against Bradford. It is more open, they play more, and better. If you play against Manchester, the guys talk to each other, but if you play Bradford, the guys shoot from anywhere, you feel that you are going back 20 years in time. Over here, ball or not, if they can get you, they do, but it is not a question of being mean, it is their way of playing, their physical commitment, their temperament. In those games, it is not an asset to be a technical player, because the physical aspect is much more important. If you cannot impose yourself physically, it is not even worth bothering coming to play in England.'

A few years later, how does he feel that he has improved personally, by playing in English football? 'I've improved in my physical commitment, definitely. Now, even if the game goes slightly over the top, in terms of tackles and duels, I'm used to it, and I can answer that, because I've improved on the physical side. The first season I was here, I was shocked. Now, it does not bother me any more.' And how does he rate English football? 'It is good as it is. I say that because I am a striker. There is a lot of space, and it's an attacking football, so it's great to play here. But a defender might say that Italy is ideal for him, because everybody protects him, the midfielders are just in front of him, and sometimes even the strikers, so it must be easier to defend. But for me, it's good here.'

Talking to Henry about football is great, because he can't stop answering questions, and instead of piling up clichés, he prefers to reflect and analyse, avoiding generalisations. 'I don't like to talk about my life, even if you sometimes have to open yourself to the people, because they want to know, but you have to keep certain things to yourself. What I want most is to focus on my football, it's what I like most. I am not too much into going to the TV shows, and so on. I want to play, and if people like what I do on the pitch, that is the most important thing.'

In London, people appreciate what Titi does on the pitch, even if they don't support Arsenal. One day, a Tottenham supporter talked to him in the street, and told him of his admiration, very simply. But you cannot generalise, so Thierry tells a funny story: 'One day, I am at the airport and I see a couple of Tottenham fans running at me. The lift is going to close, so I put my hand, to prevent the door from shutting on them. They are in a hurry, the husband is running, he puts his hand as well, but without looking inside the lift, and his wife makes a little sign to him, raising her eyebrows. He turns back, looks at me . . . and they go to the stairs. They did not abuse me, but they did not share the lift with me.'

It is already the end of the afternoon, almost teatime. One last question is about these signs and gestures that Titi, Nico and the others do when they score a goal. For example, the V-sign, two fingers pointing at the heart: 'This sign was "yes". Nico started it, after seeing it done by a baseball player; I think it was Sami Sosa. At the beginning, everybody was going crazy about that sign. When we won Euro 2000, listen, we went to the Hotel Crillon [in Paris on the Place de la Concorde], the square was full of people, and they all shouted: "The sign, the sign!" So we did it. "Wow," everybody shouted, I can tell you.' Another sign, the connecting fingers, just like E.T: 'This came from Robert [Pires] and Sylvain [Wiltord]; you will have to ask them.'

PIRES, ALL THE WAY TO THE TOP

Enter Pires, not in the restaurant, but in this chapter: 'I don't want to be recognised as the big brother. At Arsenal, everybody has his own character. With Sylvain [Wiltord] and Pat [Vieira], we have almost the same age. Titi [Henry] is from the previous generation, the one of Nico [Anelka]. There is a good communion between all of us and everyone tries to bring his own qualities, and his own little bit of experience. What makes a group strong is that everybody has a different personality, and it works rather well for us.'

Just like Wenger, Pires is now a master of the understatement. And just like Henry, he cannot stop talking, and he also has an anecdote about Tottenham fans: 'During my first north London derby at White Hart Lane, a Tottenham fan took time to give me the ball back. When I got it, I pretended that I was going to throw it back in his face. It was a little bit of play-acting, and people liked the fact that I answered the fan, but without any aggression. It was part of the show. In the end, I laughed, people clapped their hands, even a few Spurs fans did. It was a joke, it was nice.'

Wenger also has a story about Tottenham fans: 'I meet people when I go to buy my loaf of bread or while I refill my car who say to me: "Hi, how are you? I'm sorry I'm a Tottenham supporter." Here, a man or a woman defines himself or herself by the club he or she supports. It is like belonging to a clan. English society is made of clans: it is a form of identity.'

Petit too has a story about Tottenham, dating back to his arrival: 'Monaco allowed me to go to England to talk, and that same day, President Campora [the chairman of AS Monaco] must have received an offer from Arsenal. I arrived on a Thursday, but at Tottenham, the great rival. I talked to the vice-chairman, he told me that the club wanted me, made an offer. I found it very unsatisfactory so I told them that I was going to think about it. I asked for a cab, Tottenham ordered it and paid for it . . . and I went to Arsenal with that cab. A few hours later, I signed with Arsène and the [vice-]chairman [David Dein]. I have a lot of respect for Arsène, so I appreciated that he was present. I worked with him at Monaco, and at the end it was sometimes electric between us, but then I admitted I was wrong. It was like him holding out his hand to me, and I was very pleased.'

Wenger is very good at holding out his hand to a player, whatever his origin. He did it for Kanu, after his heart problems; he did it for Henry, after a bad six-month spell in Turin; and he did it again for Pires, at the end of the nightmare of a second season at Olympique Marseille: 'When I arrived at Arsenal, it was like heaven for me. Before that, at Marseille, I had seven very tough months, for all sorts of reasons. Some fans had abused the team and the players. I had this opportunity to go to England, and Arsenal. For me, London was the ideal place, quiet and serene. Everything I heard, from players such as Emmanuel Petit and Nicolas Anelka, was very positive. And to link up with Patrick Vieira, Thierry Henry, Gilles Grimandi, Arsène Wenger, it was ideal for me to regroup, and find my shape again. Here, I can really do what I want. For me, it's the top.'

The top . . . of his profession. Pires reached it on a regular basis between June 2001 (Best Player in the Confederations Cup) and May 2002, when Arsenal completed yet another Double, thanks to his efforts all season . . . until that unfortunate game against Newcastle and the twisted knee incident. A few days after the injury, Pires was elected Footballer of the Year by the Football Writers' Association. Two months later, he was smiling on the big podium at Highbury, after the last game of the season against Everton (4–3). When he lifted the Premiership trophy, all of his teammates were bowing in front of him, to show their gratitude, as the ultimate act of allegiance to the new king with a number 7 on his back.

DIXON WRAPS IT UP . . .

Among them, good old Lee Dixon, who had just played his 619th official game with an Arsenal shirt on his back, before retiring at the end of the season. As such, he was perfectly entitled to comment on the latest achievement, and on the spirit behind it: 'The spirit of this team reminds me of the Arsenal of '89 rather than the Double-winning side of '98. I think the spirit of the English players has rubbed off on these foreign players. Many of them are now much more like English players. They have taken something from us, and we have taken a lot from them. The blend has created a quality squad.

'"Winners" are what Arsène says he is always looking for, and he handpicks his players very carefully. The emphasis is on them not only as footballers, but as people too. What he has done in five years deserves the highest praise. The revelation we have seen with Wenger, and the likes of Gérard Houllier and Sven Goran Eriksson, is that a different type of management, more cerebral, more sensitive, perhaps, can work in English football. You cannot fluke two Doubles. I grew up with the disciplinarian managers, an arm around you one day, and a rollicking the next. I'm totally convinced by the Wenger way, and I think it is a total change for the better.'

Daniel Ortelli
(with Xavier Rivoire)

CHAPTER 4

Liverpool: Houllier – A Great Mind and a Big Heart

Anfield has had lots of great nights, but this one was probably the most moving of them all: 'Gérard' was back home, back where he belongs, back from a no-man's land between life and death, to test Bill Shankly's famous words: 'Football is not a question of life and death, it's much more important than that.' As always, Gérard the perfectionist wanted to check for himself, so he almost died, of a dissection of the aorta, and then came back to life, at Anfield, for a crucial Champions League game against AS Roma, on 19 March 2002. No human being could have written a better script, so maybe the Great Director had a hand in this one.

That night at Anfield, Houllier was as white as the bedsheets had been at the Broadgreen Cardio-Thoracic Centre where he had spent two months, but he had a small light in his eyes, when he glanced at his wife, then Dr Abbas Rashid, the chief surgeon at Broadgreen, and finally to all his friends behind the bench, before sitting next to his assistant Phil Thompson, as if nothing had happened. There was also a long and warm embrace with Fabio Capello, the Roma coach, and a long look at the Kop singing 'Gérard Houllier' better than ever. The Kopites had also spread out a 12,500-piece red and white cardboard mosaic with the word 'Allez' and the famous liverbird. The lucky charm was back, and there was no way Roma were going to ruin the party.

'The Kop will sing, the Vatican bells will ring, arrivederci Roma', claimed one of the placards in the crowd. 'Aim for the moon, and we shall land in the stars', advised another one. At Liverpool FC, team orders are not taken lightly, so Steven Gerrard and Co. did the job, perfectly, and Roma went home, beaten by a couple of goals (a penalty by Jari Litmanen and a beautiful header by Emile Heskey), on a night to remember, probably forever.

'Was this the greatest night ever?' asked Paul Eaton on the Liverpool website (www.liverpoolfc.tv) the next day, and he also gave his personal view: 'It was the night no one at Anfield will ever forget, the night we qualified for the quarter-finals of the Champions League for the first time.' The answers of enthusiastic fans came pouring in, from almost everywhere in the world:

'The sight of Monsieur Houllier walking to the dug-out was enough to tell what was to come,' as *Allegro* summed up.

'I wish I'd been there. It reminded me of 1977. The best bit was when Gérard Houllier arrived on the pitch. I had tears in my eyes. When 'YNWA' ('You'll Never Walk Alone') was played at the end, my hairs stood on end,' added *Ulstersandra*.

'I live in Portland, Oregon, USA. All the way out on the west coast. We are eight hours behind there, so I had to listen to the performance over the Internet at work (I didn't get much done, naturally). Strangely enough, I could really feel the energy, even over the Internet. I felt nervous, but I could feel the crowd pressing the team on. I could feel Roma crumbling. I could feel that we were going to win it. I remember listening to a lot of Liverpool matches over the radio in the '70s when I lived in Ireland as a kid, and this match really took me back. Truly magnificent,' wrote *Msdayrocks*.

'Got up at 3.00 a.m. to watch the game live on TV here in the Philippines. The atmosphere came across brilliant . . . the tension you could feel . . . the entrance of Houllier left a lump in the throat and tears in the eyes,' wrote *Gogo*.

'I have never experienced an experience like that in my life. It was all amazing and maybe the quickest 90 minutes of my life! All in all it was simply . . . perfection,' wrote *RedAdz*.

And to bring some perspective, 'Sunglasses Ron' wrote that: 'This is what Shanks was all about. Gérard is the new Messiah. It brought tears to my eyes to see him. We owe him everything in making us so proud of our team again. Hold on tight – the ride has just begun!!!'

Twelve months earlier, the ride had already started, and Gérard and I talked extensively, in our native French language, on the morning after another quarter-final, against Porto in the UEFA Cup. We were at Melwood training ground, work was going on in the new complex, he could show us where the swimming pool was going to be, and so on. He was completely relaxed, happy with the result of the night before. He shared his views about everything from English to European football, including Italian football: 'The Italians have been very good for a long time, but there were already some signs of a decline last year. What puzzles me in Italy is this permanent chaos, this instability of the squads. You cannot feel any sort of overall strategy, of a logical approach. However, Juventus tries to bet on more stability, and Roma is a very strong team.'

Liverpool having beaten Roma in the previous round, Houllier knew what he was talking about. Then, after Porto, Liverpool eliminated Barcelona in the semis, and won the whole lot in Dortmund, their third cup in as many months, at the end of a crazy final against yet another Latin team, Deportivo Alaves. So much for the pretend weakness of the Premiership of which Houllier is a passionate advocate: 'We have had 4 English teams in the last 12 in Europe [quarter-finals of the Champions League, semi-finals of the UEFA Cup] for two years in a row [2000 and 2001]. This is not luck, it shows that the Premiership is a quality league. There is so much intensity, it's so demanding, mentally, athletically and technically, that it is the best preparation for Europe. When you play at Sunderland, it's the best way to prepare for playing in Rome, because Sunderland knows how to play football.'

Houllier knows his English football well, so I asked him to elaborate on the characteristics of his major rivals: 'Manchester United is a more compact, better-lubricated machine, with a more fluid game. They are flourishing, whereas at Liverpool we are still in a building phase. We are more solid than before, we worked a lot on this aspect of our game, but we still need to work on the efficiency. With the same half as us against

Porto, a team like Man U would score two more goals, they are more clinical. Leeds is a little bit like us, they have a potential, they are difficult to move around. But they also have a certain form of fickleness. Arsenal are more creative, they have a greater football potential. Pires and Wiltord have just arrived, they will be even stronger next year.'

Again, Houllier was spot on when he talked of Pires' and Wiltord's success, one year in advance. But not only is he a visionary coach, he is also a great tactician; it's one of his fortes: 'In my team, I have them playing 4-5-1, traditional 4-4-2, yesterday we did 4-2-3-1 from the beginning. I work on the tactical flexibility of the team, we can change immediately if the other side starts playing 3-5-2. There is false prejudice about the English tactical rigidity, they have evolved. They keep the same philosophy, but it is possible to change a game plan without changing the style.'

Mikaël Silvestre, now at Man U, remembers when Houllier was the coach of a gang of young French footballers with names such as Thierry Henry and David Trezeguet: 'For me, he was the first coach to go so much into detail, he was very meticulous. The set pieces, the blackboard, we could spend a whole session on free-kicks and combinations, first on the paper, and then on the pitch. Even in Italy, where I had four different coaches, they did not go that far into detail. He was a teacher, you could see that, and I think that he applies a method. After missing World Cup 1994 [when France failed to qualify following two disastrous performances at home to Israel and Bulgaria in the autumn of 1993] he was looking for some sort of revenge. He started from scratch, with youngsters; it was different. We had super strikers, but we were not especially offensive or defensive. There was no big mouth in the group, we knew he had some experience behind him, he had managed Paris SG, we respected him. Everything went well, we won the European Championship, it was a good way to start again, for him.'

Under Houllier, the Under-18s won their own Euro in Besançon, ten years after Houllier's last trophy, the French title with Paris SG. They continued to shine at the World Under-20s Championship, in Malaysia, were beaten by Brazil (3–0) in the first match, but made it to the quarter-finals and lost a penalty shoot-out to Uruguay. Young Nicolas Anelka, 17, missed his penalty and then blamed the whole failure on Houllier's coaching, although Gérard had been brave enough to play Anelka, Henry and Trezeguet in the same team. Anyway, Houllier was hoping to continue with the same age group and manage the Under-21s. It did not happen: 'Had they given me the Under-21s, I would not have left for Liverpool.' Instead of that, Houllier got back to his office, and planned the French triumph at the 1998 World Cup, as a national technical director. Even today, at Melwood, he sits down every morning under a huge picture of four hands, his and Aimé Jacquet's, holding up the World Cup.

'I don't believe so much in a charismatic leader. A coach is not only someone who motivates players, but rather someone creating the ideal conditions for motivation. Our role is to create an atmosphere, an environment, a spirit, for players to express themselves. So that only by looking at the quality of the pitch, they want to train. It's all about the people around them, the facilities. Before the World Cup in France, we refurbished the offices [at the French Football Federation], and the secretaries worked better, it struck me. Even the people who are in charge of the material environment participate in the motivation of players.'

When Houllier arrived at Liverpool in 1998, and started as a co-manager with Roy Evans, there was a lot more to do than just refurbish the offices. David Fairclough, the Red supersub of the late 1970s, recalls that 'before his arrival, Liverpool, as a club, was somewhat lax, the players were having a good time. With [Graeme] Souness, there was discipline, but when Evans took charge, everything went down the drain, the injured players did what they wanted. Houllier's arrival suddenly meant more professionalism, the start of the twenty-first century. The supporters accepted that very well, whereas previous coaches, such as Souness and Evans, did not seem to touch the fans in the same way.' 'Focus', according to Fairclough, is Houllier's most French quality. 'The British never were as focused as the French or the Europeans. Houllier brought his sense of detail, his culture of work, this application that the players can see every day. Houllier is at the training ground every day, and nothing is left to fate. Everybody likes him here, starting with the gardeners at Anfield.'

At Anfield or Melwood, everybody speaks English, and the gaffer leads by example, when he asks 'Everything all right?' to French players or journalists who cross his path. 'There are quite a few foreigners,' says French World Cup winner Bernard Diomède, 'so it is important to speak

English. When I am with Pegguy [Arphexad, the French reserve keeper], and if Emile [Heskey] is around, we speak English. The coach was very clear about that, right from the beginning.' Diomède continues: 'Houllier kept his way of looking at things. He watched, and little by little, he is changing things which appear fundamental to him. But he leaves a certain leeway and the English coaches also have their say, so he is not alone in changing things. I don't think it is like that everywhere in England. A guy like [Phil] Thompson is very strict, so they get along well. He found an Englishman who is slightly French.'

'I am an Anglophile, but I am not a revolutionary,' reckons Houllier, 'I try to convince rather than impose. We have a clever mix of English and foreign players, who know each other well, who get along well, a sort of unity in the team, a very good staff behind them. It is important to find, and keep, this balance between English and foreign players, especially here. In London, it may be different. I have a very eclectic staff, everybody is in the right spot. A foreigner working in a foreign country has to be very strong, because there will be no mercy. The most important is the trust of the board.' As soon as he arrived, Houllier made sure that he would eventually win over the board, and soon ended up the only chef in charge of the Liverpool kitchen, but with a lot on his plate.

"There were some difficult moments. We had to digest the end of the first season, and sack some of the buggers ['Governor' Paul Ince was one of them, and his anger at Houllier was splashed over all the tabloids]. There were some orthodox things that had to be jostled, mentalities that had to be changed. This is not a job where you can develop self-assurance. The first summer here, I had twelve million pounds to spend, so if I bought for fifteen I had to sell for three. I looked to recruit within the financial limits that were set for me. There is no striker under ten million, that's the way it is. In the summer of 1999, seven foreigners came, but as soon as I could sell, I bought Heskey and Barmby. I was the only one to buy English.'

Houllier knew exactly what he was doing, right from the beginning: 'I knew the history of the club. I lived here in 1969. I was a French lecturer, I wrote a thesis here, entitled "Growing up in a deprived area". At that time, Everton was in better shape than Liverpool. Here, with football, you touch 95 per cent of the people. The only thing is that you have to announce your colour: blue or red. Here, some players are "blue". Two years ago, [Jamie] Carragher got off the pitch and turned to a guy who takes care of players, but supports Everton. He asked him: "Do we stay [in the Premiership]?" Sometimes, I meet people who tell me: "It is a problem, because in our family there are Liverpool and Everton supporters, for life." Even with [Nick] Barmby, who is from Yorkshire, there was some controversy when he came from Everton.'

'Players like Carragher, Owen and Gerrard are children of Liverpool. For Houllier, it is very interesting to build his team around people like that,' says French football historian Claude Boli. 'In the long term, it will be interesting to work on Houllier, because he knows the background, the history of the family, the club, the city; he is like a remote cousin. He tried not to change everything, to bring his French Touch, but without doing a French Connection. His dream was to have German, English, French and Czech players, a European club but Reds-style. Because at Anfield, the people want to see the Reds, not the rainbow.'

Houllier tried to buy French players, but apart from Jean-Michel Ferri's brief passage, and Bernard Diomède, who never got the chance of a long run in the team, most of them were contacted in vain: Thierry Henry, Olivier Dacourt and Mikaël Silvestre, among others, had talks with Houllier, and then they signed respectively for Arsenal, Leeds and Manchester United. 'The club tried to sign Marcel Desailly before I came,' Houllier confirms. 'I tried Laurent Blanc, but Robert Louis-Dreyfus [then the president of Olympique Marseille] did not want to let him go, and Marseille had a good season. I did not need Karembeu. I would have been interested by [Robert] Pires, but Arsène [Wenger, Arsenal's manager] had already progressed with him, and I was not going to play a bad trick on a friend. It is also a question of opportunities. I like Didier Deschamps, and he would have helped me to save one year in the process, thanks to his maturity. Instead of taking a Deschamps, I took a Biscan [Igor, a Croatian].'

Some were signed, but rarely played, such as Diomède: 'Bernard was unlucky, he started well and then he got injured. When he came back, he had to undergo surgery. He is in the train, with us, he has great physical qualities, he is very skilful in front of goal, and he has a good attitude. It is a question of opportunity and patience. But in football, things go very fast. God knows, maybe he will be the hero next season.' Others were signed, but got impatient and tried to play it clever against Houllier. Bad idea: 'Titi Camara tried to be smart, the Kop liked him, but it all turned against him. He told me: "I don't want to play any more." Bye bye! We waited . . . and nobody came, except West Ham! It is true that I can be ruthless if the guy tells me that he does not want to play for Liverpool any more.' Houllier also had an argument with Christian Ziege. Not surprisingly, the German was the one who left, not the Frenchman.

Asked about the French Revolution, Houllier dates it back to Eric Cantona, of course, and points to a couple of other landmarks, Wenger and Wembley: 'For me, the revolution, the French Touch, is first and foremost Cantona. He showed the difference between training and practice. He opened the doors, because he was successful at Leeds and then at Manchester. The first foreign coach was Josef Venglos at Aston Villa. Then came Arsène at Arsenal, all the way from Japan. Arsène's Double sent shockwaves through English football. The Wembley game [England–France 0–2 in February 1999] was a revelation. I had five Liverpool players in the [England] team. They came back with *le moral dans les chaussettes* [literally: morale low down in the socks]. This was after the World Cup, England had gone out after a penalty shoot-out [against Argentina, for those who don't remember]. It looked like a bit of bad luck, so the English still thought that they were strong enough. But they lost 2–0, at home in Wembley, after a Zidane–Anelka demonstration.'

As an expert in international football, and a regular member of UEFA and FIFA technical commissions, Houllier also provides a new angle, and a wider scope to the debate: 'The foreign revolution really came from Middlesbrough, because they bought lots of foreign players. As they did not train properly, the guys were unhappy and started opening their mouths in the press. When a player like Ravanelli says: "Training is not right," and when the team is relegated at the end of the season, this must have led certain clubs to think that maybe something has to be done.'

Talking about the limits of training at Middlesbrough is clever, because it prevents Houllier from criticising the Liverpool set-up when he arrived. This should rather be done by Professor John Williams, sociologist and Liverpool fan, who wrote *Into the Red* among other football books. Professor Williams knows his Liverpool as well as Prof. Houllier knows his football, and is always ready to give some interesting insight about Houllier's arrival at Anfield. The last occasion was a football conference in London, entitled 'Two failures = One success', about French successes in English football, at the Institut Français in May 2002.

'When Houllier arrived, he was appalled by the lack of connection between training and play, and part of his argument was to say that English players seem to think that training was something that you did in between matches, to fill in the time, and that there was no connection between doing things in training and what you will do on the field. He was amazed by the talent of Michael Owen, but appalled by the quality of coaching that Owen had had with the club. Owen arrived at the club as a child, with three great strengths: he was very fast, very strong on his right side, and he was nerveless in front of goal, even as a young boy.'

Williams continued his argument: 'When Houllier arrived at the club, Owen was on the brink of the first team, but he was still a raw talent. What Houllier has done with Owen is to make him work on his left side, on his heading, and he is now a good header of the ball, although he is rather small. Houllier refused to accept this as an excuse. He said that he had to learn to head the ball. He is now a terrific header of the ball, and Houllier is now keen to prepare Owen for the time when his pace will not be as good, and he will play in a withdrawn role. He has begun to add a repertoire of skills to Owen.'

Not only does Houllier help Owen to improve, he also looks after every detail of Michael's job. A few days before the 2001 FA Cup final, Owen was training at Melwood with a brand new pair of Umbro boots. Gérard saw that and told him: 'You just cannot wear these boots for the final, you have to keep those which allowed you to score all your goals.'

Michael answered: 'But I feel really good with them, better than in the old ones!' Later, Owen explained: 'First, I thought he was joking, but then he really insisted, so I decided to keep the old ones. We won the Cup, so he must have been right. After the game, the first thing he told me was: "I told you, these boots bring you luck."'

Owen scored both goals of a 2–1 win, in the last seven minutes, with his old boots. Then Houllier justified his piece of advice: 'It has nothing to do with superstition. There is a technical reason for not using new boots in a big game, because you can get blisters on your feet. I learnt that from Michel Platini.'

With Houllier and Owen, we eventually get to the core of the matter: the huge input of the French master with a big English heart in the renaissance of the England team. If Sven Goran Eriksson deserves to be knighted for services to English football, then the least Gérard Houllier can expect is an OBE. The roots of England's renaissance can be found in France as much as in Sweden, and while no one doubts the positive influence that Eriksson has had on the young squad, Houllier has also played his part in the national team's renovation.

In September 2001, Robbie Fowler's goal against Albania was the seventh consecutive international strike by one of Houllier's men. No wonder, then, why the red half of Merseyside suggested, at that time, that the last two England scorelines should have read: Germany 1, Liverpool 5; and Liverpool 2, Albania 0. At that crucial time for England, in the qualification campaign for World Cup 2002, Houllier's players were beginning to exert the same kind of influence as the Liverpool stars of old. Eventually, one month later, a Man U player, David Beckham, clinched the valuable ticket for Asia at the end of the Greece game (2–2), but he could have thanked his Liverpool teammates for all the good work done beforehand, especially against Germany in Munich.

Faced with the choice of watching his native country play a friendly against Chile, or England take on Germany, Houllier opted for his adopted nation. He told Alex (Hayes) a few days later: 'I was in Paris with some friends on the night of the Germany–England match, so I took them to the offices of *L'Equipe* to watch the game on the big screen. Well, I'll tell you what, it was really exciting. Whenever one of my players scored for England, I felt as if they were scoring for Liverpool. All my friends were saying, "God, your players are good." When you hear compliments like that, you can't help but feel extremely proud.'

Houllier is proud, but modest, and he tries to shy away from any personal praise. However, much of the renewed Red vigour can be attributed to his intelligent style of management. Whether it be nursing Steven Gerrard through injury, moving Jamie Carragher to left-back, honing Emile Heskey's raw talents, keeping Robbie Fowler on the straight and narrow for a long while before eventually losing patience and selling him to Leeds, making Nick Barmby a better right-footed left-midfielder, or filling the boy-wonder – Michael Owen – with the confidence he needs, the Frenchman left an indelible mark on the England pre-World Cup set-up. Unfortunately, a series of injuries – Gerrard, but also Jamie Carragher and Danny Murphy – prevented the Red contingent from being much stronger in Asia.

'Sven is the one doing a great job,' Houllier added, and he admitted that there were some parallels between Liverpool and Club England. 'I think that Sven has tried to mirror what we've done here. He's attempting to create a good atmosphere and a positive environment for the players. I'm all for that because I know it works. As a club manager in this country, I want England to do well. It is not my duty to help the national team, but I am very happy to see England getting close to reaching the World Cup finals next summer [2002]. I think it has a very positive effect. You always want your national team to do well, because there is nothing worse than your players coming back from internationals really depressed.'

So far as Houllier is concerned, success breeds success, and it is perhaps no surprise that the young English players who form the backbone of his Liverpool team have blossomed on the international stage at the same time. 'I always said that I wanted the core of my team to be English,' he explained. 'So I guess it is rather flattering for me to see that policy be rewarded by so many of my players being selected for the national side. But England are lucky, you know. Not many countries have such a wonderfully talented generation of players between the ages of 19 and 24. I can name 40 who are good players, and at least 20 who are good internationals. That is very rare.' Then Houllier quoted some names: 'Frank Lampard, Joe Cole, Jonathan Woodgate, Lee Bowyer and Alan Smith. It's incredible how many promising talents England possess.'

Back to Professor Williams, with an interesting parallel between Houllier and Wenger, in their Anglophile component: 'The reason why they come to England in the first place, particularly for Houllier, is that there are things about English football that they deeply admire, that they feel are lacking in French football. They are very much Anglophiles, they are very committed and interested in English football culture. One day, Houllier visited Liverpool to spy on players while he was still a club manager in France. He came to watch a European club match, and he said to a young French coach: "There is something fantastic about where the stadium is, the passion of the people for the game, and the fact that there is a very strong working-class local community interest in the sport."

'The kind of passion of both the public and the players for the game here seems to be the main attraction for both Wenger and Houllier.

Houllier said to me: "In France, the players may be better and more technically educated, and you may be able to have conversations with them, but they don't have the heart, and it's wonderful to come and work with players who have this real belief in their local club, and to introduce them to new ideas." What is interesting is that both these managers bring a very English style to their club. Plenty of people in Liverpool were not happy with the style of play Houllier brought, they did not see an intellectual, Continental influence. They saw a very direct, very scientific, very well-prepared approach, but they did not see poetry, people re-inventing the game, an intellectual's input in the way they imagined. What we get is a very organised team, which is kind of interesting.'

An organised team is often the best option to win trophies, especially if its defence is awesome, such as Liverpool's during season 2000–01 and 2001–02. It's even better when the manager makes sure that players rotate, especially up front, so as to cope with 50-plus games a season. 'Freshness comes from managing it,' Houllier stresses. 'The press uses the term rotation, I never use it. The idea is to be cautious, to see the signs when the player begins going down, to take into account the development of the player. It's also a question of tactics, to make sure that the players don't spend too much time running after the ball.'

'The amount of work that Gérard can do is fantastic. He is very conscious of what works better, tactically, for the team and for each player,' acknowledges Patrice Bergues, his long-time friend.

'Patrice came over with his "yoghurt pot", a Fiat 500, when I lived here, in September 1969,' Houllier recalls. More than 30 years later, Bergues was Houllier's number 2 and next to him on the bench when Liverpool won three cups in three months. He then became the general manager of RC Lens, the most English of French clubs.

Houllier continues: 'Here, at this club, tradition is to bring back silverware, I realised that when we won the Worthington Cup. It's in the culture of the club, but I would be very disappointed if we did not manage to qualify for the next Champions League. My priority was the League last year and will be the League again this time around. But it's not just me saying that. Players like Michael Owen are also desperate to win the Premier League with Liverpool. As a foreigner, this has particularly struck me, because I would have thought that winning big European trophies was the dream for most, but my players are more interested in the domestic titles. I can tell you, they were happier to win the FA Cup than the UEFA Cup in May [2001].'

Every year in August, *The Guardian* publishes 'The Season, a supporter's guide'. For 2000–2001, in the Liverpool section, there was an interesting recommendation, in the 'Hot seat' column dedicated to managers: 'Job security: Houllier starts on safe ground, but he has spent a lot of money and will be expected to deliver at least a cup this season. Failure – anything but Champions League qualification and a decent cup run – could prove fatal.' On the same page, Steven Gerrard added: 'We must do better in the cup competitions. You watch the FA Cup and the other trophies being handed out and I just know it would be brilliant to be part of a Liverpool team that collected something. That's what I am aiming for.'

Promised, and delivered. One year later, the trophy room at Anfield was filled with five new items of silverware, and a Champions League spot on the top of it all: the League Cup, the FA Cup, the UEFA Cup, the Charity Shield and the European Super Cup, against Bayern Munich (3–1), as a prelude to that amazing Munich night. 'England benefited from our good win against Bayern Munich, and we always benefit when the players are on a high from their time with England. It works both ways,' Houllier stresses. It was still working at the end of the year [2001], when Owen, thanks to his amazing year with Liverpool and England, became the European Footballer of the Year, elected by the . . . *France Football* jury. England, France, it's a never-ending story.

At that time, Houllier was in Corsica, recovering from his 11-hour heart operation, with his friend Guy Roux, the Auxerre manager, who also had a heart problem a few weeks after him. 'We were like two pensioners,' Houllier joked later. Actually, he had never stopped joking, even on that mid-October day, when he felt pain in his chest at half-time, during the Leeds game, and wanted to talk to the club doctor, Mark Waller, in the treatment room: 'Unfortunately, he was looking at Emile Heskey who had been injured, so I went back into the dressing-room. It felt worse, but not unbearable. When I returned to the treatment room, he was still with Emile. We actually had a bit of a laugh and a joke. I said: "Don't worry, he is worth more money than me, but I am more urgent." As the doc looked at me, Emile was peering up with worried eyes at what was going on. He has since told one of my friends that he did not sleep that night.'

Houllier was then rushed to hospital, and operated on from 7 p.m. to 6 a.m. by 'an absolutely brilliant team, led by a wonderful surgeon, Abbas Rashid, with support from Elaine Griffiths, Dr Jim Murphy and Dr Rod Stables', in Gérard's own words. In terms of timing, there was also a little help from upstairs, as Houllier was supposed to fly to Kiev the next day for a Champions League clash against Dynamo, and nobody seems to know whether Ukrainian hospitals are used to performing urgent operations to repair dissections of the aorta. 'Let's just say that somebody up there must like me. I personally feel I was in the right place with the right people with the right expert hands. It was not luck that things happened the way they did. It was fate.'

When Houllier recovered, he also told the tale of the two Robbies, one being the nurse who was on duty on his first night of intensive care, and the other a famous Liverpool player, named Fowler, who scored a hat-trick at Leicester (4–1) on 20 October, an original way to send a message to his French coach in his hospital bed. He also explained how, four days later, he got permission to watch Boavista v. Liverpool on the condition that his blood pressure would be taken regularly, to monitor his heartbeat. The doctor called just after the Danny Murphy goal, to check if everything was fine. He had two nurses with him: 'There was David the Liverpool fan, and an Evertonian called Brian. I couldn't believe it. Everton and Liverpool, with all the banter.'

The whole Houllier situation also had an interesting consequence: Liverpool chairman David Moores, who very rarely goes public, reacted on the official website to his manager's illness, by telling of his 'admiration' for the man in a revealing interview: 'He's a real fighter, a real battler. He said to me before he went in [the op room] that he's got a job to finish here and he's only halfway through it. He'll be back. We want him around for a long time to come. The Liverpool supporters know their football and they know just how good a job he's done, and how much work has gone into doing that job. He's as passionate a man as I've ever met in any walk of life, never mind just football. His passion for this club and his love of this club is something I just don't think many people realise. His ideal, he's said to me, is to produce *the* best Liverpool side ever. That is his number one priority.'

The difference with other clubs, is that Houllier wants to achieve this by using his mind and his work, rather than the money in the Liverpool

FC bank account. It's another sort of challenge, and he was ready to face it in May 2002, when he explained that 'money doesn't mean everything in football. I know Manchester United, Arsenal and Chelsea will spend to improve, but we have to think differently if we are to go forward again. And we will do it. My riches are already in my team. Half of the team are under 24, many are going to the World Cup and there would have been more but for injury. These players will develop. They have progressed this season. When you don't have the same amount of money to spend, you just need to be clever when you buy, which is what I've always tried to be with players like Sami Hyypiä and Stéphane Henchoz. Even last summer, not many people had heard of John Arne Riise. To be clever is to be on the go all the time. Nicolas Anelka was a good signing, that proved a good move for us. That's how I spent my Christmas.' For the record, Houllier then spent more than £20m in the summer of 2002.

Back to Corsica then, where the 'old pensioner' Houllier, recovering from a long heart operation, met Anelka, the young rebel, somewhere around Ajaccio, just before Christmas 2001. The loan was then agreed, thanks to Houllier's good relations with his former club, and Nico got back on track, scoring 5 goals in 22 games, and repeating week after week that he was 'so happy' at Liverpool, that he could 'walk in the streets without being bothered', and so pleased that he could score again. He even smiled on the pitch, and almost made it to the World Cup with the French team. At the end of the season, Anelka wanted to stay, Liverpool were interested in buying him, and everything looked rather smooth and easy, for the first time in Anelka's career . . . until Houllier asked for extra time, a few more days to think about his final decision. Then came the answer: 'No.'

Didier Anelka is one of Nicolas's brothers. In a special edition of *But*, the French football tabloid, dated June 2002, he gave his version of Houllier's change of mind: 'Nicolas called me on a Monday morning. He was disappointed, because it was a surprise for us. A bad surprise for Nicolas, but also for Paris St Germain. Luis Fernandez [Paris SG's manager] counted on this transfer to build his team for next season. Gérard Houllier had even said that Nicolas was his priority, so we did not expect such a decision. I don't think it's that bad for Nicolas. We know his qualities, he felt good at Liverpool and helped the team to move up to second place in the league.'

Then Didier elaborated, explaining that 'Houllier's attitude had been strange for a while,' but that he was 'confident, because Nicolas did a very good second part of the season, scoring six goals [five in fact; four in the league, and one in the FA Cup]. His integration was good. For the last meal at Liverpool, Gérard hardly talked to Nicolas, acting as if he was already in the team for next season. If he did not want him, why did he act without talking to us? Even the players, when they left, thought that Nicolas would be back in July. Houllier had confirmed that an agreement had been reached with Paris and the player.'

Didier also acknowledged that 'there were negotiations about the salary. We had a discussion, it's normal. But the problem was solved, we had a deal, everything was normal. I have no explanation. Houllier surely needs another striker, but he did not want someone who would have cast a shadow on Michael Owen and Emile Heskey, who are English. That's what Nico would have done.' There we are. The ultimate element of proof, coming from one of the Anelka brothers, and the reason why, probably, Houllier stalled on the transfer, at the last minute: Nicolas Anelka is not a team player, not yet, and six months at Liverpool were not long enough for him to become one.

We can only speculate, because Houllier will never tell us the truth about his decision, but after he almost died for the club of his life, because of too much passion for his job, too much work, not enough sleep, he surely had second thoughts about setting the foxes to mind the geese, in a Liverpool farm that he had taken so much care to clean up. After a good transfer, and with a long-term contract, anything was possible with the Anelka brothers, and the odds were not good. You always marry for 'better or worse', but with the Anelka family, the worst happens more often than the best. You only have to look at Arsenal, Real Madrid and Paris SG, these past few years. Anelka created chaos and controversy in all of them, and they are big clubs.

It's one thing to choose Puma boots because your team has a deal with Nike, and you want to be singled out, or to drive a Ferrari when the main sponsor offers you an Opel, free of charge, because you love fast cars and can afford to buy one. It's much more serious when a footballer, within a couple of years, manages to fall out with two coaches who really cared for him, such as Arsène Wenger and Luis Fernandez. It is just impossible that Houllier did not think of that before signing for Anelka's transfer fee and offering him a contract that Nicolas had been hoping to sign since the beginning of March, according to his own personal website.

At that time, Houllier may have had other strikers on his mind, such as Frédéric Kanouté (West Ham), another Frenchman, who was likely to be cheaper than Anelka. Last but not least, Houllier was more interested in finding wide players anyway, who could play on the sides of the Liverpool frontline and provide options, such as crosses and assists for Owen and Heskey, rather than trying desperately, in the same position, to score more goals than the two England internationals. This is the most logical explanation, and Houllier, being from the country of Descartes, is a very logical man. So he bought El-Hadji Diouf, the Senegalese star who had flourished at Lens and was warmly recommended by his friend Bergues, the general manager of the French club.

Will Diouf and Bruno Cheyrou, a £5m signing from Lille, add more to the team than Anelka? Time will tell, but for a series of reasons, Nicolas was not the best candidate for this job: too expensive, not versatile enough (he does not like to play in midfield or on the wing, whereas Diouf does not mind), too unpredictable, and coming with a lot of baggage.

There were strong words for the fans, from a man who once said that he would prefer to play in an empty stadium. There were few thanks for Houllier, who had held out his hand to Anelka, when he was stuck so deep in his Paris hole, and when no club in Europe was interested. On the whole, the strategy was good, but not good enough. Once the Anelka matter was cleared, Houllier continued his holiday.

The former French lecturer then came back to Merseyside to pick up an honorary doctorate in law from the University of Liverpool. A few days later, he was spotted at the French Embassy in London, coming out of a ceremony with a brand new title: Chevalier de la Légion d'Honneur, the highest civil honour for a French citizen and the equivalent of a knighthood. It was the 200th anniversary of an institution created by Emperor Napoléon Bonaparte, so, again, as often in Houllier's career, timing was perfect. 'It is the proudest personal honour I have received. I am pleased and proud because it is recognition for a career that has been spent in both England and France. That is why I wanted it to be presented to me at the French Embassy in London. I am French by heart and by nationality, but I have spent much of my working life in England

and Liverpool. I like the people very much and I consider myself an adopted scouser.' The man has such a big heart, no wonder he was adopted by the people of Merseyside. And the battle between the two best French coaches in England continues: Wenger was also awarded the Légion d'Honneur in July 2002: 1–1!

Daniel Ortelli

CHAPTER 5

Chelsea: A Bridge Too Far?

Soon after Sir Alex Ferguson had transformed his team with the signing of Eric Cantona, most other clubs decided that a sprinkling of French players could only lead to glory. Witness Arsène Wenger, who, long before he was released from his contract with the Japanese side Nagoya Grampus Eight to take formal charge at Arsenal, had instructed the club to buy a young kid called Patrick Vieira. A year later, he brought his long-time protégé Emmanuel Petit over from Monaco, and then pinched the 17-year-old goal-scoring sensation, Nicolas Anelka, from under Paris St Germain's nose.

Chelsea, too, realised the importance of the Gallic flair and invested in a number of French stars. Five have come and gone since the summer of '96, when England hosted the European Championships, and football in the Premiership finally seemed cool. And all five have had very different experiences in the blue of Chelsea: some good (like the two FA Cups and the Cup-Winners' Cup), some not so good (like the defeats to St Gallen and Hapoel Tel Aviv), some promising, and some frankly disappointing. None, though, has been dull.

BIG-TIME FRANKY

First to join the Stamford Bridge revolution was Frank Leboeuf. The 35-year-old, who ended his five-year stay at Stamford Bridge in the summer of 2001 before signing for his home-town club of Marseille, remembers the day he was called by the then Chelsea assistant manager, Graham Rix, and offered the chance to join the Blues. 'I was in England with the French team for Euro '96, when Graham rang. He spoke French because he had played for Caen in the late 1980s and he just said to me: "Hey, I'm Ruud Gullit's number 2 at Chelsea and we would like you to join us. What do you think?" So I asked him: "Go on, tell me more." I mean, I didn't even know where Chelsea was. I thought it was a small town near London. I had never been to England before the European Championships. So Graham told me that Chelsea was a chic neighbourhood, that the club was going places with players such as Mark Hughes, Dan Petrescu, Dimitri Kharine and David Rocastle. I don't know, the prospect seemed attractive and I was hooked. They had just signed Gianluca Vialli and I thought: "Yeah, they're really keen to do something good here." So I signed.'

It was not long before the new kid on the block had his nickname: 'Lovely Boy'. It was not long, either, before the way Gullit's Chelsea played had its own label: 'Sexy Football'. 'For 18 months,' Leboeuf recalls, 'that's exactly what it was – great, attractive football.' Not that Leboeuf could have predicted such an outcome after his first Premiership match against Southampton – a 0–0 draw at The Dell. 'God I remember that game,' he says. 'Here I was playing in front of 15,000 delirious fans, all crammed into this small cauldron. Just as the match kicked off, I heard the crowd go wild and I had to give myself a couple of slaps on the face. "Don't let yourself get taken in by the whole atmosphere," I thought. Trust me, it wasn't easy.'

If Leboeuf thought that was tough, he had another thing coming. His baptism at Stamford Bridge was even more memorable. 'We played Fabrizio Ravanelli's Middlesbrough and won 1–0. Robbie Di Matteo scored the goal and, afterwards, he dived onto the ground with his head resting in his hand. Lots of the players joined him on the turf and copied his actions. People suddenly realised we were a bunch of guys who were going to entertain. The Chelsea legend was born there and then.'

Soon, Leboeuf's performances were being noted by the media. 'Because I was unknown and hurting no one, the tabloids decided to get hold of me. Sometimes I would not play all that well, and yet the papers would do double-page spreads on me. I think a lot of neutrals were getting excited about Chelsea's potential; I think there was a sense that we might be a new, fresh face in the hierarchy of English football. As for me, I feel that I surprised a few people. I'm not sure they had seen many *liberos* who could play confidently. It was clear early on that I would not be able to match a lot of my opponents with my heading ability or body strength, but I proved that I could get by if I anticipated well and used my superior technique.'

Gullit's eclectic mix was quick to produce results. By the end of Leboeuf's first season, Chelsea were heading to Wembley for an FA Cup final against Middlesbrough. Chelsea won 2–0 and, to this day, that remains Leboeuf's favourite memory of his five years in England. 'It was my first ever Cup final, the weather was incredible, the crowd was fantastic, and then, after the final whistle, Pelé came and embraced me. Pelé! I was like a kid. I've still got the picture at home. In so many ways, this meeting with the greatest footballer of all time summed up why I loved England. Had I stayed at Strasbourg, I doubt Pelé would have been watching me play. But at Chelsea, anything was possible.'

Anything in the domestic Cup competitions, that is. Leboeuf won three more trophies at Wembley – the League Cup in 1998, and then the FA Cup and Charity Shield in 2000. 'The first FA Cup win in 1997 was particularly special,' Leboeuf explains, 'because it was the club's first trophy for over 20 years. The guys, like Peter Osgood, who had won the FA Cup and Cup-Winners' Cup in 1970–71 were legends. The supporters had waited 27 years for more success, so, when it came, you can imagine that there were a lot of emotions towards us: respect, glory . . .' And jealousy? 'Yes, I think that there were some people who didn't like the fact that we were having fun and winning trophies.'

The fun, though, ended almost as abruptly as it had started one day in February 1998. Gullit went into a meeting with the then managing director, Colin Hutchinson, to discuss possible transfers, and came out with his P45. More shocking still, Vialli was named as the new player-manager. Leboeuf recalls how, almost overnight, his relationship with the Italian changed dramatically. Suddenly, 'Luca' and 'Franky' were no longer the two jokers in the pack. One was now the boss. And that boss was making decisions his old friend did not approve of. 'One of the first things Gianluca tried to do was make us stay in a hotel the night before home matches,' Leboeuf explains. 'We all kicked up a fuss and the idea was quickly abandoned.'

Like all good Frenchmen, Leboeuf liked to have his say. It made for good copy during his time in England, but it also got the defender into trouble. Leboeuf's repetitive outbursts also embodied everything that has been wrong with Chelsea in the last few seasons. The club's fun, carefree image has been fine when everything is going well, but it has demonstrated a lack of internal discipline at all other times. Claudio Ranieri, the Italian currently in charge at the Bridge, has tightened things up a little since he took over in November 2000, but the dissenters remain. Witness the decision by several of the club's senior players, including Emmanuel Petit and Marcel Desailly, to stay at home for the UEFA Cup second round match against Hapoel Tel Aviv in November 2001. Somehow you doubt Sir Alex Ferguson would have allowed such chaos at Manchester United.

Leboeuf, though, is unrepentant. 'I have never minced my words,' he admits. 'It has caused me problems in France and in England, but that's life. I just happen to think that I am right to be honest with my feelings. Not many footballers are. Most prefer to keep their mouths shut and go with the flow. I can't be a hypocrite. The few times I have been, it has really embarrassed me.' Leboeuf became such a recognisable figure during his time in the Premiership that he was a regular columnist for *The Times*, became one of only a handful of foreign footballers to speak at the Oxford Union (others include such luminaries as Pelé and Maradona), and was invited no fewer than three times to 10 Downing Street. 'I don't believe any other French players have ever been invited there,' he says proudly. 'I think I was approached because I made an effort and tried to immerse myself fully into the English way of life.'

Leboeuf adds: 'I love everything about the English system: the education, the sense of respect and duty, but also the sporting attitudes. In a sense, that is perhaps my greatest disappointment at Chelsea. When I first joined the club, everything was done *à la British*. OK, the manager was a Dutchman, but he was very much an Anglophile. We were less caught up in tactics and the like, and that was what I loved. That was the reason why I came to England. In more recent years, Chelsea have tried to be a Continental club, which I think is a mistake. I would say that is part of the reason why I left.'

Leboeuf might not have marked English football in the same way as his fellow Marseille-born friend, Eric Cantona, but he did unquestionably pave the way for the arrival of several big names from France. And he did also move to London before it was fashionable to do so. 'Let's not forget that when I first came to England in 1996, the pound was exchanged at FF 7.50,' he says. 'It was the end of the economic crisis but it was not all bright. London is now the international financial centre, all those who were living in New York, working on Wall Street, are now coming to the City. For now, London is the stronghold. Most of the [French] people have moved to London because they found a way to make big money and to pay less tax. It was not my case since when I came I discussed my salary in net figures and the question of tax was not raised. I didn't even ask myself the question. It was not the point. We understood we were better off over here. When you look at the rise in currency, you know you're better off in England than in France, where the currency stays at a low level. Those coming over knew why they were moving.'

All in all, Franky had a good time in England. 'Hey, you know, I came to Chelsea as an unknown player with no silverware,' he says, 'and I left a World and European champion, and a household name. I think you'd have to term my time in England a personal success.'

MR MARCEL

The case of Marcel Desailly is less clear-cut. Unlike Leboeuf, Desailly came to Chelsea with a big profile and a cabinet laden with trophies and medals. Like Leboeuf, though, the current French captain clearly believed that Chelsea were going places. Indeed, Desailly signed for the Blues more than a month before *Les Bleus* had achieved their historic triumph in the World Cup final on 12 July 1998. He genuinely wanted to be part of the Chelsea ride. 'I remember having different emotions,' he says of the moment the £5.5m transfer was completed at the French training centre of Clairefontaine outside Paris. 'On the one hand I was very sad to be leaving AC Milan and ending my Italian adventure, but on the other, I was very excited about the prospect of playing in England.' As someone who had a natural affinity with England (Desailly was brought up in the English-speaking country of Ghana), and had studied in England as a teenager in the late 1970s, Desailly knew that the Premiership was the right place for him. 'I had the feeling that Chelsea wanted to become a super-power. They had developed an aggressive strategy with the Chelsea Village project, the renovation of the stadium, the encouragement of children joining the supporters' club

. . . all these individual factors helped me make my final decision.'

He did, however, also receive a little help from a friend – someone called Patrick. 'Vieira was already in England,' he recalls, 'and he told me that I would love London and the people. Patrick particularly spoke to me about life in England. If he feels so happy and relaxed in England, it is for a reason. There are always little rumours circulating about Pat, but he, like many of us, has shown that this is the place for him. Italy is a passionate place, but rarely are the stadiums full. And the fans are far too powerful and can lack respect towards the players.'

Not so Londoners, who have amazed Desailly with their charm and good manners. 'You can live in London without hanging out with true Englishmen, because the city is so cosmopolitan. The English are open, able to enjoy life and willing to party in pubs or anywhere. Their culture is a little different from ours, because once they finish work they don't go home. They'll go to the pub for a drink and they'll stay talking forever. They'll drink copious amounts, talk football, and then go home. Although English people will talk to you, they always keep a natural distance, which is something I like. They never interfere with your private life or what's going on under your roof. After a match for instance, it's possible to go out and walk in the middle of the crowd. Okay, they might ask you for an autograph but it is essentially children who ask you. And they're polite, too. It's all so different.'

Listening to him, you can understand why Desailly chose London after the heat of Milan. But why Chelsea? 'I wanted to sign for one of the big four clubs in the country,' he explains. 'Manchester United, Arsenal, Liverpool, or Chelsea. Then, there was the fact that I fancied bringing my children to London so that they could learn a new culture and language. In many ways, what attracted me was the history of the club, as opposed to its silverware. I knew that Chelsea had not won the title for many years [since 1955 in fact], but I was tempted by the sporting and mediatic challenge.' What, you might wonder, is a mediatic challenge? 'Well,' Desailly says, 'I just felt that I would get more global coverage by playing in England than, say, Spain, where I was also thinking of going before I decided to sign for Chelsea. I realised that people in Ghana, but also Hong Kong and other places, would be able to follow my career if I was in the Premiership.'

Desailly's original motives for joining Chelsea are not in question, nor are his performances in his first two seasons, which culminated in that historic 2000 FA Cup win at Wembley with his French chums Leboeuf and Deschamps. But in the seasons since Chelsea last won some silverware, Desailly's performances have often failed to live up to his reputation. Is he getting too old? Too complacent? Or, as he himself admits, has the English style of football never been all that easy for him to grasp? In a sense, his first match in English football perfectly sums up his time at the club. 'We played Coventry, and it didn't go too well,' Desailly recalls. 'It was all so new for me and a lot of the European guys. We arrived in a tiny stadium, packed to the rafters, and we were simply not used to this sort of match.' Coventry won 2–1.

Most observers agree that it is this inability to defeat the typical British teams that has cost Chelsea so dear in recent seasons. And yet, whatever accusations can be levelled at the Chelsea teams of the late 1990s, no one can doubt Desailly's joy at playing his first league game in England. 'It was tough, but also really exciting,' he says. 'One thing that really sticks in my mind is the smell of the burning sausages as we approached the stadium. The trail of the cooking was drifting into the bus as we drove up the road, and I remember thinking back to my days as an amateur. Back then, I would send someone off to buy me a *merguez-frites* [sausage and chips] just before my match ended, so that I would have something to eat afterwards. That's when life was really simple. You never get that sense of simplicity in Italy. The realism around English stadiums is so striking.'

Desailly says he retains mixed emotions from his English baptism. 'It was a surprising match rather than a pleasurable one. I never thought it would be this way – with such total physical commitment. I received quite a thorough education during my time in Italy, where you have to learn how to hold your defensive lines and you must not step out of your specific role. But this was something completely different and new to me. For that match against Coventry, I remember that we had a rough plan, but I am convinced that they were just doing anything and everything that came into their heads. But it works in England. I think that teams that show determination often do well here.

'In fact, I think that that is what the fans want more than anything else. If you show willingness for the cause, you'll be liked. Crowds at football matches are so eclectic. You have guys in suits sitting next to builders, and they are all chanting the same songs. All they want is to see you sweat. It's unique to England and it is very strange for a foreign footballer to get used to. It's very primitive in many ways. The supporters' view is that it is better to encourage a player, even if he is having a bad day or is down, rather than boo him and make things worse. It's incredible really, and it explains why the Premiership is so difficult to win. Every match is a battle.'

Desailly adds: 'The English approach is sometimes a little amateurish. In the way they sometimes train or eat, it is certainly less professional than what I've found on the Continent. But besides that, there is a positive culture. There is passion without exaggeration. Italy is very much at the other end of the scale, going over the top. England, for that reason, is sensational. Things have evolved greatly since the foreigners decided to play here. The way football is perceived has really changed, as well as the way of playing. One does not do the kick-and-rush any longer. Nowadays, teams play much more with the ball than in the past. That is down to the French. Think of guys like David Ginola. In my eyes, he has epitomised the Frenchman. He has done things in his own way, with a bit of class: the talented player, available to the public, yet a bit sensible. He has surely been someone who has contributed to improve the image of the French in England.'

So how does Desailly feel he has been received by the Chelsea supporters? Is he regarded as a fearless battler? 'I'm not sure,' he admits. 'As a footballer, and therefore always in the limelight, it's difficult to know exactly what people are thinking. There is a natural distance that exists, a form of respect for me because of what I have achieved during my career. I didn't start as a kid at Chelsea, so it's harder to judge me.'

What is not difficult, however, is for Desailly to name his most memorable moment in English football. Winning the FA Cup final against Aston Villa in May 2000. 'Now that is winning a trophy!' he exclaims. 'It's something special for the English because the Cup represents so many things for them. I think the main thing has always been the venue. Wembley Stadium for the English represents so much: it is the mythical stadium where they won the World Cup in 1966. The FA Cup is part of that special history. You visit small clubs, take every match seriously, and try to win it at all costs. It's nothing like the Cup competitions in other European countries. And then there's the final at the famous Twin Towers.'

It is impossible, when talking of Wembley Stadium, not to pause for a few seconds to reflect on the night of 10 February 1999. More than any other, that confrontation between England and France on a cold night in north London stands out as the seminal moment. Until then, and even allowing for France's World Cup victory on home soil the previous summer, French players were seen as great individuals – luxury items that supplemented hard-working Premiership teams. And then France won 2–0 in England's back garden (Nicolas Anelka, then of Arsenal, scoring both goals), and attitudes suddenly changed. France gained the respect of the old English enemy.

'It was a sort of confirmation,' Desailly explains. 'It's true that the English, and in particular the press, said that we had won the World Cup thanks to an easy route to the final. Even in France, there were those who questioned the quality of the opponents we met. I think everyone thought it would be interesting to see us play in the cauldron of Wembley. This was supposedly a test for us. Well, we just laughed. I mean, we were the champs and we didn't give a damn. And it showed during the match. We were awesome and it proved how good this generation of French internationals was.'

WILL THE REAL DIDIER DESCHAMPS PLEASE STAND UP

The quality of the French players Chelsea purchased has never been in doubt, and yet the club's supporters might wonder why they have rarely seen the best of a lot of them. Leboeuf and Desailly have impressed in patches, but how will two other World and European champions be remembered at Stamford Bridge? When Didier Deschamps arrived in SW6 in the summer of 1999, he was the captain of the all-conquering French team. He was also an experienced club campaigner, who had won the Champions League with both Marseille and Juventus. But, in his 12 months at Chelsea, Deschamps did little more than fall out with his one-time friend Gianluca Vialli.

The two had been close during their time together at Juventus, but it did not take long for their player–manager relationship to break down. 'Even before I came to Chelsea I always felt it was a big mistake for someone to try to continue playing while they are the manager,' Deschamps says. 'Having seen what happened with Luca at Chelsea, I would definitely stand by that assessment. You either do one job or the other well – not both badly. Apart from anything else, it makes relationships with players very difficult. How can you be a teammate one day and the boss the next? He trained with us and warmed up with us, but then he went away and decided on team-sheets. That's not a solution.'

Deschamps is speaking from experience, after deciding to hang up his boots at the tender age of 31 to concentrate on management. He had a difficult first year with Monaco in the 2001–02 season, but says that he enjoyed applying all the different lessons he learned during his time in Italy and then England. 'I've had a lot of managers in my career, so I've taken in something positive from all of them. Even Vialli had good ideas. The key now is for me to combine things to get results.'

During his brief spell in England, Deschamps says he learned more what not to do in management. This is significant, not least because it tells us something about the way in which top French players view England's managers. Indeed, how many Frenchmen have found success with an English manager in the Premiership? Ginola impressed under Kevin Keegan's tutelage, but that Newcastle United team won nothing. 'The most significant difference with English-style management is that the man in charge takes care of everything,' Deschamps explains. 'Sure, he gets some help, but the manager in England takes care of every aspect of the club, from the first-team tactics to the menu for lunch. The most important power that the manager has in England is the control of the purse-strings. If you want a player, you go out and buy him. In Italy, Spain or France, someone else deals with the money side of things. You can't just do what you want in other countries. It is a difficult and time-consuming job in the Premiership, and one which I do not believe can be executed properly by an inexperienced man.'

Why, then, did Deschamps leave one of the most successful clubs in Europe to sign for Chelsea? 'Well, I did have other possibilities when I left Juve, and, had I been given a special offer from one of the big clubs in Spain, I think I would have gone there. I knew that English football would require specific qualities, but I felt I could do it. It would be a challenge but that was all right because I fancied something different.'

At first, it seemed as if Vialli had found the missing link to stiffen up his midfield and challenge on all fronts. 'In our first match, we played against Sunderland and beat them 4–0,' Deschamps recalls. 'It was a really good start.' But it was not long before Deschamps looked out of his natural habitat. Like many of his compatriots, he played well only at home or in Champions League matches, but failed to impress in away Premiership fixtures. It remains a mystery to Chelsea supporters, even today, how the man they watched struggle most of the season then went on to lead France to victory at Euro 2000. At least Deschamps acknowledges his failures. 'That season, Chelsea played two types of games. There were the ones at Stamford Bridge when we were almost always able to stamp our authority on proceedings, and the ones away when we, quite literally, got stamped on. We had good technical players, but we never had the strength to do the business.'

Despite the team's failures in the Premiership, the Class of 1999–2000 still managed to win the FA Cup and reach the quarter-finals of the Champions League. 'I'm like Marcel [Desailly],' Deschamps says. 'My favourite memory is winning the FA Cup, the last final in the old Wembley. It's nothing like the Cup competitions in Italy or France – it's so much more important. Perhaps too much so, in fact. I wonder whether winning the Cup hasn't become the "easier option" for Chelsea.'

Deschamps also believes that, just as the Chelsea players have sometimes settled for winning Cups, so too the management have often cut corners over the years. 'One thing that always amazed me at Chelsea,' he says, 'was that the training ground did not belong to the club. People walk in and out willy-nilly, the wind affects the practices, the pitches are frozen in the winter, and Concorde goes just overhead at 10.10 every morning. Conditions there were . . .' Deschamps pauses. 'I know that there are plans for a new training centre, but a club like Chelsea, with all the money available, should have proper facilities. Arsenal did it under Arsène Wenger's instructions, and Chelsea should follow suit.'

Deschamps stops just short of blaming Chelsea for his poor performances with the Blues, but he clearly feels that the conditions there are not right for top players to do their best. 'Even the smallish club I started with in France, FC Nantes Atlantique, had a fabulous training ground. It was so much more agreeable for the players and helped many of us [Deschamps graduated from the academy with the likes of Desailly and Christian Karembeu] become top professionals. I'm not saying that's why we didn't win trophies at Chelsea, but it didn't help.'

So does the multi-garlanded midfielder feel he acquitted himself well at Chelsea? 'I played more matches than people think and I had some good performances,' he says. 'But you know, I was used to a certain role for five years in Italy, and suddenly I had to change everything in my game to try to succeed in England. It was tough. If I had come earlier in my career, it might have been easier. I mean, look at guys like Pat Vieira and Manu Petit: they came directly to England without stopping off for any significant length of time in Italy. If you start off in England, it makes life easier to adapt to the style.'

Deschamps' views are supported by the vastly superior quality of his performances in Europe during his time with Chelsea. 'In the Champions League, I had no problems at all,' he recalls. 'And in the Premiership, I was fine in four or five games during the season, because they were played against top sides that had a more Continental approach. The rest of the time, though, matches were being played at 100 mph and it was tough to get involved.' Should a player of his quality not have been able to make the necessary adjustments to succeed in England? 'I don't know if I could be expected to do that at 30,' he says, before adding honestly, 'but I do know that it was very depressing and frustrating to come off the pitch after most matches feeling like I had only played at 50 per cent of my capabilities. That was not very pleasant, but I think it is something which a lot of the older French players have felt.'

PETIT'S SECOND COMING

Witness the second coming of Petit. Here is a player who was supreme for three years at Arsenal, then sat on the substitutes' bench at Barcelona for a season, before making a big-money return to London in the summer of 2001. It would seem that even those who know the rigours of the Premiership will not necessarily deliver in the blue of Chelsea. What, the fans might wonder, happened to the big Petit of Arsenal? Petit, like his fellow compatriots Leboeuf, Desailly and Deschamps, is an honest professional. So why has he failed to deliver at Chelsea?

It is clear that no one has the answer. Equally, it is clear that the Chelsea manager, Claudio Ranieri, has been looking for it for some time. Before the 2002 FA Cup final against Arsenal, the Italian launched this cry: 'Manu and Marcel are good players and great men. They're an example for the rest of their teammates. It's very important.'

It was a stirring message for Petit, and, though he and Desailly failed to deny the Gunners the Double, as Chelsea lost the final 2–0 at the Millennium Stadium in Cardiff, it is interesting that they both had their best games of the season. Then again, perhaps you would have expected nothing less from Petit when faced by Patrick Vieira, once his midfield partner at Highbury, still a close friend and a player with whom he hopes to defend the European crown in Portugal in 2004. Together they form what Petit calls the best partnership of his career.

Watching the match, you sensed that Petit saw the final as a chance to confirm the resuscitation of his club career after that wasted year with Barcelona. The 31-year-old has insisted he has no regrets about going to the Nou Camp but it would be only human if he wondered what might have been at Highbury. He rates the current Arsenal side as the 'best in England', stronger than the one that did the Double in 1998. 'I think probably they have a better team than we used to have in 1998,' he says. 'This team don't play as we used to play. There is more and more movement. They have more options in the team. It's very difficult for any opponent.'

Early in the new year of 2002, Chelsea had been forced to deny stories that their £7.5m signing would be sold that summer. Was his heart in it, some had wondered? Was he saving himself for the World Cup? 'We [certain players] were the target most of the time because people thought we weren't giving what was expected from us at the beginning of the season because there was a World Cup at the end,' he explains. 'But it wasn't because of the World Cup, not at all. We were not scared. I was not scared about injury. If you think about that, you are going to be injured. Injuries happen all the time during training and during a game. You never know if you are going to be injured.'

Petit offers various reasons for his disappointing early form. Changing clubs twice in two years, he says, was not easy. Then there were injuries to cope with and the task of acquainting himself with new teammates. Things were 'very difficult' to begin with. 'The first six months were not very good,' he says, 'and the last six months I am happy with. I find I did better.'

Whatever people can accuse Petit of, at least no one can question his honesty. Only a brave man or a foolhardy one says 'no' to Sir Alex Ferguson. Although he insists he is neither, Petit did just that in the summer of 2001. Following rumours that the Frenchman was about to sign for Chelsea, Ferguson launched an audacious bid to try to prise the World Cup- and European Championship-winner away from the London club's grasp. 'I was flattered,' Petit admits, 'but I told Alex Ferguson that I had already given Chelsea my word and would not break it.' That is Manu all over.

Promises can often mean very little in modern football, but Petit is a man of honour. Thoughtful and intelligent, he has never been the type to change horses at the last minute. 'I had lots of contacts,' he says, 'but if you tell somebody you're going to do something, you owe it to them to honour that pledge.' Most major European clubs coveted Petit's signature. Having decided he would leave Spain, three firm options presented themselves: France, where the league is of an average standard; Italy, where Petit feels he would not fit in; or England, where he enjoyed the best three years of his career. There was no contest. 'My heart was set on a return here very early on,' he says. 'I realised in that year in Barca how much I missed England. Irrespective of football matters, it is the way of life which I enjoy. Within weeks of arriving at Chelsea, I felt more at ease than I did in my ten months at Barcelona.'

Ranieri may have his detractors, but the Italian is clearly a skilled negotiator. He first decided to approach Petit in May 2001 and, though he was warned that the Frenchman was not interested in discussing his future, he still managed to speak to the player face-to-face. That meeting all but sealed the deal. 'A number of clubs had been trying to reach me to find out what I was planning to do,' Petit recalls, 'but I had decided to ignore all the calls because I felt I should finish the season with Barcelona and give them a chance to shed some light on my situation. But then Claudio came out to see me, at a time when Chelsea were busy, and I was very touched. I sensed there and then that the club had serious ambitions, so I gave them my word.'

The other Premiership clubs to show an interest included Tottenham and Petit's former employers, Arsenal. Although keen to work with the man he used to worship in his early playing days when they were both at Monaco, Petit had to tell Glenn Hoddle that he could not sign for the Gunners' oldest rivals. 'I like Glenn a lot, but I could not bring myself to join Spurs,' he says. 'Coming back to a London club was difficult enough without me making life even harder for myself.' Sol Campbell is only too aware of that fact.

So far as Arsenal are concerned, Petit says he never seriously considered rejoining his mentor, Arsène Wenger, at Highbury. 'They did come into the bidding,' he says, 'but, to be honest, I couldn't see myself returning to a place where I'd had so much success. I still have fond memories of Arsenal and their wonderful fans, but going back is always dangerous because people then make continuous comparisons.' Petit may have chosen not to rejoin his old club, but he was keen to rediscover London. 'It's a city which I know well and appreciate,' he says. 'My life is different now that I am married, and London allows me to be as anonymous as I choose. I love the fact that I can go cycling with Agathe in Richmond Park on a Sunday without being disturbed by anyone. That's important to me.'

FRENCH DISCONNECTION

The moral of the Chelsea tale is simple: just because you buy French players does not mean you will necessarily win every competition you enter. Not convinced? Take a walk down the streets of Chelsea Village, and you will be greeted by a legion of fans scratching their heads. They have a multi-million-pound stadium, a multi-million-pound team, an ambitious chairman, and . . . and, well, little else really. There have been numerous Cup successes in recent years, most notably during Gianluca Vialli's reign, but the league title has continued to evade the Stamford Bridge trophy cabinet.

No wonder, then, the Blues have the blues. What, you can hear the supporters ask, do we need to do to win the Premiership, let alone the Champions League? Their frustration is all the more pronounced because of the triumph of Manchester United and, in particular, their London rivals, Arsenal. On paper, Chelsea have matched their two rivals, and yet the results have been poles apart. *Les Bleus* bought by the Blues over the last six years read like a Who's Who of 1990s French football – Leboeuf, Desailly, Deschamps and Petit – a list arguably more impressive than those of Manchester United or Arsenal. And yet it is doubtful whether any of their World and European champions will ever be remembered as Chelsea legends.

So what is it about Chelsea Football Club that often prevents it from getting the best out of France's best? Why have four of the pillars of the all-conquering French team failed to impose themselves fully on English football? One thing is for sure: none of these players became bad overnight. Indeed, most of them are capable of putting in Man of the Match performances, as Desailly proved in the 2002 FA Cup final – but only when it suits them. According to John Reeder, a long-time season ticket holder (home and away), whose name has been changed for the purposes of this book, the main problem is the difference in culture. 'The thing is that we signed too many players who were bigger than the club,' Reeder says. 'Apart from Leboeuf, these players came from bigger, more successful clubs. Chelsea was their swansong and they never really managed to play their best stuff in England.'

Examining the four French World and European champions one by one, it is clear that a pattern emerges. 'Leboeuf, in his first season, did OK,' Reeder recalls, 'but that was because Ruud Gullit [the manager at the time] was playing three at the back. Once he won the World Cup in 1998, though, his attitude really stank. He became arrogant and over-confident. I would say that the World Cup was the worst thing that ever happened to Leboeuf. Desailly was the first Serie A player at the height of his powers to sign for Chelsea, but he has never really met our expectations. In his defence, though, he would probably argue the same about Chelsea.'

Reeder, who holds a season ticket in the Upper Matthew Harding Stand, continues his French tour. 'Deschamps was just a bad buy,' he says. 'Not because he was a bad player, but because he was the wrong sort of player for Chelsea. After five years at Juventus, playing at the pace of the Italian league, the Premiership can be a big shock. Even for a talented guy.' Last on the list is Petit, a midfielder who so impressed at Arsenal, but has looked 'scared and uninterested' since his arrival in SW6.

These views are shared by many, and yet no one would question the quartet's genuine enthusiasm for English football. Whether or not their times on these shores will ever be viewed as resounding successes remains to be seen, but one thing is for sure: when you talk to the four actors, you quickly realise that they always dreamed of playing in England.

NEW KID ON THE BLOCK

There is genuine hope that, following the not-entirely-convincing showings of his more illustrious predecessors, a young defender called William Gallas may yet become a French Chelsea legend. Bought for a fee of £6m from the club where Desailly and Deschamps made their names, Olympique Marseille, Gallas had an impressive first season in 2001–02. Even more so when you consider that he has been played in every different position across the back four.

'Whenever anyone sees me, one of the first things they mention is the fact that I play all over the place,' he says. 'It must mean that it is very obvious. Yet again in my career, the label of versatile is attached to me. It's actually really hard to accept, and even if it is for the benefit of the team, it is a pain to be moved around constantly from position to position. Sometimes, I get the feeling that I'm reliving my Marseille years.'

Gallas continues: 'Let me give you an example. Lilian Thuram plays in the centre of defence for Juventus but on the right flank for France. He knows exactly what he is expected to do depending on which shirt he is wearing. For me, though, it's always up in the air. Before the 2002 FA Cup final, I worked hard for two weeks playing at left back. I played there against Manchester United and Middlesbrough and I was sure that I would be there against Arsenal in the final. But, then, on the morning of the match, the manager told me I was going to be at right back. Can you imagine? You are in a stadium in front of 80,000 fans, you know that there are millions watching around the world on TV, and you are completely lost. You have prepared yourself for one role, and then you are given another at the last minute. I was really surprised.'

All the moving around might explain why Gallas did not have the best of beginnings to his Chelsea career. 'To start off with,' Gallas admits, 'that was tough. People never really understand when you tell them that you need a little while to find your feet. But, when you arrive in a new country, and a new city, you are looking for a house and living out of a suitcase in a hotel. You have no attachments. That's tough and it's only normal that it showed in my performances on the pitch. Once you have sorted your personal life out, the professional side of things follows very easily.'

He spoke about the matter with Ranieri in the summer of 2002 and asked the Italian to set him one task. 'I broached the subject during pre-season training [which started in the first week of July 2002],' Gallas says. 'I knew Claudio would be the manager for the 2002–03 season, so I needed to know what he planned to do. I couldn't go on like that for another season. The years go by and nothing changes. After a while, you just need to know what your position is going to be.'

Gallas's uncertain start was, in many ways, a microcosm of Chelsea's entire 2001–02 season. As a result, the under-performing has not surprised the Frenchman. 'This tendency to alternate the good with the less good is nothing new,' he says. 'Like in years gone by, we play really impressively against the big guns and then play really poorly against the teams we're expected to beat. For some reason, we lose our faculties. The manager had warned us at the beginning of the [2001–02] season, because the club had had the same problem the year before, but the lesson was not heeded. Quite frankly, I don't understand why all this happens.'

The net result of Gallas's maiden season in England was that Chelsea finished a disappointing sixth. 'It was not good enough,' he says. 'We did not win any trophies and, for a club like Chelsea, that should not be possible.' Gallas cannot blame himself for anything that went wrong at Stamford Bridge. He was, by some way, the most consistent French performer in the team. He was also, rather ironically, the only one not to be selected for the World Cup squad, even though he proved his worth. 'For a first season,' he says, 'it went quite well. I had a few physical problems, but these days it is rare for a player to go through an entire year without picking up an injury. We saw that with Robert Pires. He was at his peak and was cut down by a nasty knee injury. It really was his year, and I am sure he would have shone with France had he gone to the World Cup.'

The same could be said for Gallas, who returned for pre-season training with his club in July 2002. 'Every day, I worked hard on my fitness,' he says. 'These days, you cannot stop working out for two whole months. Especially when you have Italian coaches and fitness instructors. They make you suffer real hard. It's so tough, you often cry.'

Perhaps now, Gallas knows how the Chelsea faithful feel about the myriad of French stars who have tended to under-perform for years.

Alex Hayes
(with Xavier Rivoire)

CHAPTER 6

Leeds: Dr Wilko, Canto and Mr Oli

Long before French became the coolest word in football; long before nearly every club in England employed a player from the other side of the Channel; and even long before the Football Association realised it was time to ditch their old-fashioned views and methods; perhaps the most unlikely of coaches had predicted the benefits of the Gallic system.

Forget Arsène Wenger's revolution at Arsenal and Gérard Houllier's transformation of Liverpool; it was an Englishman who first implemented the French methodology. Howard Wilkinson is a bag of contradictions. As a coach, he has always favoured the English 4-4-2 formation. As a manager, however, he has always been open to the Continental viewpoint.

This two-pronged approach was never more apparent than when Wilkinson was manager of Leeds United. Appointed in 1988, when English football was still in its post-Heysel, pre-Hillsborough, Neanderthal days, Wilkinson quickly instilled a tough-tackling and long-ball system. It says everything that he surrounded himself with players such as Vinnie Jones and Lee Chapman to help Leeds out of the then Second Division. The Yorkshire club played a no-nonsense game, rejoined the elite, and then won the last-ever First Division championship in 1992 with a brand of combative football.

And, yet, in amongst the very British traits of Wilkinson's side, one man stood out like a sore thumb. Tall yet technically gifted, foreign yet physically strong, individualistic yet the perfect team player: Eric Cantona made all the difference. There can be no doubt that Cantona's arrival midway through the 1991–92 season gave Leeds the *je ne sais quoi* they needed to pull away from Manchester United and win the title. It was a brilliant piece of vision and business by the manager, a sign of Wilkinson's knowledge of the French game.

Wilkinson deserves credit for his decision. In many ways, he took a chance on a maverick who nobody wanted either side of the Channel. Having called the former French national manager, Henri Michel, a *sac à merde* (bag of shit), and then been kicked out of Nîmes for throwing his shirt at the bench when he was substituted in a league game, Cantona was an outcast. Ostracised by club and country, turned down by Trevor Francis after a week-long loan spell at Sheffield Wednesday, King Eric was little more than a footballing pauper.

IN AND OUT OF LEEDS

It is worth pausing for a second to recount Cantona's bizarre spell at Leeds, not only because it served as the catalyst for the arrival of other Frenchmen such as Henry, Petit, Anelka, Vieira, Barthez, Blanc and Ginola, but also because it made Wilkinson realise how well French players were educated. Cantona may have been a difficult character, but no one could question his talent. It is ironic that Cantona's arrival in England owed more to circumstance than careful planning. His adviser, the former French international striker Dominique Rocheteau, had enquired about the possibility of sending his protégé to Japan, but the J-League was closing its doors in March. England seemed the only logical, not to mention remaining, place for Cantona to ply his trade for the last three months of the season.

The player may have been desperate for first-team football, but it is often forgotten that his country was desperate for him to return, too. Gérard Houllier, then assistant to the French national manager Michel Platini, played a pivotal role in the negotiations to take Cantona to Leeds. 'Michel went to see him [Eric] and tried to convince him to come back,' Houllier recalls. 'Then he asked me to see whether we could get him into English football. He went first to Sheffield Wednesday, but Trevor Francis delayed signing him. Then I was on a trip somewhere and my secretary asked me to call Howard Wilkinson very quickly. Howard asked me about Eric and I told him what I thought. Howard was clever. He signed Eric very quickly and they won the title.'

Indeed they did. Cantona made his debut on 8 February 1992, in a game which Leeds went on to lose against Oldham. Less than 12 weeks later, Wilkinson's side were champions. Cantona was a firm favourite with the crowd, and his future in Yorkshire seemed assured. But then came the typical Cantona breakdown in communications. Wilkinson knew he had a special talent on his books, but also realised he could no longer keep him.

The Southampton manager, Gordon Strachan, a teammate at the time, recalls: 'Eric had made up his mind that he couldn't relate to big Lee Chapman [the club's centre-forward] as a player. He found it hard to understand how Chappy played and Chappy found it difficult to understand him. We had to play a certain style . . . it was very hard . . . we didn't have megabucks to change the whole side just to suit Eric Cantona. Hard work made us tick – and no lack of skill – but sometimes when we went away from home, Eric just couldn't understand what we were at. It frustrated him, there's no doubt about that. He had just made up his mind he wanted to leave; there was no way he wanted to stay. Nobody had anything against him personally. He wasn't a problem to get on with.'

Cue the return of Houllier. 'When the Leeds problems arose, I stepped in once more to find Eric another club,' the Liverpool manager says. 'I knew Alex Ferguson. I appreciate Alex very much and had known him for many years. So I phoned him up and Eric duly joined Manchester United.' The rest, as they say, is *histoire* – for both Cantona and Wilkinson.

HOWARD'S WAY

Cantona's five incredible years at Old Trafford are now legendary, but what many people have forgotten is the impact he had on Wilkinson while at Leeds. Indeed, it was not long after his departure that Wilkinson totally re-shaped the Yorkshire club. Wilkinson had always planned to model Leeds on a French club like Auxerre, but Cantona's brief spell seemed to give him the impetus he needed to implement the radical changes.

Academies were but a distant thought in all the top clubs' minds when Wilkinson started his. Seeing what a good footballing education did for French players, Wilkinson revamped the Elland Road set-up. He moved the youth team away from the dilapidated training ground that they used right next to the stadium and, after months of negotiations with the council, moved the players to new facilities away from the ground. Trainees would now be groomed away from Elland Road, so that they would then appreciate their first visit to the stadium more. In time the new facilities in Wetherby would be used by the first team as well. Wilkinson's decision seems obvious today, but, like his signing of Cantona, it showed incredible foresight a decade ago. One thing is for sure, David O'Leary and then Terry Venables would not have worked with such quality players at Leeds had it not been for Wilkinson. And, in a funny way, Cantona.

Equally, though, had Cantona not decided to swap premature retirement for Howard Wilkinson's Leeds in 1992, it is highly debatable whether Wilkinson would be the current technical director of the Football Association or indeed whether he would have implemented such a radical overhaul of the English football system. Eric Cantona was unique in that he served as a model for the players and the managers in England.

By 2004, a 350-acre site in Staffordshire at Burton upon Trent will be transformed into England's centre for footballing excellence. On completion, the project will be the grandest, boldest and most advanced of its kind in the world. There will be an indoor arena with a full-size synthetic pitch, which, with television cameras implanted in the ceiling, will enable coaches to use instant video replays via a large screen on the wall and have access to Prozone, the equipment used to track the movement of players. Video playback facilities will be available on the 11 outdoor pitches, too, either at pitch-side or in seminar rooms nearby. As well as accommodation for 300, the £50m centre will provide space for a lecture theatre, a video-viewing library and archive, analysis and research facilities, a gymnasium, hydrotherapy suite and the latest in sports medicine and science.

Wilkinson explains his brainchild: 'We have tried to design something not for now, not for 2004, but which is still at the cutting edge in 2010 and 2015,' he says. 'You've got to try and leave the present behind and it's very important to project. It's about looking at what it is that players and coaches need in order to do their job better. We have left no stone unturned in finding the best facilities and the best site, which was critical.'

No one, not even Wilkinson himself, could have predicted that his actions at Leeds would be mirrored at a national level five years after Cantona's departure. But that is what happened when, in 1997, he was appointed as the Football Association's technical director. It had taken England what seemed like an eternity to realise the importance of grooming the youngsters. Wilkinson's plan was simple: create a legion of English Eric Cantonas.

Throughout the 1990s, French clubs had made steady progress in European competitions. And, after a rocky patch at the end of the 1980s and in the early part of the last decade, the national team were following suit. Wilkinson was convinced *Les Bleus* were the ideal model to relieve England's blues. Ron Atkinson, one of English football's liveliest characters, but also a man of great football knowledge, applauds Wilkinson for his decision to copy the French. 'The French league may not be internationally renowned but the structure of their game is second to none,' the former Manchester United and Aston Villa manager says. 'You can see how strong they are just by watching a match on the box – the players may not be internationals but there's quality all over the pitch, lads with brilliant technique whom you wouldn't know from Adam.'

Atkinson continues: 'France's domestic game underwent a renaissance after they failed to qualify for the 1994 World Cup and, thanks to their academy system, they can now pluck brilliant players out of the ether.'

THE LONG ROAD AHEAD

If Wilkinson and the FA thought all they needed to do was buy the French model, assemble it, and then put in a couple of batteries, they were sorely mistaken. As Claude Dusseau, the man who runs the INF (Institut National de Football) at the French Federation's headquarters in Clairefontaine, explains, the machinery takes time and effort before it really gets going. 'In France, we started the formation process nearly 30 years ago. The French football association drew up a plan that would, in the first instance, bring us up to date and then, in the long term, perhaps help us lead the way. The idea was never to become the best side in the world overnight, but rather to create a charter that all the professional clubs would adhere to.'

Dusseau adds: 'In effect, we wanted to create a common goal, to which every player and manager could aspire. Because that is something which is important as well. There is no point developing the players if you are not doing the same with the coaches. Otherwise, you end up with dozens of excellent players but nobody good enough to teach them.'

England's cowboy approach to football education has finally run out of steam. Nobody, not even the most loyal national supporter, still believes the old methods were the best. But neither the realisation that things need to improve, nor the FA's recent changes, are likely to produce any tangible results for some time. 'It took our national team 26 years to reap the rewards of the work we had put in,' Dusseau says. 'The first centre for excellence was opened in 1972 in Vichy and, although a few good players [Jean-Pierre Papin and Jean-Luc Ettori, to name but two] emerged, it was not until we moved to Clairefontaine in 1988 and took the formation process a step further that France made its mark.'

He adds: 'The important thing is not to panic. In the early 1990s, there were plenty of critics in France. Gérard Houllier's team had failed to qualify for the World Cup in America and there seemed to be no high-profile candidate when he resigned. But the federation stuck to their principles and, against the wishes of media and public, continued with their policy of promoting from within, as Aimé Jacquet moved up from assistant manager.'

Franck Sauzée, one of France's midfielders during the early 1990s and, more recently, a player and manager at Hibernian in Scotland, recalls: 'Progress takes time. Like any business, you have to give the plan a chance to blossom. If it is in a healthy state, it will come good. You have to allow the managers several years to build a competitive youth structure and then they will reap the benefits.'

Dusseau agrees: 'If you want a truly elite band of professionals, you need a large base to choose from. But that base takes a while to form. Once you are producing only good players, though, exceptional ones are certain to emerge.'

FOREIGN EDUCATION OR FOREIGN INVASION?

While there is a minority of highly gifted foreign players in the English domestic game, the majority can be characterised as solid professionals. The attraction of signing the latter type seems to stem from the managers' need for a quick-fix or the fact that an equivalent home-based player is likely to cost more. One outcome of this influx of foreigners is a decline in the opportunities available to young players to establish themselves in the first team. Wilkinson, though, is not unduly worried. 'High-class performers are role models and examples for youngsters,' he says. 'Look at Eric Cantona. However, it is true some foreign players are also employed because they are cheaper and more accessible, more experienced and, in some cases, short-term safer bets than an untried youngster. Young talent requires opportunity to develop. This will not happen if first-team squads are packed with older, more experienced foreign players.'

Wilkinson adds: 'This points to the need for more enlightened leadership. Alex Ferguson at Manchester United is the manager, the coach and in a football sense, chief executive, all in one. I performed a similar role at Leeds. But the industry is abrogating its responsibilities if it thinks that this is how it should be. That's not how it should be. If ICI have a good head of sales, they don't then assume that he has the skills to determine the rest of the company's policy. That's a matter for the chairman and the board.

'In football, we are beginning to move in this direction, but we have still got a million miles to go because it seems to me that the chief responsibility of the board is to determine policy. They have responsibility for establishing the vision and the broad objectives, short- and long-term. They then have to plot the pathways to the achievement of these ends. They must then have the fortitude to stick with them and the flexibility of mind to overcome the inevitable problems that will be encountered along the way. At the moment, not enough club boards are adopting this approach.'

Wilkinson gains much inspiration from Auxerre, the small-town club run by the legendary French manager, Guy Roux. The club has a tiny budget, and yet has managed to win the Double as recently as in 1996. They have, more pertinently, groomed the likes of Laurent Blanc, Christophe Cocard, Basile Boli, Stephane Guivarc'h and, yes, you guessed it, our very own Eric Cantona. 'This club is *la reference*,' Wilkinson explains. 'A relatively small club, like Auxerre, has a well-defined and successful policy on youth development. When I took over at Leeds, the club was in the old Second Division, but this didn't prevent us from establishing a sound youth development policy.'

Those who have watched English football for many years are constantly struck by the failure of many professional players to work at the weaker points of their game. The excessive one-footedness, poor balance, poor heading technique, and poor kicking by goalkeepers seem to plague the leagues. Are these French-style centres for excellence going to remedy these failures? 'English footballers have not been as dedicated to practice and honing their skills as players in certain other cultures,' Wilkinson concedes. 'Practising and coaching hasn't been an important part of our culture. In some countries if a youngster wanted to play football, he would go to a club with a coach who was held in as high esteem as a teacher. We are fighting against this attitude. It has its roots in the old notion of the "gentleman sportsman", that practising was in some way unfair, and in the era when professional players were looked down upon. Things have changed and this change can be traced to the 1950s when educationalists began to approach sports in a more scientific way.'

DACOURT IN THE FOOTSTEPS OF CANTONA

No one proved Wilkinson's theory more powerfully than Cantona. Here was a player blessed with talent and yet always prepared to put in more work. He was never embarrassed about wanting to be the best. His success in Yorkshire, however brief, left a long-standing legacy for a whole new generation of Frenchies. Just ask Olivier Dacourt, who joined the club from Lens in the summer of 2000, having spent one season with Everton two years previously. 'If Eric could play in Leeds,' Dacourt says, 'why shouldn't I? That was my theory, anyway. Eric made it OK to play here.'

Dacourt's journey to Leeds was a slightly tortuous one – and his exit may yet prove to be a swift one if he decides to join Juventus for £15m – so let us start at the beginning, in the summer of 1998, when Everton came knocking at the door. 'I had been at Strasbourg for nine years,' he says, 'seven of which were in the first team. So you can imagine I was ready to go elsewhere. I needed something new. Actually, I needed to improve. I was due to join Bordeaux – everything had been done, I had found a house and the manager had all but done the deal. But then a new man came in, Claude Le Roy, and he said that I would only be allowed to leave if they got £4m. I had planned first to take a step up to a bigger club in France and then move abroad later on in my career, but it quickly became apparent that only a foreign club could afford me at the time.'

England seemed the logical destination. 'As we had had a good run in the UEFA Cup with Strasbourg, the Everton manager, Walter Smith, who had just arrived from Glasgow Rangers, decided to take a chance and offer the full transfer fee. He had seen me play at first-hand against his Rangers team and keep Paul Gascoigne quiet, and then watched as we eliminated Liverpool and took Inter Milan very close in the quarter-finals, so he felt he knew my qualities.'

Dacourt says that he could not wait to ply his trade in England. 'I've always loved the country,' he explains. 'My uncle worked in a press distribution company, so I always had access to footie magazines. I loved Kevin Keegan – it's odd, but I think it's because he had the same name as my cousin. All I know is that we always kept up to date with what he was doing. My older friends knew English football even better because of Liverpool's repeated success in Europe. Where I lived, there was a mate who, whenever he scored a header, would scream: "Paul Mariner" [as in the Leeds striker of the 1970s]. There are lots of English bits and pieces like that in my early life.'

Dacourt's first visit to these shores came in the summer of 1993, as he competed in the European Junior Championship. The Frenchman was immediately impressed by what he saw, and vowed, one day, to return. 'I especially remember how the grounds were packed,' he says. 'The grounds have always attracted me to English football, and the atmosphere inside them. When I watched Canal Plus on Sundays, it was a football that I always adored. In the tournament, we lost to England in the first match, but we should have won. Their team was full of the guys who are superstars of the English game now. There was Paul Scholes, Robbie Fowler, Nicky Butt, Sol Campbell. I remember I changed shirts with Campbell.'

When Dacourt finally arrived back in England at Everton, he had developed a reputation as a fearsome tackler. It did not take him long to show why. 'I was booked eight times in my first eight games,' he says, 'so I remember that period well. It was weird. I was booked five times, suspended, and then booked three other times. I never tackled from behind, but it was a snowball effect, I had a label, a bad reputation, and I was always the one to be booked. It was very impressive, and so frustrating. It was systematical: one or two fouls in a game, and I was booked, sure thing. One day, before Christmas, I was really fed up, so I said: "I'm leaving." But the bosses were behind me. The proof was that I should have been fined, but was let off. Walter Smith told me not to worry. He told me that he had hired me for my commitment, so that I should play my game. Then, it calmed down a bit, but I collected 18 bookings for that first season. As I often tackled, I had the image of a butcher. It was a rather bizarre period.'

Not that Dacourt was afraid to get 'stuck in'. 'When you arrive, you should not be worried about contact,' he says, 'otherwise there is no point coming here. At Everton, it was like that, and we could also count on "Big Dunk", Duncan Ferguson, a monster header of the ball. There were also a few guys able to play with the ball, so we trained with that in mind, but as soon as things went bad, we would send the ball to Duncan. When they sold Duncan, we were forced to play, because the big guy was not here any more, and it helped us develop a better quality of football.'

Dacourt does not have many memorable moments from his solitary season with Everton, as the club struggled again in that 1998–99 season, but two images still stand out four years later. 'I remember a game against Liverpool, for the tenth anniversary of the Hillsborough tragedy,' he recounts. 'I scored in the first minute, Fowler sniffed the touch-line; it was a crazy derby, and in terms of emotion, one of the biggest games I've ever played in. I also remember my last game for Everton; people knew that I was going to leave, some booed at the beginning of the game, but at the end, the whole crowd was singing my name. It was weird; I almost cried.'

Looking back, he says he found adapting to the English way of life rather difficult the first time around. Perhaps this had to do with the club he joined, and the particular culture that reigned there. 'I did not speak that much English,' he recalls, 'and that did not help. It was a strange time. I was trying to learn, but John Collins spoke French. I never went for a meal with the players, except with Slaven Bilic and Danni Cadamarteri. Kevin Campbell arrived at the end, and we had a few nights out together.'

Still harbouring international ambitions, Dacourt felt he had no choice but to leave a sinking ship and rebuild his career elsewhere. Lens, who had just been crowned French champions the season before and had money to spend ahead of the Champions League, paid £6m to bring Dacourt home. On leaving, though, the Frenchman uttered those famous three words: 'I'll be back.' And he meant it. The Everton episode may not have ended happily but Dacourt still loved England football. 'I prefer English football to any other style,' he says, 'even if sometimes the football is less pretty than elsewhere. No game is won beforehand, you always know it's going to be a fight, and I really like that. When I get on the pitch, I want to give it my all. What's great is that the moment you give your all on a pitch, then the fans will respect you. The English public is knowledgeable – it knows how to recognise that. It's different in France: after two minutes, they are ready to boo.'

The divorce with Everton was done on friendly terms. 'The board and the manager did not want me to leave,' Dacourt says, 'but there was no more money available and the club needed funds. In March, just before the end of the transfer window, I was supposed to be sold to Aston Villa. But Everton decided that would be suicide. The club were struggling at the foot of the table and felt that they needed me to have a chance to survive. So they told me that if I could help them save our Premiership status, then I would be allowed to leave at the end of the season.'

Dacourt continues: 'I wanted to stay in England, but the clubs were waiting for my valuation to come down. Then, one day just before pre-season, Gervais Martel, the Lens chairman, invited me to have a chat. I went over and we got on really well. By the end of the afternoon, I told him that I was not particularly keen to come back to France, but that if I ever did it would be to join Lens. I honestly didn't think it mattered much what I said, because Everton had put this high price-tag on me. Then, out of the blue, Martel says: "Hey, these English people are not going to break my balls. They want £6m – fine, I'll get them £6m." So he went in his office, made a few calculations and then came back out to ask me if I wanted to sign. He slammed his fist on the table, and yelled: "I'll pay." So I signed at Lens and we cracked into a couple of bottles of champagne.'

But the fizz soon died down. Dacourt's new manager, Daniel Leclercq, did not see eye-to-eye with his star player. Arguments started, the group split in two camps, and results suffered. Only once Leclercq was replaced at the beginning of the winter of 1999, did Dacourt show his real potential. He finished the season in style. But the breakdown had already taken place, and Dacourt had his heart set on a return to England. 'For the last four months of the campaign, the Lens fans loved me, but I knew some English clubs were interested in me. I was determined to go back to the Premiership. Not just because I love the football and get well paid, but also because the attitude of the players and managers is so much better than in France. Back home, people immediately get jealous of you if you are successful. Here, the respect is much more profound.'

Dacourt waited patiently. He knew he would get his wish and come back to his 'spiritual home'. Early on, the indications were that he would probably end up at Leeds or Newcastle. 'I started looking at results and gathering information,' he says. 'I was asking people what they thought and building a portfolio on the various clubs in England. The press were getting more and more interested and could sense that I was about to go, but I insisted that I had four years left on my contract. It is the standard line. In fact, as early as May 2000, I knew I was signing for Leeds. I told Gervais and he accepted, but on the condition that I would not tell anyone.'

Dacourt continues: 'I had to go for my medical without anyone noticing. It was funny, because on that very day there was an Everton v. Leeds match being played. I spoke to David O'Leary, who was keen to introduce me to the public, but I was true to my word and said I couldn't yet reveal publicly that I had left Lens. I'll tell you what, though, it wasn't easy selling my house in France and doing all the travelling while still keeping up the pretence.'

Was Dacourt ever tempted to join his old chum, Patrick Vieira, at Arsenal? 'I did speak to Arsène Wenger on the phone, but the deal was never done. There were already quite a few Frenchmen at Arsenal, so in a sense, joining Leeds was a more exciting challenge. In fact, when I signed, I didn't even know we would be in the Champions League, which shows I was more interested in proving myself on the pitch rather than participating in big competitions.'

When Dacourt arrived in Leeds, he was the only foreigner who was not fluent in English. The first person to call him was Michael Bridges. 'I didn't know him at all,' Dacourt recalls, 'because when I was at Everton, he was with Sunderland. But he told me he was very happy I was joining the club, and that was really nice. It made me feel welcome and I knew then I would love Yorkshire.' What were Dacourt's first impressions of the county? 'Yorkshire?' he asks, before pausing. 'I say: "Yorkshire pudding!" That is my first reaction when someone asks me about the county I live in . . . More seriously, I think this area is quite spectacular. The Yorkshire I know is a green land where I enjoy playing golf. Me, the city boy, I live in the countryside halfway between Leeds and our training ground and I love it. I also enjoy visiting York for all its medieval history.'

He adds: 'I am a Parisian, I love Paris and London, but one has to know what one wants in life. I came here for the football, for my passion, not for the city. Leeds just so happens to be a really nice place, which is good, but if it was not nice, it would not bother me. I often repeat it, but when things go well here, it is extraordinary, it is fantastic. Most [French] people are like children facing food when it comes down to geography: they are scared to taste it and they will say, "I don't like that" before even trying a place. That's why Eric Cantona was so cool. He had the courage to go places and not worry about the weather or the shopping. He was a real pro.'

Speaking of influences, how does Dacourt think history will remember the important French signings? 'French players have brought something extra to this country,' Dacourt says. 'I think it had something to do with timing, but you cannot take anything away from some of these guys. The simple fact of the matter is that Manchester United started playing well thanks to Cantona, who was an excellent footballer. And the same can be said of Pat [Vieira] and Manu [Petit], who both brought a lot to Arsenal as well. Three-quarters of the French have succeeded in the Premiership, so it's not a surprise any more. Arsène [Wenger] has changed mentalities, Houllier has done the same, but at the beginning, it was not that easy, because the English are very conservative. Two years later, Houllier wins three Cup finals, everyone applauds him, but he really did have to fight for success. Houllier brought the Continental know-how, Arsène did just the same, and Vialli did it to a certain extent at Chelsea, too. Ferguson also brings a lot, because he is very open-minded.'

While Dacourt is a proud Frenchman, he is also aware of his roots. Like so many France internationals of the current generation of 'blacks, blancs, beurs', Dacourt has a 'foreign' history. In his case, he is part Caribbean. 'In the French Caribbean,' he says, 'the Premiership is followed closely. All my friends and family have a satellite dish, and they follow everything. They all wait for the Sunday night programme, because there is Titi [Thierry Henry], myself, and Nino [Sylvain Wiltord]. They really watch it faithfully. And now, thanks to our journey in the Champions League two seasons ago, they know what Leeds United is about. Even in France, you can find the Leeds United replica kit these days – that says a lot. All the French fans are beginning to discover Leeds United. The adventure starts here.'

One wonders if, bearing in mind his colour and the problems that have plagued British football for the last 20 years, Dacourt has ever encountered any racism? 'I've heard that it exists in England,' he says, 'but I never experienced it myself, never felt anything like it. At Everton and Leeds, everything has always gone well in that respect, but you need English players, so that the team has an identity. In France, if there were teams with foreigners only, it would not go well at all.' Dacourt's awareness of racism on the Continent explains why he rejected the advances of Lazio, a club renowned for its fascist supporters.

Dacourt's love affair with Leeds clearly took no time to be consummated, but it is interesting to hear him talk about the difficulties, often ignored because so many Frenchmen now play in England, that a foreigner can experience in England. 'The young player who wants to come here has to be very strong in his head, because it's not easy every day,' Dacourt explains. 'It's easier to come here at 25 than at 18, because it's tougher than people realise. It's better to come here with a little bit of experience, and to be someone already. However, when you get here, they don't care what you have done before, so you have to show them that you've got balls. What you've done before will give you confidence, but you will have to prove it again at the training ground.'

And the pressures go beyond the dressing-room doors. 'A foreigner has to be irreproachable,' Dacourt says. 'He has to be an example, and even more so at Arsenal, Manchester United, or Liverpool. You have to make efforts, so that the other players accept you. You should not stay in your corner, you have to speak English. When I arrived in Leeds, I had not spoken English for a year, nobody spoke French, so it was a bit of a jungle, but I immersed myself right away, and spoke with the guys. Now the words come to me in English first.'

What people appreciate most about Dacourt is his honesty. Not just in his opinions, but also in the way he plays football. Tiburce Darrou, the

Monaco-based physical coach who has trained with the majority of the current French squad, is full of admiration for the Leeds midfielder. 'What I like most about Oli,' he says, 'is that despite his lack of power, but thanks to his controlled aggression, he has managed to forge a wonderful career. He really is the French player who has impressed me most in England, when you consider his talent and footballing education. To be so consistent when you have not had the training of a big club early on in your career is something else. *Chapeau*!'

Apart from his unquestionable personal qualities, Dacourt clearly enjoyed becoming the leader of the young Leeds team of the turn of the century. He may only have been 25 when he signed, but so much was expected of him. 'I've been lucky in Leeds, because the youth of the squad means that there are no airs and graces. Everyone is immediately accepted in the group. For a player, it is very important to arrive in a club and feel that you are wanted. That's particularly true if you are a foreigner.'

Oli's performances undoubtedly helped facilitate his smooth integration, as Leeds swept all before them during an incredible 2000–01 season. The greatest achievement, of course, was reaching the semi-finals of the Champions League. 'Playing in the Premiership is cool,' Dacourt says, 'mainly because there is less defensive rigour than when playing in Europe. England has everything in place to succeed, and an extraordinary fish-tank of young players. But nothing compares to those big European games, when you are up against some of the biggest guns in the world. In those situations, you have to be at your very best in every department or else you will lose. It's much more organised and less chaotic than domestic English football.'

And yet, it is that chaos that Dacourt loves most. And it is a quality he says comes out most in FA Cup matches. 'For the fans,' he says, 'it's as big as the World Cup. The supporters love the FA Cup. When we were knocked out by Liverpool, there was absolute dismay and consternation in Leeds. People live for football, even the old lady is mad about football. The proof of this is that people will bet on everything to do with the game: who will score, in which minute, etc. . . People will spend hours studying the stats before making their decision. It's like a science or a religion.'

Dacourt has made it abundantly clear that he loves England and its football. Wilkinson may be trying to bring the French methods to England, but Dacourt, like Cantona before him, has come to Yorkshire to taste the English game in its truest, rawest form. Plenty of different quirks have struck Cantona's successor at Elland Road, but it is the strength of the bond between clubs and their supporters which will never cease to amaze him. 'I've been here for more than three years,' he says, 'and still I find the loyalty amazing. In France, we like the fashionable teams. One season it is Bordeaux, and the next year it is another team. In England, this is not possible. When children are born, they are born fans. If they are born Blues, then they will die as Blues. I had never seen anybody tattooed to the colours of his club, but I've seen that at Everton. And I've seen it at Leeds. It's very impressive. It's England.'

And who knows, with a new manager now in place, Dacourt may yet be part of a Leeds team that finally recaptures some silverware. After all, it has been ten years since that other famous Frenchman lifted their last trophy. 'We all know what the fans expect,' Dacourt says. 'They have been waiting for a long time and are crying out for success. They are so devoted and loyal, that I feel they deserve everything they can get.'

Just like those many tattooed supporters he refers to, Dacourt has quite obviously been marked for life by English football.

Alex Hayes

CHAPTER 7

Newcastle: Sir Bobby and the French Rebels

Statistics can be twisted, but they don't lie. According to the final stats of the Premiership, Laurent Robert was one of the best providers in 2001–02, with 11 assists in 32 games, to which you can add 4 Alan Shearer penalties awarded after Robert was fouled in the box. He also scored eight goals, hit the woodwork quite a few times, but when another Robert, Pires, got injured in March, nobody in France thought of the Newcastle one as a more than able replacement in the French squad. In Roger Lemerre's catalogue of errors, this was a big one. The former France coach sometimes said that he was a big lover of English football, but he rarely came to London to see a game (three hours on the Eurostar is a lot of time wasted for someone whose favourite line was: 'Tomorrow does not exist'), and he never cared to go to Newcastle to see Robert's influence on a Premiership game.

As Lemerre did not care for the statistics either, he could not find out that Robert was also one of the best shooters and crossers of the ball in the Premiership (see Opta stats in Chapter 16): first for shots (85), most of them on target, and second for crosses (340), dribbles and runs (257). To his credit, Robert had also won the Confederations Cup with France, in 2001, and then he took the chance of moving to England, instantly having one of the best seasons of his career so far, but he went AWOL on the screens of the French Federation. It must be that the French Football Federation (FFF) hard disks were saturated, or even bugged, with all the data about Christophe Dugarry and others. Ideal for the job, but forgotten, this was another common feature between Laurent Robert and David Ginola.

It is easy to see why people are quick to draw parallels between Robert and Ginola. Both played for Brest and Paris St Germain before signing for Newcastle United; both have fallen out with managers; both have a wonderful left foot; both, at the peak of their powers, would walk into most international teams but have strangely struggled to make an impact on the French side; and both will always be remembered on Tyneside for the influential first six months of their respective Black-and-White careers. How long, one wonders, before Robert, although his hair is much shorter, receives a call from L'Oréal?

Although flattered, it is at this point that the new boy would like the comparisons to end. Robert has obviously been studying the history of the Premiership. While Ginola and Newcastle had a start to the 1995–96 season to shout about, the second half was largely forgettable. To this day, that crop of Magpies are still seen as the ones who played pretty but could not fight dirty when it mattered. Top of the league at Christmas, they eventually surrendered the title to Manchester United. Ginola, who had announced himself as the new Cantona, was incapable of stopping the rot.

'His first four months at the club, I couldn't believe how good the Frenchman was,' Kevin Keegan recalls in his autobiography. 'He was playing so well I thought he could become the European Footballer of the Year. While he was causing our opponents problems going forward, it did not matter so much that his defensive work was found wanting. After Christmas, he hit a brick wall, along with a lot of the others,' the former manager of the Magpies, and then England, adds.

No wonder then, that Robert, knowing the history of his predecessor in the same club, kept a low profile after a great start to his first English season. The 26-year-old wanted to be top of the pile in May, not just during the festive period. 'It will not be much good if we just fall away from here on in,' he said around Christmas. 'We want to maintain our good form to the end. What we have achieved so far has been great, but who, outside Newcastle, will remember that we played well for a bit, come the final day of the season? This has to be the beginning of our title challenge, not the end.'

Five wins out of five before a defeat by Chelsea had gone a long way to bolstering Newcastle's title credentials, although Robert insisted that the championship has always been within the team's grasp. 'We've been in the top five since the first day of the season and never played badly twice in a row,' he said. 'That shows how consistent we are. The media might not talk about us or give us any credit for what we have achieved, but we're in no doubt. After our 4–3 win at Leeds United, all the papers were talking about Lee Bowyer when the real story was our incredible second-half performance.

'We are a tight-knit group who play good football, possess a massive stadium and have the greatest supporters. People out there might not take us seriously, but every single member of our squad believes that we can do it, and that's all that matters.' It is no surprise that the experienced Robert believed Newcastle still had to improve if they were to maintain their challenge. A little more unexpected, though, was to hear the former Montpellier and Paris SG player saying that the key to the Magpies' success is to give him the ball as often as possible.

'The thing about Newcastle is that they haven't had a natural left-winger since Ginola,' he explained, 'so the team are not used to playing down that side any more. This is why most of the action over the last four or five years has taken place on the right. But that has to change if we are to progress. If I get the ball more, I am sure we will score more. There needs to be more balance. At the moment, I often have to go to get the ball because it rarely comes to me. It is a problem which I have discussed with the manager and I hope will be resolved soon.'

Alan Shearer, as the main recipient of Robert's assists, does not mind confirming that Robert has revolutionised Newcastle as an attacking unit: 'We had become predictable because 75 per cent of our play was channelled down the right to Nobby Solano [Nolberto, the Peruvian international]. Laurent has given us the ability to attack from both flanks.' But this was not enough for Sir Bobby Robson, so the veteran of managers asked Robert for more, early in the season: 'Maybe he was able to play as a winger and hang upfield in France but you cannot play that way in England. You have to tackle back. Sir Alf Ramsey said that you have the ball for two and a half minutes in a match, so you had better spend the rest of the time doing something pretty sensible. We had to teach him that. We encouraged him, moaned at him. He thought it was easy when he came here. He arrived with a determination to put on a bit of a show, did well and then did not put in the work. He had to be worked on constantly. Full-backs will get past him and he has to respond.'

A few months later, Robert was making progress, but he still had his ups and downs. At the end of April, after another game of two halves, against West Ham (3–1), Sir Bobby summed it up nicely, and with his eternal sense of humour: 'Laurent was poorish first half, but scintillating in the second half. We told him what to do in French, Latin, everything! Not just get the ball, I can do that. Get the ball behind the full-back. When he's like that, he's the best in the country.' Being much more confident than a few months earlier, he added: 'Robert's ability is not in doubt. He's very talented, exciting. He's a goalscorer, like John Barnes [the former Watford, Liverpool and England star]. On his day, he's the best in the league.'

Robert is clearly not a player who suffers from a lack of confidence, but he can sometimes come across as being arrogant. It has always been a fine line with Robert and might explain why he, like his friend Nicolas Anelka a few months later, was shown the door by the Paris manager, Luis Fernandez. It might also offer an insight into his failure to hold down a regular place in the French team. In truth, Robert is simply being honest. Brave enough to move from his native Réunion Island, in the Indian Ocean, to Brest in the north-west of France at the age of 13, he was not going to shy away from a few constructive comments, now that he is a £10m professional. Whether it be speaking his mind or taking a nap most afternoons, Robert does things his way. But never, he insists, to the detriment of the team.

'I might have been a little big-headed in the past,' he said, 'but now I am just offering my honest opinion and concentrating on doing well for club and, if I am lucky, country as well. I feel part of a Newcastle side who are firing on all cylinders. We had some injuries to start with, but everyone is fit again and ready to make a serious push in 2002. Having someone like Kieron Dyer back is so important, because he is a player who brings so much to the team. In many ways, he has been the missing link, and I feel that we are now better equipped for a title bid. Getting into the French team for the World Cup is my obsession, but the only way to get there is to help Newcastle do well first.'

Eventually, Newcastle made it to the fourth spot in the Premiership, and a preliminary round of the Champions League, but Robert, after being the 23rd name on a list of 22 for the European Championship in 2000, also missed the plane to Asia for World Cup 2002. This was all the better for Newcastle, who could count on a fresh Robert when training started, at Drayton Park, at the beginning of July. Fresh, but rusty, and as honest as ever, he explained this to his fans, on his personal website, as soon as 8 July. Unfortunately, the interview was picked up by some sort of translator working for *The Sun*, who made a meal of it all, claiming that there was a big crisis brewing between Robert and Sir Bobby Robson. Immediately, the Geordie fans' website (www.nufc.com) reacted, with style, and explained what happened, under a very funny headline: 'Dodgy Translation: Le Miserable? Mais non!'

Then, the webmaster explained what happened: '"Readers" of today's *Sun* might be under the impression that Laurent Robert has had a big fall-out with Bobby and is sick of pre-season training already. To coin a phrase, his words have lost a little in translation. The *Sun*'s resident interpreter has obviously resorted to a GCSE interpretation of Robert's latest website musings, whereas you'll see our expert linguist's version gives the interview a very different slant:

> *What's happened to you, you sound exhausted?*
> I've just finished training, I'm in a right mess. I swear, they nearly killed us out there. At the end, I couldn't go on. It hurt so much, I wanted to throw up. What a nightmare! We ended the session with 500m races that had to be run in 1 min 50 secs. Six pitch-lengths at a time, twice. It was incredibly hard.
>
> *Getting back is tough then?*
> Tough, but good. We're working hard. It's hurting at the minute, but we know it'll pay dividends in the season ahead.
>
> *You rejoined the squad last Thursday. How was it, seeing everyone again?*
> Well first off, there's the new facilities. The club has completely refurbished everything and it's amazing. Then we were straight into training, hard training. We've been at it two times per day since last Thursday. The hardest is the afternoon session, it starts only an hour after we've eaten, so it's tough on the digestion.'

End of quote. Good translation, nothing major, except a couple of words for *The Sun* ('they killed us', 'what a nightmare') but it reminds me of something Alain Goma, the French centre-back who moved on to Fulham, said about his arrival at Newcastle, under Dutch manager Ruud Gullit, Robson's flashy predecessor, and about the pre-season preparation: 'I got along well with Gullit, but he did not stay long. His preparation, Italian-style, was too hard, so we lost the first six games. But the atmosphere was all right, because the crowd was very positive, always there to say: come on, we are going to win. At that time, there were five Frenchmen at Newcastle, but we never played at the same time. We tried not to speak French all the time, because the English can become somewhat paranoid sometimes. Because of the bad results, the team was split in various clans. Everybody was on the same level, but English key-players felt aside a bit, so they would not give it all for Gullit. There was also a problem between Gullit and Shearer, because they are two strong characters. One day Gullit tried something, he left Shearer on the bench, for a derby against Sunderland, and we lost 2–1. So Gullit was kicked out . . .'

This was an interesting moment in Newcastle's history, with so many foreigners including five French players on the salary bill: Goma and full-back Didier Domi, both coming from Paris SG; two other defenders, Franck Dumas and Laurent Charvet, plus a reserve keeper, Lionel Pérez. In the *Observer Sport Monthly*, Goma recalled his 'great memories' of Newcastle, starting with his very first game at St James' Park: 'Didier Domi had told me about the Newcastle crowd, saying: "It is really something. Two or three seconds before kick-off, they will shout like crazy." I got to the pitch, the crowd was already boiling hot, the stadium was full, and just before the ref blew his whistle I could not hear a thing. It was against Aston Villa, Shearer got sent off, and I put a header on the crossbar. The first time I heard them booing was when we lost to Manchester City at home. There was no football, nothing. But before that, there had already been some bad games.'

When Robson returned to Newcastle, the team was second from bottom, with one point from seven games. 'Don't panic!' Robson said, with all his legendary optimism and sense of humour. He even quipped that he was following a car with SOS on its plates, on his way to St James' Park. Goma recalls: 'Robson arrived, he did not even know our names, he kind of looked down on us, and instituted a new discipline. He

LEFT: '*L'esprit Ginola*', *L'Officiel Homme*, issue number 1, March 1996. Less than a year after David Ginola's arrival at Newcastle United, this new French magazine chose him as cover boy for its very first issue.

RIGHT: '*Ils sont complètement foot!*' (They are absolutely crazy about football), *Il* (He), issue number 6, a supplement to *Elle*, 1997, a series of stories about Eric Cantona and English football.

BELOW: 'Made in England – Tony Cascarino on the Premiership's role in the French Revolution', *The Times Football Handbook*, 13 April 2002, with a picture of Pires, Vieira and Henry celebrating after an Arsenal goal on their way to the Double.

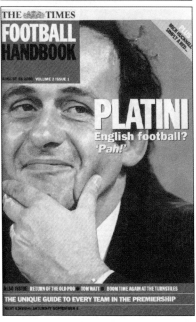

ABOVE: 'Platini: English football? Pah!', *The Times Football Handbook*, 18 August 2001, with an interview of Michel Platini, the former French playmaker, striker and then coach, who had almost joined Arsenal in 1982.

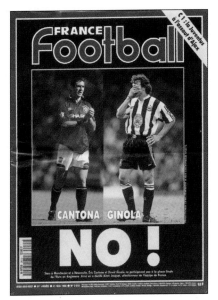

LEFT: 'Cantona – Ginola – No!', *France Football*, issue number 2615, 21 May 1996. Cantona and Ginola, currently at the top of their game in English football, were not selected by Aimé Jacquet, the French coach, for Euro '96 in . . . England. No comment.

RIGHT: '*A nous les grands Anglais*', *France Football*, issue number 2628, 20 August 1996, a reference to *A nous les petites Anglaises*, a cult movie in France, in the '70s, the story of French teenagers enjoying summer holidays on the south coast of England, and discovering love, among other things. The three pictures were of Eric Cantona, Frank Leboeuf, then at Chelsea and with hair, and Patrick Vieira who joined Arsenal that summer.

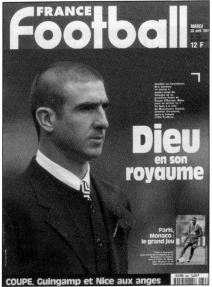

LEFT: '*Dieu en son royaume*' (God in his kingdom), *France Football*, issue number 2663, 22 April 1997. The picture of Eric Cantona was taken before the final of the FA Cup at Wembley one year before, and published before the second leg of a European Cup semi-final against Borussia Dortmund. One month later, Cantona announced his retirement.

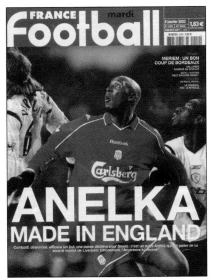

LEFT: 'Anelka – Made in England', *France Football*, issue number 2909, 8 January 2002. Two weeks after Nicolas Anelka's arrival at Liverpool, on a six-month loan deal, the cover story insists on how happy he is at Anfield. Six months later, he moved to Manchester City.

RIGHT: '*Real Madrid – Objectif Vieira*' (Target Vieira), France Football, issue number 2911, 22 January 2002. In the middle of renewed rumours of a departure for Vieira, the next summer, a cover story about the will of Real to create a dream team, with Vieira next to Zidane. Six months later Vieira was Arsenal's skipper.

LEFT: '*Blanc – Le chant du départ*' (The departure song), France Football, issue number 2916, 26 February 2002. In this cover story, Laurent Blanc explained why he intended to end his career at the end of the season. Four months later he announced a one-year extension to his contract with Manchester United.

RIGHT: 'Worshipped, Damned . . . and Gone – Cantona' – '*Un dix-page célébration du Roi Eric*' (a ten-page celebration of King Eric), *FourFourTwo*, issue number 35, July 1997, two months after Eric's retirement.

LEFT: '*Vive la Revolution*', *FourFourTwo*, issue number 48, August 1998, about France winning the World Cup in France, and with a cover picture of Laurent Blanc holding the trophy . . . three years before he moved to England to finish his playing career at Manchester United.

RIGHT: 'David Ginola – I came, I saw, I conquered', *FourFourTwo*, issue number 57, May 1999, an exclusive interview of David, then a Tottenham player, after winning the League Cup and a couple of 'Player of the Year' awards, his very first . . . and last trophies in England.

LEFT: 'Vieira – Hard, mean, a little bit tasty . . . don't you wish he was English?', *FourFourTwo*, issue number 76, December 2000, a cover story revealing 'why Tony Adams might be handing over the captain's armband soon'. This eventually happened, 18 months later, when Adams retired.

LEFT: 'Knowing me . . . Knowing you . . . Saha !', *FourFourTwo*, issue number 87, November 2001, a cover story on 'How the Fulham French connection put the smile back on the face of football', and Fulham star striker Louis Saha, the best scorer in the First Division the season before. It was not to be so easy in the Premier League . . .

RIGHT: 'The enemy within – Thierry, Petit, Trezeguet, Pires, Platini . . . on how France are going to do it again', *FourFourTwo*, issue number 93, May 2002, a whole series of articles about France before the World Cup, including an exclusive interview with Thierry Henry and Emmanuel Petit. One month later, France was out at the end of round 1, after failing to score one goal in three games.

'Cantona Story', *L'Equipe Magazine*, issue number 586, 24 April 1993.

The sub-heading read 'in England, "Canto" has taken, in the space of one year, a new dimension. His talent will be very useful to the French team'. Less than two years later, after the Selhurst Park kung-fu kick, Cantona was kicked out of the French team for good, and never came back.

'Du ballon, vite!' (Gimme some ball, quick), *L'Equipe Magazine*, issue number 696, 15 July 1995. After David Ginola's departure for Newcastle, in the summer of 1995, after a long transfer saga. The cover story was about the transfer stories of that hot summer, but also refers to Ginola's impatience to kick a ball with the Magpies.

'Les enfants de Canto!' (Canto's children), *L'Equipe Magazine*, issue number 803, 23 August 1997. Three months after Eric Cantona's retirement, the cover story was about his French followers at Arsenal, Petit, Vieira, Grimandi, Garde and Anelka, asking 'is Arsenal the best French team?'

'Sur les traces de Cantona' (On Cantona's tracks), *L'Equipe Magazine*, issue number 829, 28 February 1998. Less than one year after Cantona's retirement, the cover story was about the fact that his younger teammates at Manchester United were at a loss without him. That year Manchester United did not win one single trophy – for the first time in five years.

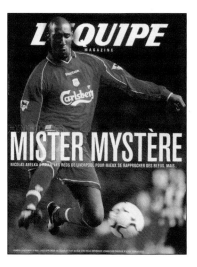

'Anelka – Mister Mystère', *L'Equipe Magazine*, issue number 1036, 23 March 2002.

Three months after Nicolas Anelka's arrival at Liverpool, the cover story asked whether his consistent effort under a Red shirt would be enough for him to be selected for the World Cup and play in Asia in a blue shirt. Eventually, the answer was no.

'French stars' final glory', *WSC* (*When Saturday Comes*), issue number 162, August 2000, after Chelsea's win at Wembley in the final of the FA Cup. 'Now, let's win the Premiership,' Desailly 'says' on the cover. 'Nah, can't be bothered,' Deschamps 'answers', next to Leboeuf.

'Wenger stays calm', *WSC*, issue number 164, October 2000, when Arsenal was in the middle of yet another controversial spate of yellow and red cards, as well as brawls in tunnels. 'Take it easy on the pitch, I'll get them in the tunnel,' Wenger 'says' on the cover, to his skipper Adams.

'Man Utd ease up', *WSC*, issue number 169, March 2001, after a vain effort by French goalkeeper Fabien Barthez to make Paolo di Canio (West Ham) think that he was offside. The Italian striker did not believe him, scored, and Man U was out. 'Come in closer, anywhere you like, go on, shoot,' Barthez 'says' on the cover.

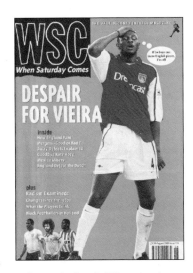

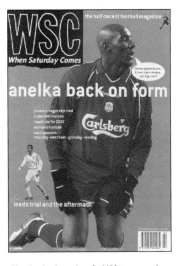

'Despair for Vieira', *WSC*, issue number 174, August 2001, when Arsenal manager Arsène Wenger was in the process of buying a series of English players, to change the balance of the team. 'If he buys one more English player, I'm off,' Vieira 'says' on the cover.

'Anelka back on form', *WSC*, issue number 180, February 2002, when French striker Anelka was on loan at Liverpool. 'No one passes to me, I want more money, can I go now?', Anelka 'says' on the cover.

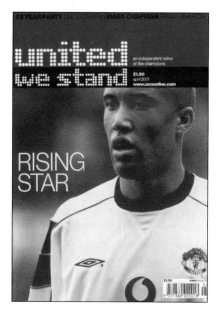

LEFT: 'Rising star', *United We Stand*, an independent voice of the champions, April 2001, with a cover story on French Manchester United defender Mikaël Silvestre.

RIGHT: 'The year ends in a one, but we still beat the scum!', The Gooner, issue number 112, May 2001, with a cover picture of Vieira, after beating Tottenham at Old Trafford, in a semi-final, to qualify for the 2001 FA Cup final.

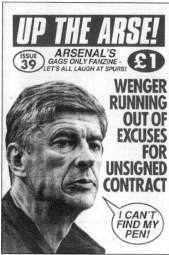

'Magnifique – Does it get any better than this?', asks *The Gooner* in the summer of 1998, after Arsène Wenger's first Double at Arsenal, at the end of his first complete season at the helm of the north London club. What nobody knew at that time is that Wenger would hold the same two trophies again, four years later, after yet another incredible season.

'Wenger running out of excuses for unsigned contract', *Up the Arse!*, issue number 39, November 2001, about Wenger taking over six months to find the time to sign an extension to his contract with Arsenal. He eventually signed, until 2005.

tightened everything up, but very tight, it was almost like the army. Robson gave the English players their confidence back, he made them play again, and the others, the foreigners, we were supposed to serve the group, that's all. It was the contrary to what Gullit had done.'

Now for Robson's version, in *The Independent*: 'I said "Is there money?" and they said "Not a penny". Morale was poor. [Stuart] Pearce went on a free [transfer] and a month later was back in the England team. Rob Lee didn't have a number. Shearer was out of favour. There was no discipline. Players were going upstairs to eat whenever they wanted, using mobile phones whenever they wanted. The whole thing needed an overhaul.'

Robson won over Shearer by restoring him to the team. 'I'd never even met Alan, but he's a top lad. I could see straight away that he'd lost the movement in his game. He was playing with his back to goal and just working the 18-yard line, not coming deep and spinning, not making diagonal runs. We got the movement back, and he scored 30 goals for us last year. Who's going to get us 30 goals this year?'

Goma appreciates that Shearer is important for Newcastle: 'In a town where everybody is fanatical about football, the fact that Shearer came back, with such a big name in English football, is great. At the club, no decision is taken without consulting Shearer. And Robson knows that his interest lies in having a good relationship with Shearer.'

Goma is a professional, he had a contract, so he waited and watched: 'At the beginning, training sessions were interesting, because he [Robson] had learnt a lot by working abroad, he had diversified. Then, progressively, they became sort of a routine. He tried to institute a system, we started from basics again, it was a mix of English and European football, but closer to British football, with two sturdy strikers up front, Shearer and Duncan Ferguson. However, there were deficiencies, especially on the physical side. There were two physiotherapists, but an *ostéopathe* was missing, someone higher qualified. In France, we have that *ostéo* culture; as soon as things go wrong, we have a look at the pelvis, etc. There was also a lack of tactical work in training, which we paid for in the games. I sometimes felt that Robson didn't take enough responsibility for things. He gave me the impression that he blamed the players, and especially the foreigners.'

However, Robson's plan worked, and Newcastle were saved: 'You know, when I came, the chairman said that he didn't think I'd be able to do it, to keep them up. He was investing in a super stadium and had visions, with respect, of Stockport and Crewe playing there every week. But from the eighth game we scored 51 points and finished 11th. By the beginning of March we couldn't go down. I saved the club, really, because if you go down will you ever come up? Look at Notts Forest. You'd have thought they'd come straight back up, but they haven't, have they?'

Newcastle's revival included some vital away wins, achieved, says Robson, as a direct result of his experience of Continental football. 'I used to watch how teams would come to Porto and play defensively. And if a team plays defensively and it's your job to break them down, you won't do it with two players, or four, or even six. Sometimes you need eight going down there, and those eight get sucked in, and then the other lot get possession and they're taught how to break quickly and suddenly you're losing. You think, "Jesus Christ, we've got done on the counter-attack." I used to watch that, particularly in Portugal where they play counter-attacking football, and I learnt from it. We went to Leicester and won, we went to Aston Villa and won . . .'

Robson saved Newcastle, but Goma was on his way: 'One day, I had a very average game, and soon after that, there was a bomb in the papers, they said that I wanted to leave, and people thought I was a traitor. The club bosses control the local press. When a player needs to be criticised, they use the press. There was more and more tension, and no real dialogue with Robson. Eventually, I had an argument with Robson, and everything accelerated. We lost at home to Manchester City; I was not very good. On Monday, we had a lousy training session, four-a-side, small goals, lads shooting from everywhere, no work at all, no fun, it was a catastrophe. At the end, I left before the stretching session, and I went directly to the locker-rooms. After lunch, Robson did a speech about professionalism, and started raising his voice when talking to me, saying that I was not a good pro. I got worked up, I criticised training, I was very nervous, it was "broken English". He tried to justify himself, it was really tense, and from there something was broken. The English looked at me strangely, because I was answering the big shot. Everybody was surprised, because I was not that extrovert before. The English, with regards to Robson, they try to keep their self-control, because the manager is untouchable, whereas the French tend to say what they think. And I was the only Frenchman left at that time.'

Goma was the only Frenchman left, because his good friend Domi had already left, not long after a story appearing on a website (www.football365.com), which was then picked up by news organisations, claimed that Domi was ready to pack his bags and head home after failing to claim a regular starting berth at St James' Park. In addition, the former Paris St Germain full-back was reported as suggesting that Robson's methods on the training pitch were old-fashioned and not what he needed to get himself back to top form. Robson called the 22-year-old into his office for urgent talks, and then summoned the media to a hastily arranged press conference at St James' Park. There, with Domi sitting stone-faced on his right, he read an agreed statement from the player: 'The stories are a total distortion. I have not made any such statements to any members of the press criticising the training methods of Mr Robson, who is highly regarded throughout the world of football. The extracts which appeared [on the website] are a total fabrication of an interview I did with [French daily] *Le Parisien*. The contents of that website are neither fair nor accurate and I think it only right that the public should be made aware of that.'

Domi was Gullit's second signing after the Dutchman's surprise swoop for Duncan Ferguson, and the £4m that United paid PSG for his services was thought to be an astute investment for a then 20-year-old who had come through the French ranks with Nicolas Anelka. Eventually, Domi went AWOL, and Goma cannot help laughing when he recalls his friend's disappearance: 'He was in the team, he started the games, but Robson was very demanding with him. He was fed up and he did not feel like working hard any more. One day, he had an argument with him, and he left. He left for France! We had a home game the next day, he never showed up. He did not tell us, and we never saw him again. He came back, "like a submarine", to take care of his removal.' Domi refused to return, prompting United to cut their losses and sell him back to Paris St Germain.

For Robson, respect is paramount. He explained that to the *Observer Sport Monthly*, in a lengthy and fascinating interview: 'Before, the players' respect for the manager was unquestioned. Now you have to work harder to get it, because top players, the ones you really don't want to lose, can threaten to leave. Ronaldo is the perfect example. He had an eight-year contract with Barcelona and after a year he was gone. But he was a good lad, all the same. He treated senior players with respect. He always listened to what I had to say. Except when I asked him to stay at Barca. But that was the agent's fault. Some agents are good, but many are a nightmare – perpetuating the player's unrest, never satisfied. Always looking to get a bigger cut, even if it is against their player's long-term interests. As happened, tragically, with Ronaldo. I'll never forget what he said when I asked him, during the negotiations before he left for Inter Milan, what his agents' view was: "They said, I need to play football and they need to make money. I have to listen to them."'

Sir Bobby elaborated on how the manager's job has changed through the ages: 'You've got to be so meticulous in your preparations. There's a lot more one-to-ones with players, analysing their games, trying to personalise their coaching to make them better players – which is now what the coach's job is supposed to be, in large measure. As for team talks, the sorts of things I'd say in my Ipswich days were much more general. Like, "They take the long throw, watch out for the long throw." That's not sufficient now. Now I say that for the long throw I want you in front of that player, and you get behind him and, between the two of you, sandwich him in. I spend about 90 minutes preparing the charts, about 16 pages in all. I mark down each player for each particular duty: for an attacking corner and defensive corner; how to line up against a lateral free-kick, where precisely each player should stand; how far back or forward the last line of defence should be, depending on the angle of approach of the ball. I have a separate sketch for each permutation.'

The former England coach knows his international football well. Contrary to what Domi may have implied, Robson is aware that things are changing, but he wants to keep a grip on the evolution: 'You'll never get a Newcastle team with 11 Geordies now. The best you can do is retain a British nucleus. I am trying to do that at Newcastle. But beyond that, you're dreaming. We're getting used to it now, but it's bad for the national side, no doubt about it. We've even got, disastrously, some clubs whose reserves are full of foreigners, so where is the English player getting a chance?' Robson has his reservations about foreigners, but he is still shopping abroad, buying Paraguayans, Argentinians, Portuguese, Congolese and Chileans: 'I am a hypocrite. But I am trying like everybody else to get success. It's a Catch 22, but I, like everybody else, have to start buying foreign players. And we'll do so till the country starts producing good ones of its own.'

What did Robson find had changed for the better when he returned to English football? 'A lot. Much greater professionalism. More attention to diets, to getting just the right protein and carbohydrate intake at just the right time. More scientific monitoring of fitness levels. Greater seriousness from the players, greater awareness that their careers are short and they had better look after their bodies.' However, Robson was shocked to discover how deep the English culture of drunkenness remained, not just among the fans, but also among the top players. 'You try to stop them from drinking alcohol but they still like a drink, more in England than in any other country I know. In Portugal they never drank, in Barcelona they never drank. It's a cultural thing. It's been in the game a long time, and the young players come in, meet it, get the swing of it, and become the same. Not every player, but there is far too much drinking of alcohol in English football, far too many players getting drunk at weekends.'

Robson has travelled a lot, he's coached lots of different clubs in Europe (PSV Eindhoven twice, Sporting Lisbon, FC Porto, Barcelona), so there could be no trace of xenophobia in his conflicts with Goma, the quiet centre-back from the French Caribbean, and Domi, the fiery full-back from the same area. On the top of that, Sir Bobby is a long-time fan of French football: 'It was not so long before that we thought of France as a poor footballing nation. We played them in my first game as an England player. I scored twice and we won 4–0. But look at that team, so unlucky not to win the 1982 World Cup. What the coach [Michel Hidalgo] did was really imaginative. He played with one winger, one front player, and no player on the right at all.

'The team was built on the midfield trio of Platini, Giresse and Tigana. Platini, who could thread the ball through the eye of a needle, was in the hole, looking for the counter-attack, doing next to no defensive work. When France regained the ball they passed it to him. Behind Platini was little Giresse, knitting the midfield with the back four. Tigana had amazing pace and endurance. He did not operate wide, but he worked the right channel up and down. What you had here was a clever coach who was aware of his weaknesses and found a way of playing that suited his players, while at the same time causing confusion in the opposing team.

I mean, what do you say to those two guys playing on the right in the other team who have no one to mark? No one mastered that problem.'

Not only is Robson a long-time fan of French football, he also tried to sign David Ginola when he was still the boss at Barcelona. Ginola recalls the whole episode, and his disappointment at not being able to leave in the end: 'What happened? I got a phone call from Bobby Robson. I was in Sainte Maxime. The phone rang: "Hi, David? Bobby Robson! FC Barcelona!" He called me to tell me that he was going to contact the Newcastle people, because he wanted me to come to Barcelona. And then I had Kevin Keegan on the phone, and all the other bosses at the club: "David, you want to go, and the fans, what are they going to think? You cannot do that."'

Ginola continues to explain the aborted move: 'Barcelona made an offer, but Newcastle asked for £12m, to block the move. Barcelona was ready to give £4m, went up to £6m, Newcastle went down to £7.5m. There were supposed to be huge commissions for agents, the deal did not happen. In my mind, I was almost there, I was ready to go and find a house in Barcelona, but I think Keegan reacted. The previous year, he had made a mistake, letting Andy Cole go to Manchester, and he had the fans on his back. He realised that if he let me go after my first season, he would have the same problem.'

Ginola at Newcastle is another interesting episode. In fact, it was the very first episode of the French saga on Tyneside. And to write that Gino's arrival in the North East was a cultural shock is an understatement, according to the player: 'To land in England and start the journey in the North East was not an obvious thing to do. Newcastle is a working-class city, a bit like Lens. There was such a difference with Paris, where I had spent the past four years. Suddenly, I was in the working world of the North East. With training every day, matches to play, I was often away from home, and it was very tough for my wife. In Newcastle, there are very rich people, and very poor people. The rich ones, of course, are around the club. When they came to pick me up at the airport to drive me to St James' Park, in a Rolls-Royce, and then when the same person drove my wife around the city, to show her the area, she started to cry when she came back.'

In Paris, the Ginola family lived next to Saint Nom La Bretèche. 'We had a nice house with trees, a swimming-pool, we were close to our friends, we could go down to the south of France whenever we wanted, by car or by plane. It was such a change for her, and it was summertime, but the weather was incredible: the good weather must only last 15 days over here. But I cannot criticise that choice, I did it at one point in my life, I went to the North East and I had to face the situation, to try and be as good as possible, that's what I tried to do. My wife has been very strong, and when we left, I could feel sort of a resurrection [he laughs].'

The weather was only the first surprise, there were more to come: 'My first season at Newcastle, we played on New Year's Day, at two o'clock. I found that completely staggering. The English were in the stadium, it was a party for them, a celebration. On Boxing Day, it's also very important for them, they go to the stadium with their children. It's like a ritual, you cannot take that away from them. If you took away a tradition in France, suddenly, one day, millions of French people would be upset.'

Ginola also had to cope with the English game: 'The game is fast and furious. At the beginning, it was hard to cope with the pace of the game, the way the English mark another player. I often had two or three players on my back. It is very difficult to move, to find a way out of this situation, and this is what surprises them: to see the skills that we have, the difference in the game, with the English. We are much more skilful, technically, which allows us to show more ease in the game. It's true for lots of French players, because there is a French education, and one has to recognise that it is a quality education. French players are recognised as quality players, and it's all very well. As a Frenchman, I am proud to hear: "You are French, it's great. I love the way you play. It's good for our country."'

David is proud of his French football education, but as a father of two, he was also interested in the education of his children when he moved to England: 'English education is a very good education. One year, I put my son and my daughter at the French school, in Sainte Maxime, during my holidays, in May and June. The profs were stunned by my son's ability to sit down and listen, while the other children created an uproar. Private education demands this sort of commitment, of respect. When you see all the children at school with their uniforms, it may appear snobbish, but I find this absolutely logical. When I was a kid, I remember that we always had a close look at the last model of Nike sport shoes, or so and so's shirt.

Here, everybody is the same, there is no jealousy. My son goes to a school with Hindu, Japanese, Chinese, Pakistani and English children of a certain social hierarchy. They are all friends, some of them come to the house, and I think it is a good thing.'

So much for English education, but what about English football? 'The quality of the leagues is not really a matter for debate. It's always the same; in all the leagues, there are great teams, and teams that are slightly less good. In Italy, in the Serie A, there is the top of the table, and the bottom of the table; all teams are not excellent. The styles are completely different, there is a football education in each country. In England, it is a football with no interval, the game for the game, and even if there is some waste of energy, there is huge commitment.'

Huge commitment from the fans, as well: 'When I am in a park, my son on my shoulders, my daughter holding one arm, my wife on the other side, the English would come to me and ask me for an autograph. With respect, but they want it, because it is important for them. They will return home with the autograph, it's an important moment, it will be an immense joy for their child. So they tend to forget that I am also a father, they don't think: it is his free time, I am going to leave him alone. Some do, but not all of them. Most of them are real fans, and they don't care about the free time. It's the other side of the deal.'

Ginola is good at deals, although they often take time to materialise, and to get the final green light and rubber stamp of Chantal Stanley, his cautious and faithful advisor. After Kevin Keegan's departure from Newcastle, Ginola moved to Tottenham, won the Worthington Cup in 1999 and was elected Footballer of the Year by the Football Writers' Association. Then things turned sour with George Graham and he made his way to Birmingham, where things turned even sourer with John Gregory at Aston Villa (see Chapter 13, The French Sceptics). Eventually, he ended up at Everton for three months, at the end of the 2001–02 season. Back to the north, closer to Newcastle, as if the wheel had come full circle for Ginola, the great French Romantic of English football.

Everywhere Ginola passed, he left a mark, for all sorts of reasons. At Newcastle, his mark is on the pitch, not on the bench: 'Ginola was part of a unique combination of talents,' remembers Mike Bolam, editor of www.nufc.com, the leading Geordie fans' website. 'His crosses were so good that you could forgive him not tackling back or the odd Gallic shrug. I almost feel the same about Robert. If he was from Blakelaw, he would be getting savaged, but Newcastle are playing so far above our expectations that there isn't more than a murmur of disapproval.'

No wonder Robert wants to follow Ginola's path, and go even further. In one season on Tyneside, he has even managed to convince Robson that he was the right man for the job. Robson went where Arsenal and Liverpool feared to tread when he signed Robert. Standing by his enigma, he vowed, in the spring of 2002, that the Premiership would soon see the best of Laurent Robert: 'Look at Robert Pires compared to the player we saw last season. He has shown us what a talent he is. Laurent can be the best player in the Premiership next season. That is when you can judge him. He is the kind of player who can do something special and win a game.'

After another great game from Robert, and in the euphoria of securing the first Champions League spot in Newcastle history, Sir Bobby continued raving about his French winger. It took some time for Robert to learn how to defend, but eventually he got it right: 'You need that type of player, but sometimes he seems to be out of the rhythm of the game. That's his style. Don't forget he played in a very different league and is used to a more attacking role but to be a winger in the Premiership you have to defend as well. All the lads are trying to tell him to work hard and he showed today that he knows that, which is a good sign. We know we all have to try for each other and a team like Arsenal shows that. They have good individual players but they have the determination to win games by working hard for each other. He has to learn the culture of the game. We don't want him to defend all the time. His main job is to create, but there are times when we need him to help out.'

Eventually, Robson seemed to be happy with Robert's achievements and improvements, but he was not finished with his French contingent. The latest to find himself on the wrong side of the former England boss was young Olivier Bernard. The 22-year-old arrived at St James' Park from Lyon in October 2000. After a loan spell at Third Division Darlington, he forced his way into the first-team picture, scoring three goals in a dozen games. However, disgruntled at his lack of opportunities, he was happy to accept West Ham's overtures in June of 2002 and prepared to pack his bags and head for London.

The furious Magpies reported the Hammers to the Premiership alleging an illegal approach, and succeeded in their attempts to block Bernard's departure. In a statement released through the club's official website, www.nufc.co.uk, Newcastle stressed that 'West Ham were reminded again at the end of the season that the player was under contract to Newcastle United until 2003.' At one point, Bernard stated his position: 'Whatever happens, I do not want to play for Newcastle United and would find it very difficult to go back.' The player said he was 'disappointed' at his 'lack of first-team opportunities', his reason for turning down 'the offer of a new contract'.

Eventually, Bernard signed a new three-year contract and reported back at training before mid-July. However, the whole affair was a case of *déjà vu* for Robson, who in his time at St James' has seen Frenchmen Franck Dumas, Alain Goma, Didier Domi and Sylvain Distin all leave the club under a cloud. More than once, Robson was even left uncharacteristically speechless by the antics of the young Frenchmen. The Goma and Domi incidents have already been described but there were other instances. Robson did not want to lose the experienced Dumas either, but had little choice in the matter after the solid centre-back insisted that he wanted to return home. Last but not least, in the summer of 2002, Sylvain Distin's £4m move to Manchester City, after a spell on loan at United, was the subject of a separate complaint by the club.

Since Ginola's arrival in England, Newcastle have had 11 French players under contract. It's the same score as Arsenal, but for the amount of time they spent on Tyneside, and the number of games they played, the French Magpies have a much greater record of arguments and controversy, from what we can gather. And as Damian Spellman, a reporter for the Press Association (PA), once pointed out about Sir Bobby Robson, 'English football's most experienced manager has a grasp of several different European languages after his time working on the continent, but there is one phrase he is unlikely to utter when contemplating his dealings with some of his French stars: "*C'est la vie!*"'

Daniel Ortelli

CHAPTER 8

A Fulham of Two Halves: Too French to Win?

January 2000: 'Jean Tigana's skill, his patience and foresight – now available in bottles.' The tongue-in-cheek advert, placed on page five of Fulham's programme notes for an FA Cup tie against Manchester United to advertise the 1999 white wine made at Tigana's vineyard in France, told you everything about the esteem in which the French manager was held in West London.

In the early part of his reign, Tigana was a hero. He introduced a new breed of footballers, a new brand of football and, most importantly, repaired 33 years of hurt within 12 months of his arrival, by guiding Fulham back into the promised land of the top flight.

Cynics said then, and might well repeat now, that Tigana only succeeded because of the millions of pounds made available to him by the club's eccentric but devoted chairman, Mohamed Al Fayed. But that would be unfair to Tigana and the French revolution he started on the banks of the Thames. We use the word started – and not finished – because the jury is still out. Unlike Arsène Wenger and Gérard Houllier, both of whom have silverware to show for their efforts, the new kid on the block is still finding his feet.

Following the incredible rise to success of the Fulham team during Tigana's first season in charge, a year during which the club won the First Division title in record time, the wheels have come off the Fulham machine. Has permanent damage been caused? Only time will tell.

THE TIGANA TEAM ETHIC

If one word were needed to sum up Tigana's thinking, it would have to be 'sharing'. Indeed, the greatest strength of the Frenchman's approach to management is his ability to create a nucleus of generals to help him fight his campaigns. It might seem strange to mention other names when discussing Tigana's football methodology, but the truth is that John Collins, Christian Damiano and Roger Propos can take much of the credit for the Fulham revolution.

The 'other Jean', in particular, has been inspirational since he became Tigana's first Fulham signing in the summer of 2000, both on and off the pitch. Not only has the Scot been pulling the strings in the heart of midfield, he has also become a vital cog in the workings of the Fulham machine. No wonder, then, Tigana calls him 'my special player'.

'I don't know if you can call me special,' Collins says. 'It's simply that I know what Jean expects. I'm familiar with his methods and, most importantly, I know they work. That's why I decided to leave Everton and the Premiership at that time to join Fulham. I was moving down a division, but I just felt it was a case of taking one step back to take two steps forward. To be honest, I wouldn't have come had it not been for Jean.'

Tigana signed Collins once before, in the summer of 1996, when the Frenchman was in charge of Monaco. Collins says he learned more in those two years in Monte Carlo than he had in the previous 13 of his professional career. 'What Jean has done here at Fulham is what he's always advocated,' Collins explains. 'He asks the players to play simple football. What we're doing is not complicated. We're passing the ball quickly and moving. Of course, in order to do that well you have to be fit and sharp, and that's why we work very hard on the training ground. It's all precision training; nothing is left to chance.'

Collins adds: 'A lot of coaches in this country think that if you train lots then the players will be fit, but that's not necessarily the case. What we do at Fulham is not too much, but not too little. It's a science. Players have been taught how to stretch properly, what dieting really means, what they should drink, how their muscles work. Everything is done for a reason, it's not just done to kill time. I've seen both sides [British and French] and I'm in no doubt as to which is the better system. I feel fitter at 35 than I ever have. I'm better now, both physically and mentally, than I can remember. There's no doubt that the things I learned from Jean have extended my career.'

Tigana's rapid revolution has been aided by two other experienced Frenchmen. Roger Propos, who worked at Marseille during their golden era of the late 1980s and early 1990s, is responsible for fitness, while Christian Damiano, once of the respected French Football Federation, focuses on technique. This leaves Tigana to concentrate on tactics and Collins to work on his translation skills. 'I've been acting as an interpreter,' says the Scot, who speaks fluent French and helped Tigana settle in. 'In the early days, if players weren't sure what one of the coaches meant, I could help.'

Collins adds: 'There's undoubtedly been a massive change in the way things are done here. It can be a bit of a culture shock, but I'm in no doubt that all the players have got the opportunity of a lifetime to learn everything they will ever need. I've told them. That's why if one of them has a moan I am here to say, "Try it, it will benefit you like it has me and others."'

Damiano was France's assistant coach to Roger Lemerre, chief scout for the former French manager Aimé Jacquet, and has been one of the key figures in the Federation's youth development over the past decade. During his time at the national training centre at Clairefontaine, Thierry Henry, Nicolas Anelka, David Trezeguet and Lilian Thuram all passed through his hands. 'We took Anelka and Henry when they were 13 and they already had good balance and coordination,' Damiano says. 'But they were with us before they had bad habits. That's the key. The way we improved them was by concentrating on technique and repeating exercises many times. Here, at Fulham, Jean and I are applying exactly the same philosophy and methods of work.'

Part of that system involves making sure that there is always a senior figure present at the club. 'Thankfully, there were three of us when we arrived,' Damiano explains, 'because alone it would have been impossible to survive. With three of us, we can share the duties, and it works very well. One person can arrive at 7 a.m. and the other leaves at 8 p.m. every day. We take it in turns. English people arrive at 9 a.m., leave at 4 p.m., and aren't even here at weekends. We are at the club from Monday morning to Sunday evening. We leave nothing to chance. In many ways, we practise more like an Italian club than a French one. We often split the players up in groups so that they can concentrate on technique and certain specific areas. Fitness is crucial.'

And fitness was Propos's first task on his arrival. Under his strict guidance, the majority of the first team lost five to six kilos, thanks to a specific regime for each player. 'That is so important,' explains Alain Goma, a purchase from Newcastle in March 2001. 'You have to cater for the individual needs of each player. Without that, footballers cannot progress to the maximum of their potential.' Goma is one of many who have blossomed at Fulham. 'In Newcastle, people were charming, welcoming and friendly,' the Frenchman says, 'but the pub culture was a little special. I was a single man and I had a tendency to get bored, because the nightlife was not exactly recommended to us, due to our job. In the spring, I wanted to move to London, but I was behind in terms of fitness. To find Fulham, with a group of Frenchmen working differently, was really the ideal for me, because we have the same approach. It is important that the coach manages his group decently, by putting all the players at the same level, and that all the French take the pain to speak the language, because the English really appreciate it. I worked a lot on my fitness with Roger [Propos], and I played the last games of the 2000–01 season. And now I am back to my best after another year under my belt and I feel excited about going into work every day.'

Like Tigana, both Damiano and Propos are workaholics. No wonder, then, they complain about the amount of holidays given to the players. 'The summer break is far too long,' insists Propos, after his club have played in an InterToto second round tie in the first week of July 2002. 'Anything more than a month is enormous and disastrous for the players, because a sportsman loses roughly 1 per cent of his physical potential every day he is off training.' The Fulham training, therefore, starts earlier than most other clubs, and is pretty rigorous. 'They are always terrified when they get back from holiday,' Damiano jokes, 'because they know they haven't done enough work.'

Damiano, for his part, never stops. 'When my day finishes,' he explains, 'I go home and start to think of the video I must compile to show the players at the end of the week. We work with the same technology as the French team. Everything is computerised and saved. I have a full-time information technology guy working just for me to compile the stats and stuff. He will dissect all our matches, and put together the information regarding each and every one of the players. It's a largely unknown, but really vital part of our work at this club.'

Another often unsung hero is the man they call 'Teacher'. Philippe Patry is a linguist, who did a lot of work on African dialects with Tigana's father in Mali. Patry's responsibility is to teach English to the new French recruits as quickly as possible. It may sound like a luxury, but language, more than any other factor, can bond or break a group of players. In that respect, it is interesting to know that he also refreshes the English players' and staff's French so that there is a genuine attempt from everyone at the club to meet halfway. 'I come to the club ten days per month,' he says, 'and my main aim is to make sure everybody is adapting to each other. The worse thing would be if clans formed, with neither side understanding what the other was saying. That would be catastrophic.'

Stories of factions are not uncommon. The Middlesbrough team of 1996–97, for example, which included the likes of Italy's Fabrizio Ravanelli and Brazil's Juninho, was clearly not a happy ship. 'It's vital to get the players and manager learning the language,' Patry says, 'but it is really tough. I have so little time with Jean. He's so busy that we will often have to do five minutes of lessons in the back of a taxi or if he's soaking in the bath.'

The Patry–Tigana alliance goes back a long way. Indeed, it was Patry who taught Collins how to speak French in record time, when the Scot joined Monaco from Celtic in 1996. 'Teacher' takes up the story: 'I had lived in Scotland for over 20 years, teaching the bosses of the big whisky conglomerates how to speak French, Spanish and Italian. It was during that time that I also met the vice-president of the Scottish Football Association [SFA]. That's how I got in touch with John and offered my services. I called him one night, as he was packing his things, and he told me to come over to the house. I did that, we got on, and I immediately taught him, his wife and his kids. There is no doubt that grounding helped him adapt as well as he did in France.'

Patry adds: 'If a player can't speak the language, he feels ill-at-ease and rejected. John, when he went to Monte Carlo, was doing interviews with French journalists after just ten days. One of the local guys came over and told me he couldn't quite believe what had happened. He said that in the three years he was at Monaco, he was never able to get a single word out of Glenn Hoddle.'

TIGANA THE DEMANDER

Part of Tigana's make-up has always been his tough-guy image. His manner may seem quiet, withdrawn, almost aloof. But he is a thinker, a tactician, and, most of all, a disciplinarian. Tigana, who remains exceptionally fit and takes all training sessions himself, says he likes to get close to his players; he is a tracksuit manager. He is also someone who treats his players like adults. 'If I'm demanding of people,' he says, 'it's because I'm demanding of myself. The things which I expect a player to do are the same things which I have always done myself. People accuse me of being harsh and tough, but I'm a communicator. Don't forget I gave several youngsters their chance at Monaco.'

Tigana can stake a claim in the development of the likes of Lilian Thuram, Thierry Henry, Fabien Barthez and David Trézéguet, all of whom he blooded young. 'I pushed those kids hard,' he admits, 'and they probably thought, "God, this guy is severe", but now they thank me for it. I prefer to bump into old players and have them come up to me and say, "You made us work but it was worth it because I joined Arsenal for £10m," rather than, "I wish you'd been more demanding."'

Goma concurs with his manager's views: 'Jean does not speak too much, and he likes to allocate a specific time for each different thing. So there will be a period when he is close to the players, when he mucks around with us; then there is a time when he will not speak at all, unless he has something really important to say. In those moments, believe me, everyone is listening to him. I think he was greeted with a degree of scepticism when he first arrived, but I also think that is sort of normal.'

Thankfully, the Fulham players responded to his ways. 'I quickly felt a great desire among the players to move forward,' Tigana says. 'Perhaps the fact that I was also a pro helped, but ultimately I just think they responded to my methods. I see the players as my kids. I'm strict with them but I'm also compassionate and understanding. I only have a go at the ones who aren't trying.'

Tigana's temper is legendary, especially if players give the impression they would rather be elsewhere. Like many a manager, particularly one with a certain pedigree, the 47-year-old demands respect. It is, he says, the only way to get the most out of a player. 'I see the body of an athlete as a business, with each individual managing his as he chooses. Either he tries to get the most out of it and can have a fruitful career, or he is only interested in doing the minimum, in which case he will not be successful. The Fulham players have been very responsive. I'm interested in building a rapport with them, not imposing my views on them. I'm available at any time; the players know that and they seem happy. It's worked.'

INSTANT SUCCESS

Pinpointing the reason for the Frenchman's instant success is difficult. Before the 2000–01 First Division season kicked off, many felt that Tigana's lack of experience of English football and his timid transfer dealings (Fulham bought only three new players, one of whom was Fabrice Fernandes on a year's loan) might doom them to failure. It did not, and Fulham grew stronger and stronger.

So far as Tigana is concerned, the key was empowering the players. 'Whether in lower-league football or the European Championship,' he told me, 'it's always the teams wanting to express themselves that come out on top. I may be proved wrong, but I simply don't believe you have to be negative or ultra-safe in order to win. Over the course of a season, the best team always triumphs.' Did he not feel he needed to spend big as soon as he took over at Craven Cottage? 'To be perfectly honest,' Tigana continues, 'no. I immediately thought that this team had a lot of potential. They were willing to learn, particularly because most English kids are brought up with that raw passion for football, and I simply shared my knowledge. English players are much more hard-working and receptive than their French counterparts.'

As a player, Tigana, who combined tidiness and tigerishness for Bordeaux, Marseille and that magical France midfield of the 1980s, never forgot the significance of ball retention. Without such an asset, the creative forces around him could not have flourished. 'Size is one thing, skill is another,' he says. 'Look at [Gianfranco] Zola, he's a little guy but when he has the ball he's immense. Why? Because people can't get the ball off him and he's in no hurry to give it away.' For Tigana the coach, the same rules apply. 'Teams that are uncomfortable in possession and are desperate to get rid of the ball will never progress. My philosophy is that power lies with the carrier.'

Lee Clark, one of the players who has developed most under the tutelage of the Frenchman, explains the ethos. 'Each and every player has the freedom to express himself, but only once he has fulfilled his obligations to the team. Everybody defends and attacks together. You need that cohesion to succeed. Jean has given us the power to play this way. Almost from one day to the next, he was able to transform the way British players play, not to mention their mentality and their habits. We suddenly became European.'

Collins has been pleased with Fulham's overall showing these last two years. The confidence which Tigana enjoys from the players has helped, but the club's success has firm roots as well. 'It's gone well, but that does not surprise me. Jean wants everyone to participate in the game. He never tells defenders, "Clear your lines" or "Don't take chances." Jean expects everybody to take responsibility but enjoy themselves at the same time. That's the way it should be. I wish all coaches thought like that, but too few of them have that football education.'

In his first 12 months in England, Tigana moulded a team in his image. Solid defensively, ambitious offensively and, most importantly, hard-working. 'He instilled a 24-hour way of life,' explains Louis Saha, the striker Tigana brought to the club early on. 'It's not just about practice or match days, it's about being a professional at all times. Jean's strength is that he knows how to strike a balance. Sometimes he wants us to be serious, sometimes he wants us to relax and have fun. That's why we did so well so quickly.'

Much of that early success was owed to the goal-scoring feats of Saha. The Paris-born player remembers the day he decided to join Fulham. 'I wanted to come to Fulham,' the 24-year-old says. 'The club were starting to make a name for themselves when I was last here in 1998. Kevin Keegan was manager and one of my Newcastle teammates at the time [Philippe Albert] was at Fulham on loan at the club. I didn't know much about English football when I arrived, but Fulham were one of the first clubs I heard of. People talked about them. I was intrigued.'

Saha is honest enough to admit he probably would not have come to Fulham had it not been for Tigana. But when the former French midfielder, who happened to be Saha's agent at the time, called in July 2000 to offer him the chance to join his London-based revolution, his client signed up instantly. 'It was a bit like Newcastle,' the Frenchman says. 'When somebody like Ruud [Gullit] or Jean invites you to their club, you must say yes. I was so flattered. And I knew that if Jean was at

Fulham it was because he felt that the club had potential and he could take them somewhere.'

That somewhere was the Premiership, after an incredible first season in charge, during which Saha shone. 'Statistically, 2000–01 was an incredible season for me,' the striker says. 'Come May, I couldn't wait for the new Premiership season.'

BACK IN THE BIG TIME

Let us return to the happy days of Fulham's triumphant return to the top flight of English football. Fate would decide that Fulham, the First Division champions, should play Manchester United, the Premiership rulers, for the opening fixture of the new campaign. We would soon know how good this Fulham side really was. Saha, who had scored more than 40 goals the previous season, looked fresher than ever, as he scored within four minutes. United equalised through Beckham just before half-time, but, shortly after the break, Saha struck again. Fulham were on the brink of a major shock until Ruud van Nistelrooy, Manchester United's most expensive striker of all time, netted twice to steal all three points.

Understandably, Tigana was more than happy with his team's showing. The season, you sensed, augured well. 'We started our Premiership lives against the reigning champions and we produced an excellent performance,' the Frenchman says. 'My team was not scared, my players kept the ball well, and we learned a good lesson. It was an exciting match, although I am never happy when I lose. All I hope is that next time, we will play a little less well and win. That has to be our aim.'

The next day, Ernest and Michael Moore, father and son supporters of Fulham, are on the train taking them back from Old Trafford to London. They will never forget the match. 'It was amazing,' Ernest says. 'We were singing: "Are you [Manchester] City in disguise?" What fun. And Saha – what a player. When he left Newcastle at the end of the 1998–99 season, his brain was not communicating with his feet. But now, under the guidance of Tigana, he is a changed player.'

Neither the Moores, nor indeed Tigana, could ever have guessed that, eight months later, the club would be in a fight for Premiership survival. Significantly, the slump started just as the goals were drying up. 'In terms of my overall game, I felt it took me a while to be a more complete player,' Saha says. 'To be honest, the whole team was not quite ready to challenge the Premiership when we first got promoted. We needed a few more months to get prepared.' During the difficult times, the young French marksman found comfort in the number of games played in England. 'That's one of the things I like most about English football; you play every three days and just get on with it. It means you get straight back into the saddle if something goes wrong.'

Critics will argue that Saha has been found out at Premiership level. For those who never believed in Tigana's personal approach, the disappointing end to the first season back in the big time cemented their fears that the club's early success was not built on firm foundations. That, insist those involved, is not the case. 'The whole club is very well structured,' Alain Goma, the French central-defender, says. 'Everything is detailed and thought out, and everyone knows what they have to do. It is a mirror image of the "Harrods way", where Mr Al Fayed has slowly built an empire without rushing or jumping any stages. This is a little like owning a vineyard: you have to be patient and caring, and then the results will eventually follow.'

The Tigana strategy was always based on a five-year plan. Two years in, therefore, the results must be viewed as positive. One promotion at the first attempt with a minimum of expenditure; one season back in the Premiership without falling into the trap of making a swift return to the Nationwide abyss; and the bonus of an FA Cup semi-final, lost 1–0 to Chelsea. So what is the problem? Tigana runs Fulham like a limited company. He is the chief executive with a long-term strategy, and he is implementing it to the letter. It may not always produce the exciting football of the first year, but it is keeping Fulham afloat.

Well, perhaps not in financial terms. Following a quiet first season in the Nationwide, Tigana went on a massive shopping spree as soon as he had helped Fulham into the elite. Edwin van der Sar, the number one Dutch keeper, was bought for a record fee of £7m from Juventus. Jan Koller and John Arne Riise were stolen from under his nose at the last moment, but that did not deter the Frenchman. He also added the Bordeaux midfielder, Sylvain Legwinski; the Lyon play-maker, Steed Malbranque; and the Lyon and France striker, Steve Marlet, to his squad, spending a further £18m in the process.

Tigana has not been afraid to use funds available to him, although he insists that he did not join Fulham because of the money. 'I have come here with my family and really integrated myself to prove how motivated I am,' he says. Michel Platini, who is a life-long friend and actually recommended Tigana to Al Fayed when he turned down the Fulham job, begs to differ. 'To be totally honest,' the French legend says, 'I don't think that he could turn down the offer that was made to him [reportedly in the region of five million pounds over seven years].' Answer from Tigana: 'I had plenty of other interesting offers, in France and abroad. But they did not grab me. What has always kept me going is a challenge, and Fulham is one. It would have been easier for me to take an established Premiership club or to accept the job of taking over the French team when Aimé Jacquet resigned after winning the World Cup in 1998, but I wanted to take a project from the beginning to the end.'

Whether or not the end is nigh remains to be seen, although the arrival and subsequent departure of Milan's Franco Baresi as director of football in the summer of 2002, might eventually lead to Tigana making a sharp move back to his native land. All in all, one thing is sure, in Fulham's case, big spending has not meant big returns. But why? Could it be that the French system has run its course?

THE END OF THE FRENCH REVOLUTION?

Say it quietly, but there are signs that the French football revolution is reaching its natural conclusion. For years we have been preached the virtues of France's training and playing methods, believing that our Gallic friends were perfect specimens who could do no wrong. Yet recent events, both on and off the field, suggest otherwise. Leaving aside the fact that Luton Town's winger Jean-Louis Valois spent a night behind bars in March 2002 following a nightclub brawl it is last season's sudden demise of Tigana's Fulham side that continues to raise most eyebrows.

Back in August 2001, the Premiership new boys were being touted as potential UEFA Cup qualifiers – and the latest incarnation of the masterful French system. Today, they stand in the no-man's land of mid-table Premiership obscurity. Was this Al Fayed's dream? Tigana's second 12 months saw the slick and sophisticated Cottagers turn into an anxious and ordinary team. Gone were the simple yet devastating passes; and gone, too, were the goals from all angles and players.

Perhaps the single most worrying aspect of their plight was that Fulham looked not only out of their depth but also out of their natural habitat. As the season progressed, it became increasingly apparent that they were, for all intents and purposes, a French League side operating in England. By the same token, it is now clear that such a team can have only limited success in the Premiership. Even Christian Damiano admitted as much after Fulham's 1–0 home defeat by West Ham on Easter Monday. 'We have arrived in the top level of football, perhaps in the world,' the Frenchman said, 'and every week there are big and tricky matches for our players. It is possible for us to remain in the Premier League, but we have players who are less experienced than their opponents.'

The French system was the brainchild of George Boulogne, who believed that young players needed to be given a complete football education at an early age. Today, the INF (Institut National de Football) is run by Claude Dusseau. He believes that Boulogne sought to create footballers, not a style that was applicable to any domestic league. 'The whole point of our plan,' the 62-year-old says, 'was to bring France up to date and then, in the long term, perhaps help us lead the way. The idea was to draw up a playing and coaching charter that all players could adhere to. We have produced many players who can travel well, but not necessarily a versatile style of play.'

In other words, Fulham can expect to make progress in the Premiership by buying good French players, not by trying to play à la française. And herein lies their problem. Whereas Arsène Wenger has bought top-quality French internationals to supplement his English base, Tigana has signed mainly average Frenchmen to form the basis of his side. How many of his compatriots has Gérard Houllier brought to Liverpool? Three, if you ignore the juniors he has picked for the future. One is the World Cup winner Bernard Diomède, a left-winger who has never managed to establish himself; another is Nicolas Anelka, a proven striker who was a wonderful luxury to have on loan until the end of the 2001–02 season; and there's also Bruno Cheyrou, a young left-footed midfielder tipped for greatness, bought from Lille in June 2002.

Tigana, meanwhile, has filled the Fulham changing-room with relative unknowns. Only Lyon's young dynamo, Steed Malbranque, has been a resounding success. You wonder, though, how long he will stay at the club. The fact that he has been continuously overlooked for the senior French team up to and including the World Cup, suggests that he might have to move to a more high-profile club if he is to break into the national side.

The player, himself, remains calm, but how much longer can he accept the rejection? 'There are just too many players ahead of me in the pecking order,' he says. These include two of the most famous Frenchmen, Zinédine Zidane and Robert Pires. 'However well I play, there is no way I will be picked at the expense of the guys who have been part of the group for years,' Malbranque says. 'This is an established set, and I don't think any youngster will be given their chance until this generation has stopped [something that appears more likely following France's terrible showing in Japan and South Korea]. But that's normal to a certain extent. These players have remained very close and have been very successful. You can't suddenly ask them to pack their bags.'

Damiano agrees with his protégé. 'I have known Steed since he was a young teenager,' Damiano says, 'and I can tell you that he is destined to do great things. For a 22-year-old, he is incredibly complete: he works hard, he's willing to progress, and he can pass and score from central midfield. He is Fulham's Gianfranco Zola, and one day he will be France's new Zidane. But for now, he has no choice but to wait his turn with the national team.'

The Malbranque signing, although deemed expensive at over £4m at the time, was clearly a wise investment. The same, though, cannot be said of the other transfers, particularly the club's most expensive signing, Steve Marlet. The £11m striker's return in his first season was poor, scoring just 9 goals in 27 appearances.

It says much that the former Fulham and Newcastle striker Malcolm Macdonald believes that weak attacking play has been the key to the Cottagers' problems. 'They sometimes get to the stage where the goals dry up,' he says, 'and people are falling over each other without even getting a shot in. It's a very difficult quandary to resolve. You can see that no one has any confidence in the front men. This means that the midfield over-elaborate and tend to pass the ball sideways a lot. They either fail to give it to the strikers or, when they do feed the forwards, they don't then support them. It's a vicious circle.'

In periods of crisis, players tend to turn to their leader for inspiration and guidance. Tigana, though, appeared to be as confused as his troops towards the end. Could the man being hailed as a managerial phenomenon just 12 months previously really have been lost for options? His refusal to change his team's style of play suggested he either genuinely believed that the system was right, or that he did not know how to alter the tactics. That seems unlikely, if only because his record is good and he is surrounded by experienced football brains. But questions remain.

Having spent more than £40m on players, and with a new stadium due to open for the start of the 2004–05 campaign, Fulham cannot afford to slip through the relegation trapdoor. The Fulham adventure has been both intriguing and engrossing so far – let us hope it does not become tragic, too. As the 'Teacher' might say, *à suivre* . . .

Alex Hayes

CHAPTER 9

West Ham: Welcome to the French Eastenders

He is close to tears, or almost. Sébastien Schemmel has trouble controlling his emotion when he remembers every detail of the ceremony when he was awarded the trophy of Best West Ham Player in 2001–02, as a result of the vote from the fans. A few weeks later, the tireless and imposing right-back still cannot get over it: 'This was the most beautiful present in my life. You have to remember that a few months ago, I was at the bottom of a big hole, I played in the French CFA [equivalent to Division Three in England].' What a recovery for Schemmel: he fell from grace at FC Metz (in the east of France, where Robert Pires started his career), but came back stronger, a much more mature player, at West Ham: 'West Ham revived me, gave me an incredible opportunity. I cannot see myself leaving this club. I owe something to the club directors, because they got me out of a big hole.'

Frédéric Kanouté feels the same; he cannot picture himself leaving the Hammers. A former Under-21 international, a pure product of the Olympique Lyonnais academy, he knows that he found, at West Ham, in London, the ideal spot for him to flourish as a player, and as a man: 'The atmosphere is something very important for me, and the people here have a very positive attitude. Football is my job, and there is a lot of effort to put in, but for me it is, first and foremost, something that I like to do; it is a passion. If you happen to land in a club where the bosses transform this into a compulsory thing, a repetitive one, the passion disappears. This is not the case at West Ham, not at all.'

Kanouté arrived at West Ham in the spring of 2000, without anybody noticing, for a three-month loan. At 24, he quickly became the Hammers' most consistent and reliable striker. So every summer, during the silly season, the tabloids make headlines about millions of pounds for his transfer to Liverpool, Fulham or Chelsea. This does not bother 'Freddie', he feels good at West Ham, and he knows why: 'This is a club where everybody is happy, from the first-team players to the subs. The training sessions are lively. It is admitted that you can get it wrong, as long as you show that you are putting in the effort. What the supporters and the bosses take into account, here, is the spirit. On the contrary, if a very good player does not try hard enough, they will be after him. At the beginning, it happened to me a couple of times. I did not have a reputation for running after the ball, so I had to change this.' Kanouté has learnt his lesson, and now it makes him laugh.

The big change for Schemmel had more to do with his attitude and his nature. Trained at AS Nancy-Lorraine, Michel Platini's home-town club, this is where he started his career as a professional, in the French Division Two. Then he joined FC Metz and took part in the glorious 1998 campaign, with Pires, when Metz missed the French title on goal difference. The turning point came some day in the year 2000, after a draw at home against Lille. Metz was now in the relegation zone, and it all turned sour. After a heated discussion with a local journalist he was suspended by his club. The chairman even talked of mental instability. A few years down the road, he is 27 and able to smile at this memory, but he insists that he has learned the lessons of this incident: 'I am a rather difficult customer, so when I left France, I was alone. Ever since I arrived here, I have not said anything, I just listen to the people. I like this mentality in the club, we all want to learn, this is West Ham's strength. All those who tried to start a revolution here, except for [Paolo] Di Canio, who is considered a god here, they took a beating, such as [Croatian Davor] Suker or [Portuguese Paulo] Futre. One has to remain humble.'

Schemmel is quick to underline that French players who have succeeded at West Ham are simple, humble guys: 'Look at Marc Keller's example. He left a very good image here, he was a big brother for the youngsters, thanks to his experience with the national team. When a Frenchman arrives in this club, thanks to Marc, there is a very favourable attitude to him. I don't think it will be that easy when another Croatian player shows up around here, following what happened with Suker,' Sébastien predicts, with a smile.

Keller is now a young retired footballer turned successful general manager of Racing Club de Strasbourg. The Alsace club, where Arsène Wenger became a French football champion in 1979, as a centre-back, have fought back to the French First Division (there is no Premiership in France) at the end of their first season with former winger Marc Keller as a manager. He remembers his arrival at West Ham, in February of 1998, a few months before a World Cup that he still hoped to play in. He was in that first group of French internationals who crossed the Channel. 'I had just spent two years at Karlsruhe [a German Bundesliga club], I was 30 years old, I wanted to discover another country, but I did not want to play in too tactical, too defensive a league. The game in Italy is rather closed, very tactical. I had contacts with Sampdoria [Italian Serie A], but nothing more. I was never attracted by Spain, so I said to myself: "I want to go to England, because there is good money, the language, and London on the top of it." It was becoming a fashionable city.'

Marc Keller spent three years at West Ham. There were injuries, frustrations, for the former international player, who had managed to score a goal against Germany. It was like paving the way for the next emigrants, as French–English football relations were only starting to develop. 'I discovered something else, another football, another way to work. It struck me, because at Karlsruhe it only took me one day to get settled. I spoke a little bit of German, we trained the same way, the schedules were the same, there was not much of a change. But when I arrived at West Ham, what a shock! Everything was different. I could also feel the difference because there were 30 to 35 players around, working and training. Wednesday was off, just like Sunday, whereas in France or Germany, Wednesday is a day when players tend to work hard. Another thing is that in Germany or in France, you train the way that you play. In England, it's a different phenomenon. Some players used to train a little during the week but managed to be very efficient on the Saturday. Training a little, often injured, but in good shape on match day. During my first season, I had plenty of physical hitches, because I trained too hard. It took me six months to adapt. It is a more relaxed way to train, *à la carte*, and if you're injured, you just don't train.'

In this new context, Keller often managed to find a spot in the first team, especially during the first two seasons, and even if he feels that he may have missed something, his final assessment is pretty much balanced, just like Marc, an economics graduate, is balanced in his life: 'At West

Ham, I signed a four-year contract, and played on a regular basis for the first two seasons, between 25 and 30 games a year. I liked it, but I have the feeling that with my skills, and how hard I trained, I could have encountered more success, maybe in another system. We played 3-5-2, and I'm more a 4-4-2 player. It was good, but not always easy, there were too many players. I should not say that, but some players, really, I had no idea what they were doing there.'

Keller knew exactly what he was doing at West Ham. Meeting and working with the manager, Harry Redknapp, changed his perception of football. Unlike most of his colleagues, but just like Wenger, Keller had managed to play football as well as pursuing a university education. As a young pro at Mulhouse FC (French Second Division), he would train in the daytime and then prepare for HEC (Hautes Etudes Commerciales), the prestigious business school, in the evening. Eventually, he gave that up, but managed to get a *licence* (the equivalent of a BA) in economics.

'I was always interested in the economics of football, the transfers of players, the strategies of the clubs, much more than everyday work on the pitch. I have had that in me for a long time. To be a coach is something I'm not interested in. Thanks to my travels, my own transfers, I discovered the world of the agents. There are so many things happening here in England, it's football business for real, lots of transfers. On that level, I learnt a lot with Harry. He was very good at transferring players in and out. He could feel the players with a good price. He bought Kanouté for £3.7m, but he can sell him for over £10m. Same thing with Foé [Marc-Vivien, a Cameroon international]; he bought him for £4m and sold him for £6.5m 18 months later.'

Keller was impressed. For the last six months of his contract, he was on loan, and on the bench, at Blackburn Rovers, with plenty of time to think about his immediate future. A few phone calls and meetings later, IMG McCormack, the major shareholders of RC Strasbourg, gave him the key to his home-town club. Blackburn were going up, and back to the Premier League, but Strasbourg were going down, to the French Second Division. Not a problem for Keller, eager to start using everything that he had learnt, at West Ham and before, to make his new job a success.

Less than one year later, Keller's Strasbourg were back in the top drawer of French football, and Redknapp announced his retirement at the end of the season. Before that, he had enough time to impress the two adopted French Eastenders. Schemmel remembers his first meeting with Redknapp: 'It must have been four or five years ago, West Ham played us [Metz] in the InterToto Cup. I was very impressed by the crowd at Upton Park; it was extraordinary. Two weeks later, they were in Metz with 5,000 supporters. This lad with red hair and a red face was shouting on the touchline. I had a couple of good games against them, so two years later, West Ham called. I talked to Harry on the phone, he wanted to put me on trial for six months. At the end of the six months, West Ham wanted to buy me, but Metz asked for too much money, according to Harry. I was almost without a club, but then Harry and Glenn [Roeder] came. He managed to negotiate with Metz, and eventually they let me go for £400,000.'

Schemmel remembers these training sessions on the Romford pitches, the often cold wind, and Redknapp's orders translated by his friend Kanouté. 'Sometimes the coach was too laid back, sometimes he did not even come to training. Before the game, other coaches would talk, they would tell us different things. I had no idea what was going on.' Schemmel laughs, and he can, because big clubs like Newcastle and Paris SG are now keeping a close eye on the former Metz outcast. With Roeder's arrival, West Ham's French Connection is now on a much more familiar ground: 'Roeder has a football culture which is much more French. He used to go and watch Paris SG on a regular basis; he admires Lille. With him, we use video, we use the blackboard, some of the preparation is done with French ideas. This is what was missing at West Ham. He managed to convince us that we could improve *à la française* and it's a plus for everybody.'

Same sort of enthusiasm on the 'Freddie' side, his nickname since his arrival, thanks to a few die-hard West Ham United fans: 'Glenn is very Francophile. He saw many French league games, he knows the players, the clubs, maybe better than me. He managed to mix the attraction of the tactical and technical culture of France, and the English tradition of physical commitment. The synthesis of the two makes for beautiful football, such as the football we sometimes play at Upton Park. Do you remember the game against Man U?' Kanouté asks.

'It was completely crazy,' Schemmel remembers. 'I would have paid to watch that game. I felt like clapping at the end, because I was so happy I had played in that game . . . although we lost 5–3. At West Ham, we play, the coach wants us to play, he wants us to enjoy ourselves, and to please the crowd. When he can see that the fans are happy, he is happy. And if on the top of that, we win, it's party time.' Schemmel's enthusiasm is beautiful to see, and he knows how to make the fans tick. Last season, he played in 36 Premiership games, scored one goal and provided six assists, not bad for a right-back. 'He was our best player last season. He is a nice guy and a very reliable defender': the summary and the compliment came from a West Ham fan from Essex, wearing an England shirt, some time in June 2002. We were in a noodle restaurant at Saitama, north of Japan, after England v. Sweden at the World Cup, and Schemmel managed to make it into our very international conversation.

Kanouté also enjoys West Ham's positive attitude, and points to the passion of the fans as one major explanation for his attachment to east London: 'What I like is the passion, the euphoria, the way people like football without going over the top. It's not like Italy, from what I gather. I can meet Tottenham or Arsenal fans, there is never a problem, they always joke. There is a good atmosphere; I don't like it when people take things too seriously. In the stands, or on the pitch, there is something different about West Ham.' Just like his mate Schemmel, he chose to live in the popular areas of east London. Every day, he can talk to the West Ham supporters in the street, and realise how much they remember Bobby Moore's goals and other feats. One day, Kanouté had to knock on his neighbour's door because he had to put a tie on. He had been invited to a gala evening, but he did not know how to tie the knot.

Schemmel also recalls a rather surprising encounter, on a motorway: 'I was driving my car, a guy overtook me, he was going full blast, but he saw my face when he passed me. Honest to God, he pushed on his brakes, like a madman, and went down from 100 to 50 miles per hour, just to show me his tattoo, a West Ham tattoo of course. And then he kept on driving, rather slowly. People respect us enormously here, they would never shout that we get too much money, as often happens in France. It is for this mentality that I play, I am very happy here. I play football to be acknowledged, to pass some advice to youngsters. I really like it. At every game, there are 36,000 spectators who only watch us, whether we win or lose, as long as we run and make sure that our shirt is wet. We know they are here, and it motivates me. At Manchester, there were 11,000 of them, and 5,000 at Sunderland. This is how I see football: we give to the supporters, and they give to us. At West Ham, they gave me everything I was looking for; I was born again.'

No wonder Schemmel, Kanouté, Foé and Laurent Courtois have flourished at West Ham. They share the same passion for football with the youngsters coming out of West Ham's youth academy. From AS Nancy-Lorraine's training grounds to Romford's, the scenery has not changed so much. The weather, the hard times, the culture of work and effort, nothing is very different from the Lorraine region. 'I feel at home,' says Schemmel, the Lorraine-born defender, on the very same training ground where Rio Ferdinand, a kid from Peckham, started his career, a few years before wearing the England shirt in a World Cup, just like Bobby Moore. Had he been born in England, Kanouté would have probably crossed swords early with Ferdinand, a teenager just as gifted as him.

Freddie started playing football in Sainte-Foy-lès-Lyon, a housing estate in the suburbs of Lyon. His father is a metal worker who emigrated from Mali, his mother is a literature professor. He made his name in London: 'West Ham launched my career, much more than it revived it. It could have been Lyon, but things were not right, on my side and at the club. I had surgery, so I lost time, and the club went forward without me. I had no reason to stay in France. I arrived here, got back in shape, and made a name for myself. My game has improved. However, I don't feel that I have a debt, I just feel good at West Ham. If I really felt that, on the sporting side, I could go somewhere else and it would bring me something extra, I would go.

'I am a professional footballer, but my goal is to live as simple a life as possible. I don't mean living like a monk, but I try to make things easy. Everything is coming together, slowly. I am confident we are able to make it to Europe.' European football is his next goal. He discovered it as a youngster, with Lyon, and remembers that win, in the 1997 InterToto Cup, against Polish side Odra Wodzislaw: 'We won 5–2, at Gerland [Lyon's stadium]. It was my professional debut, with my friend Joseph-Désiré Job [who spent some time at Middlesbrough]. He scored three goals, I scored one.'

In London, the beginnings were tough, and the tabloids even made a meal of his repulsion for British gastronomy. A few years later, Kanouté feels good in England. He likes American rap music as much as traditional music from Mali, and he feels good vibes in London: 'It's a fascinating city. From one area to another, it's literally a different world. It's also a more tolerant city, where it's easier to practise my faith. There is a strong Muslim community here, lots of mosques, lots of opportunities to know my religion better.' On the day after the 11 September terrorist attacks, his teammates turned to Freddie to try and understand: 'I just told them that it was contrary to Islam. I always try to explain the inexplicable.'

On a different level, Schemmel explains how important his friend, Freddie the striker, is for West Ham: 'Fred scores around 15 goals a season and provides lots of assists. He is full of talent, he is a hard worker, he is kind, and he is only 24. For me, he represents the future of the French team. He always finds the right words, he knows how to comfort his teammates, he is God's gift to West Ham. On the top of that, I get along well with him on the pitch. We are like two brothers, we have a complicity.' Sébastien had prestigious teammates before, especially when he played for the Under-21 French team, with Patrick Vieira, Thierry Henry, David Trézéguet and Laurent Robert.

At West Ham, another name, much more famous, is still everywhere: Bobby Moore. As a player, he led West Ham to its greatest successes: the 1964 FA Cup and the 1965 Cup-Winners' Cup. Schemmel comments: 'At the training ground, there are pictures of Bobby Moore. At Upton Park, one stand is called Bobby Moore. When I get on the pitch and listen to the official tune, I think of West Ham's past, in Europe and in the FA Cup. Someone who wears this shirt has to honour the past, so we think about it a lot. This club has a lot of ambition, wants to go forward, but without forgetting the past.'

According to Marc Keller, the attachment to Bobby Moore's memory could be a handicap: 'When I played for West Ham, I was one of the very few French players not to play under a French manager. Some were with Arsène Wenger at Arsenal, and others with Gérard Houllier at Liverpool. I was in a very English club. West Ham, in the East End, it's a very special mentality. Some fans still live in the memories of World Cup 1966, with Bobby Moore; you can feel the weight of history. It's so English, it's funny. I think that it was tougher for me than for others, but it was a good life experience. I travelled in Germany, and then in England, I met people, it was an enrichment. As a player, I improved as well. I have another vision of football, and I feel stronger today.' Kanouté,

Schemmel, and even Courtois, probably feel the same. But there is a small difference with Keller, when both 'Fred' and 'Seb', an improbable duet, say exactly the same thing: 'I can see myself ending my career in London.'

Daniel Ortelli
and Jérôme Rasetti

CHAPTER 10

The Old Vagabonds: Karembeu and Djorkaeff

The one linking factor among the successful French players of the last decade is their vagabond nature. These *Bleus* go where their hearts – and occasionally their wallets – tell them. All have played for a large number of clubs, both in France and abroad. The veteran, Laurent Blanc, has a pretty impressive list of former employers, ranging from Nîmes and Montpellier to Inter Milan and Barcelona. At the other end of the age-scale, Nicolas Anelka has had his fair share of clubs, too, moving from Paris to Arsenal to Real Madrid, back to Paris, then on to Liverpool, before settling at Manchester City. And all this before he was even 23. King Eric himself was also a vagabond, of course, swapping jerseys no fewer than eight times until he decided to make Old Trafford his kingdom.

Travelling and wanting to discover new cultures seem to be part of the make-up of any French national team member these days, so it should perhaps come as little surprise that two of the Premiership's more recent colourful characters have numerous stamps on their respective passports. Christian Karembeu came and went quicker than you could say: 'Middlesbrough did not have a good season that year.' Youri Djorkaeff, meanwhile, might have made an even shorter stop-over had he not accepted Bolton's offer of a two-year contract in mid-July 2002. Karembeu was in England for only 12 months, while Djorkaeff's original loan period lasted little over three months, and yet both made an impression on their clubs and fans.

Equally, however, English football made an impression on them, too. Even in that short space of time, the two vagabonds felt more at ease on these shores than ever before. England is close enough to France to not feel isolated, and, at the same time, removed enough that these superstars of Gallic football can live here in peace. The Premiership, meanwhile, offers these talented players the chance to shine in a combative, if not always technically perfect, league.

CHRISTIAN AID

Karembeu arrived on Teesside in the summer of 2000 under a storm of publicity. Middlesbrough had pulled off a serious coup by signing the World and European champion, and seemed destined for good things. But the dream soon turned sour. Following a slow start to the campaign, the Boro wheels came off in spectacular fashion. A run of eight defeats in nine matches, culminating in a 1–0 loss at West Ham, proved to be the final straw for Steve Gibson. The club's chairman had seen enough to persuade him that Bryan Robson's time as manager was up.

The mood in the lead-up to Christmas 2000 was anything but festive on Teesside. 'I knew and respected Bryan the player,' Karembeu says. 'He was a legend in England and someone who had done a lot for Boro. But perhaps the time had come for him to refresh his coaching skills. His biggest fault was that he trusted the players too much. He thought they would show the same level of commitment that he used to, but without ever being told.'

He adds: 'Bryan, though, is a real gentleman. I thought his decision to bring in Mr Venables was very brave and I hoped he would learn a lot and then return as manager. At the time, I didn't see any reason why he couldn't resume his duties after the summer and take the club forward.' Robson did not do so, of course, handing over the reins to Steve McClaren, while Karembeu also left, in his case to join Olympiakos in Greece.

The Frenchman's short stay has left mixed feelings among the fans. Many worshipped him and his laid-back attitude. But there are those, to this day, who blame Karembeu's supposed lack of endeavour for the poor start to Boro's 2000–01 season. 'It's funny,' says the 31-year-old Frenchman, who ended up playing 33 League matches for the club, 'but I never felt that my early performances were that bad. I thought I was playing OK, apart from the match against Newcastle. It was a derby and I was desperate to win. The night before, I did not sleep a wink. I worked myself up so much that I ended up being awful on the day.'

Those are hardly the words of a player who, as some suggested, did not care for the club. 'I was desperate to do well, but the problem was that the fans, as ever, wanted instant success,' says Karembeu. 'Players, though, have to be allowed to bed themselves in. The proof is that things got better and my performances became more consistent. But I think that's normal. I always knew I would need a while to adjust to the demands of English football. It's a very aerial and physical game, and I struggled with that early on. I was doing a lot of running around without ever really getting hold of the ball.'

Karembeu's first Boro manager supports the Frenchman's views. 'It took Christian quite a long time to adapt,' Robson says, 'but that happens sometimes. His talent was never in question, but there were doubts as to whether he could adjust to the rigours of British football.'

EL SAVIOUR

It says everything that Karembeu's performances, like those of his team, improved dramatically from the day Terry Venables was appointed. 'Mr Venables brought his great tactical nous and experience,' recalls Karembeu, over a plate of pasta in a quiet Italian restaurant. 'He's a pro and that's why we responded well. In football, you need solid foundations to work from. Once those are in place, the game becomes much simpler. The problem is that when you lose match after match for weeks, you forget what it is you are good at. Towards the end of that terrible sequence of defeats, we had often lost the game before kick-off.

'That's why Mr Venables went round and spoke to every player, reminding us what our strengths were. He took us all aside, one by one, to spell out what he expected. The name Venables is important but, more than anything else, it is his methods which kept us in the Premiership.'

Karembeu is one of only a handful of professional footballers to have been coached at club level by both Sven Goran Eriksson and Terry Venables. Before he played for Venables at Middlesbrough for six months, Karembeu had been signed by Eriksson at Sampdoria. He is, by the same token, a player who has been coached by some of the most respected figures in the game – including Jean-Claude Suaudeau in Nantes, Jupp Heynckes and John Toshack in Madrid, not to mention Gérard Houllier, Aimé Jacquet and Roger Lemerre with France.

Encouragingly for English football as a whole, the Frenchman rates both men as the best he has ever worked with. 'Eriksson was a particularly special manager in my career because he was the one who gave me my big break abroad,' says Karembeu, who was signed by the Swede in 1995. 'He brought me to Sampdoria and moulded me into the more complete and thoughtful player that I am now. He has this ability to transform a person.'

Karembeu senses a parallel with Venables. 'They both have a very similar approach to management,' he explains. 'They are brilliant communicators, people who can instantly get the best out of their players. One of the main reasons for their success is the fact they are so serene. Both men know what they can bring and, as a result, what they need from the team.

'When you have achieved certain goals, respect is something which you command naturally. Mr Eriksson and Mr Venables don't rant and rave. They are supremely confident and prefer to encourage their players to express themselves. Perhaps that constant positiveness is the one characteristic which best describes them both.'

SUCCESS OR FAILURE?

The one question that remains is whether or not Karembeu's brief sojourn on these shores was a success. Why, some might ask, had one of the most garlanded footballers at the time joined a club with a bare trophy cabinet? And why was a player who had spent two years in swanky Genoa and two years in cosmopolitan Madrid prepared to move to the industrial north-east of England? 'I am like Captain Cook,' says Karembeu, who was born in Lifou, New Caledonia. 'I have sought to travel and explore; the only difference is that I have done my journey in the opposite direction.'

The North East may be football mad but, compared to Genoa and Madrid, life in the picturesque surroundings of the Middlesbrough training ground was peaceful and sane. 'From a personal point of view, I needed this tranquility,' Karembeu says. 'My quality of life was better than ever at Boro. I never felt threatened. The local people turn to football to escape from their daily grind. I think they view the game as a spectacle. For them, matches are films and we, the players, are the actors.'

Karembeu liked Teesside so much he even learned to accept being teased. 'At first,' he says, 'when someone called me Frenchy, it sounded quite new to me. I now see it as a trademark, and it will remain so. Since the first French player arrived in England, and for those who will come in the future, the label Frenchy, on reflexion, is very positive. I am proud to be a Frenchy.'

Karembeu is a thinking man's footballer. He is quiet, thoughtful and measured. He also thoroughly enjoyed his time with Boro. 'I always liked what Bryan [Robson] had to offer,' says Karembeu, to explain why he swapped the Bernabeu for the Riverside. 'He, and the chairman, told me how they wanted to create a new dynasty on Teesside. I felt that the club could bring me a lot, both on a sporting and a personal level. Rome was not built in a day, and I never for a second thought that Boro would be a European force overnight. I just sensed that I had something to give the club and this was the challenge of a lifetime. I didn't want to miss out.'

Karembeu adds: 'Eric Cantona had a huge impact at Manchester United and transformed the club's fortunes. I'd hoped to do the same. It didn't work out but I tried.'

YOURI THE WANDERER

The stats tell you everything you need to know about Youri Djorkaeff's impact at Bolton Wanderers. The Frenchman arrived at the club desperate for first-team football ahead of the World Cup in Japan and South Korea. It did not really matter to him whether he signed for a top-five or bottom-five club – he just needed matches under his belt to persuade the then French manager, Roger Lemerre, that he was worthy of a seat on the plane to the Far East. But you cannot take the professional out of Djorkaeff.

Having put pen to paper on a three-month deal one late February day, the Frenchman went on to score 4 goals in 12 Premiership matches. Not a bad return for a player who, though he was brought to the Reebok Stadium as a saviour, had not played regular club football for several weeks before his arrival in Lancashire. Djorkaeff may no longer be the international quality performer he once was – his poor World Cup showings proved that rather conclusively – but he can clearly cut the mustard in the Premiership.

When the story of Bolton's season is retold in the future, the one match people will remember more than any other is sure to be the 4–1 defeat of Ipswich on 6 April 2002. Both clubs were sitting near the relegation trapdoor at the time and the feeling was that the winner would be safe. Djorkaeff played like the World and European champion that he is, scoring one goal and inspiring Wanderers to a famous victory.

Bizarrely, Djorkaeff's earliest memory of England and its football dates back to 1966 and the World Cup triumph of Sir Alf Ramsey's team. Just before the 2002 World Cup, a colleague of mine presented Djorkaeff with a photograph of a man dressed as a big cuddly dog with a Union Jack waistcoat. His face lit up in recognition. 'I have this,' he says. 'My father give me this. I have it. It's Willie. I remember Willie.' Djorkaeff was looking at a 32-year-old copy of *Miroir du Football*, a long-gone French football magazine. In it was a picture of Jean Djorkaeff, Youri's father, posing outside the Welwyn Garden hotel that the French 1966 World Cup squad used as its base. But Youri could think only of World Cup Willie, the tournament mascot. 'My father brought back a Willie for my brother and me. We still have him. He's in France. He was my first mascot.'

Djorkaeff might have liked to have a similar picture taken of himself next to the latest World Cup mascot, Gloomo, but France were not in the tournament long enough. Djorkaeff, alone, can not be held accountable for *Les Bleus' faux pas*, but the Bolton man will be the first to admit that he did not fill Zinédine Zidane's sizeable boots, for the first two games, with any great aplomb. Had he and his team defended their title with a little more purpose, the chances are that France would have met England in the round of the last 16. That was the hope; that was the match everyone wanted to see.

Denmark turned out to be England's opponents, but Djorkaeff still watched the match with intent. And, after his period in England, he rates the national team very highly. 'They are making a big progression and are now one of the best teams,' he says. 'Owen is very good.'

THE BOLTON EXPERIENCE

Djorkaeff, you sense, genuinely enjoys life at the Reebok Stadium. So much so, in fact, that he now takes his eight-year-old son to matches. 'He is just beginning to like football,' says his father. 'He comes to the stadium. There is a good atmosphere.' For Djorkaeff, it is the entire package of English life that appeals to him. One of his favourite hobbies is to look up other Armenians in the phone book. If you have an Armenian surname and live in the Manchester area, you may soon receive a call from a man with a French accent. He will explain that he, too, is Armenian, he is working in the area and would you like to meet up over a cup of coffee?

Although Djorkaeff's family left Armenia in 1915, and both he and his father have played with distinction for France, he remains very proud of his roots and always seeks to cultivate them.

Armenia may be in his heart, but France is his passion. The recent French presidential election, in which the National Front leader Jean-Marie Le Pen won through to the run-off with Jacques Chirac, hit Djorkaeff hard. 'In 1998 a lot of people recognised themselves in the French team,' he explains. 'They said: "I am a fan of Thuram because I am from Guadeloupe like him" or "I am a fan of Zidane because I am also Algerian." It was great. France is a mix of countries but it is a good mix. It has the culture of Armenia, Guadeloupe, Algeria all in the same country. There is a lot of respect because we showed we had respect and we played for the French national team.'

Djorkaeff has been working hard. He has already found an Armenian restaurant in Manchester. 'In America, on vacations, too. I call, I say: "Hello. I am a French person from Armenia here on holiday. Can we meet?" I meet some nice people because of this.'

It is hard to know what to make of this revelation. Does it suggest Djorkaeff is free of ego, or overflowing with it? Djorkaeff does have a reputation for arrogance. When he left Kaiserslautern for Bolton one ex-teammate said: 'The big ego has gone.' Another added: 'Now we can start training on time.' In the past he has claimed he invented the system which France, including Djorkaeff, played to win the 1998 World Cup. Knowing this, it is hard not to wonder what he really thought of Bolton's training ground when he first arrived. Until a few months ago, they shared it with a social club and players would have lunch surrounded by men drinking pints. It cannot have impressed a man who once used Inter Milan's facilities.

But Djorkaeff appears unconcerned. To judge from his interaction with his new teammates, he is popular in the dressing-room. A reported

£50,000 a week has the potential to unsettle but most players do not begrudge teammates such salaries if they feel it is earned. Money, though, was never the most important factor. 'I had offers from more famous clubs but what made the difference is the feeling I got from people here,' he says. 'I am a happy man. My relations with the players are very good. My life in England is better than in Germany. The people in this area are very friendly. In Germany they were very closed. To meet people who have a passion for football, for their team, is very attractive. It is the same in Italy but in Italy you do not have a life. Here people have respect for the player. It is good for them and their families.'

Djorkaeff settled surprisingly quickly. 'My family was with me, which was important, and I found a school for my children. It is an English school. I am French but I am coming to England and I want to do everything to integrate into the culture. To talk English with English people, to drive my car on the other side of the road. That is my mentality. I am very pleased that I will be playing for Bolton during the next two years. I can't wait to firmly put Bolton on the map.'

Mission accomplished. Karembeu and Djorkaeff may not have turned their English clubs into all-conquering beasts, but they did at least manage to make them considerably trendier. And, in this increasingly image-conscious football world, that is not to be sneezed at.

Alex Hayes

CHAPTER 11

The Young Guns: Aliadière, Vignal, etc.

Eric Cantona's legacy to English football is clear for all to see. From the all-conquering Manchester United team of the mid to late 1990s, to Sven Goran Eriksson's ever-improving England national side, and from the now common Premiership academies to the restructuring of coaching methods: Cantona has played some part – direct or otherwise.

No doubt Cantona had hoped that his decision to sign for Leeds in 1992 might encourage other Frenchmen to follow in his footsteps across the Channel, but not even he could have predicted that his actions would open the floodgates so quickly and for so long. More than 100 French players have now graced the Premiership at one time or another over the last decade. And, while some have failed to make a mark on the English game, most have brought unparalleled success for their employers. The only question left, therefore, is whether or not the French Revolution can continue from the Nineties into the Noughties. Are there genuine replacements for the legend that is Eric Cantona?

The immediate answer would seem to be yes. Judging by some of the young talents on the books of the major English clubs, you cannot help but feel that the quantity and, most importantly, the quality of French players is there. However, it will have to be seen whether the young English trainees, who now benefit from the same training methods, catch up or even overtake their Gallic counterparts. Only time will tell, although you suspect that there are still some unpolished gems to be found in La Belle France. Witness the keen buying of Arsène Wenger at Arsenal and Gérard Houllier at Liverpool.

Two such French stars of the future are Arsenal's Jérémie Aliadière and Liverpool's Grégory Vignal. Others, too, have been prised away from their French clubs. Once nearing the end of their formation, these young French pups are often only months away from making a serious impact. Look at Olivier Bernard, a 20-year-old Lyon trainee, who was attracted by the bright lights of Newcastle and, following an intense summer of negotiations, has signed a lucrative five-year deal with the Magpies. Think also of the Fulham pair of Nicolas Sahnoun (back in Bordeaux) and Fabrice Fernandes (now with Southampton). And what about Laurent Courtois at West Ham, Djibril Diawara in Bolton, Franck Queudrue at Middlesbrough, Sylvain Distin at Manchester City and Steed Malbranque with Fulham. The list is lengthening by the month, as more and more wannabe stars follow in the dust left by King Eric ten years ago, and others more recently.

Not all French kids have been a roaring success in England. Like their older compatriots, the baby-boomers can sometimes fail to make the grade. Such was the fate of William Huck, who was signed by Arsenal in the summer of 1998, and, following a short stint on loan at Bournemouth, went home pretty quickly. Djimi Traore, one of the first Frenchmen to arrive at Liverpool in 1999, left the club in 2001 to pursue his career in Lens, alongside Houllier's former number two, Patrice Bergues. Others have had to come and go only to re-emerge in the summer of 2002 as a genuine prospect. As ever, though, one disappointment can be countered by two successes, as proved by the Liverpool signings of Florent Sinama Pongolle and Anthony Le Tallec, from Le Havre in the spring of 2001, both described as 'the future of France'.

THE ALIADIÈRE TEST

Most accept that Jérémie Aliadière will be the benchmark for years to come. If the young Gunner can impose himself in England, after having done part of his training on these shores, then the continuation of the French Revolution is assured. If not, well . . . At least Aliadière's pedigree is not in question. Aliadière, the striker who has been described by many as the most exciting French prospect of his generation, was bought by Arsenal when he was still only 16. The French Football Federation were up in arms over the deal, claiming that Wenger had 'poached' the youngster away from his native land, just as he was about to finish his education and start his career with a French club. Whatever the ins-and-outs of the affair, one thing is crystal clear: this kid has a lot of talent. So much so, in fact, that Arsenal have kept him completely under wraps for the first three years of his English life. Only now that the 2002 season has begun, is the Frenchman likely to be liberated.

Aliadière used to live in a secluded house with his paternal grandparents, only yards away from the training ground of the rugby union club, Saracens. Arsenal are determined to protect their investment. Aliadière signed a seven-year contract worth an estimated £1m at an age when he was not even allowed to drive with a provisional licence. Now, he is on the brink of the first team.

The latest signs continue to be good. Aliadière was one of the key performers in Arsenal's youth teams between 1998 and 2001. He was particularly impressive during the 1999 and 2001 FA Youth Cup runs (a competition which often churns out great success stories, such as David Beckham, Nicky Butt, Paul Scholes, Robbie Fowler, Paul Gascoigne and many others). In the latter competition, he scored no fewer than nine goals on the road to the two-leg final against Blackburn. In the first of these matches, Aliadière scored two, as Arsenal won 5–0. In the second, Arsenal lost 3–1, but won the tie, and Aliadière was voted Man of the Match.

His then manager, Liam Brady, who takes care of the youth set-up at the club he represented with such distinction, described Aliadière as a 'fantastic player, who is good in the air, comfortable on the ball, quick, and always aware of where the goal is'. Not a bad résumé when you are still a teenager. Brady continues: 'It took Jérémie a little while to adapt, but that is only normal. Quite quickly, he got used to the culture and the club, and he is now making all the right noises to push for the first team.'

Aliadière, himself, is a lad (or should that now be man?) of few words. This is partly due to the fact that he prefers to let his feet do the talking, but largely a direct consequence of Arsenal's protection policy. Still, when he does say a few words, they are deep and meaningful. 'Young kids in France,' he says, 'when they see what I am doing here with Arsenal, might one day want to do the same thing. Once you have played in France for a bit, it is no bad thing to go and have a look at other countries.'

At the time of his controversial signing, Aliadière's father explained that he had accepted Wenger's offer not for the money but because Arsenal's high-tech environment would give his son an excellent education. He compared it to the elite of young French students leaving their native land to continue their education at Oxford University. So far as Mr Aliadière is concerned, Arsenal is the ultimate centre for the development of the ultimate footballing machines.

Wenger, who was much criticised by the French Football Federation at the time, has always maintained his innocence. 'The Federation are fighting something which is perfectly correct and logical in the Europe of today,' the Arsenal manager explains. 'In France, everyone is slapping each other on the back because football has become politically correct. If this kid had been recruited by an international school or university, no one would have batted an eyelid. But it's football. I'll tell you another story: a few years ago, a young English kid left Lilleshall to join Auxerre. Well, has anyone complained about that?'

The French powers that be may be unhappy, but Aliadière's grandfather is over the moon. 'I would much prefer to see Jérémie with Arsène Wenger at Arsenal than Guy Roux at Auxerre,' he says. 'I think the facilities at Arsenal make it very easy for a young French kid to make the transition. It's certainly a lot easier than a young African boy leaving home at 13 to live in digs in Auxerre.' Wenger agrees that the travelling mentalities have had to change. 'When I was growing up,' he says, 'you had to be prepared to move around France; now you have to be prepared to move around Europe.'

In truth, Wenger is just delighted that Aliadière made the short hop across the Channel. 'He is an exceptional talent,' the Frenchman remarks. 'It's funny because it is not the fact that he's a striker that attracted me to him, but rather his overall talent. I just couldn't let such a good player go missing. I would have signed him whether he'd been a midfielder or a defender.' Not that Wenger wants his young protégé to think he has made it yet. 'The danger these days,' he explains, 'is that these kids can think that they've achieved something even when they clearly haven't. They are constantly being asked for interviews or spoken about in the media, and can easily get too big for their boots. It's a difficult balance to strike.'

Wenger hopes that Aliadière will make the smooth transition from youth- to first-team player. Aliadière, who actually played for Arsenal on three occasions during the 2001–02 Double-winning season, now wants his first start in an Arsenal shirt. The passion and determination to succeed are apparent in this striker who, ironically, occupied the same room as a certain Thierry Henry at the French Federation's centre for excellence at Clairefontaine. Do not bet against the two crossing paths again soon on a football pitch near you.

VIGNAL AND THE OTHER FRENCH KIDS

Grégory Vignal has been through a lifetime of emotions in his two years at Liverpool. From the highs of signing for the club and then making his debut, to the lows of having to recover from a long-term injury, Vignal has seen it all. 'It's been busy,' jokes the 21-year-old.

Vignal had not even played an official first-team game for his former club, Montpellier, when Houllier, who had first spotted the French youngster in the 2000 Under-18 Championship, pounced. In fact, Vignal's only experience of senior football had been a 25-minute run-out in a friendly against Marseille, while the contract he signed with Liverpool was his first as a professional player. His career is still in its infancy, but Vignal has no regrets about his decision to sample the life and football of England. 'It wasn't just a case of signing for a new club,' he says. 'It was also a question of leaving my home to go and discover a new football, learn a new language and lifestyle and mentality. If I had been really scared, I wouldn't have done it.'

Surely, it cannot have been that easy for the player to leave the south of France? 'You'd be surprised,' he says. 'I wasn't likely to get my chance at Montpellier anyway, so I fancied the new challenge. I don't think the coach would've used me often. After the European Championship the club didn't even want me to sign as a professional. As soon as I heard that Liverpool were interested in me, I got it into my head that I would be leaving. I could've stayed in France, but what would I have done at Montpellier compared to here?'

He adds: 'I wanted to try my luck abroad. I liked English football and Liverpool had a French manager and some French-speaking players. I thought that all this would help me settle in easier. In fact, a lot of people said that going to England would be good for me. In France, I had a tendency to get a lot of bookings. I thought English football would be the best for me because I like playing long and I like the physical aspect of the game.'

Vignal settled in quickly at Liverpool. It took him less than nine months to make his first team debut, on 3 February 2001 against West Ham, and, predictably, he impressed. Houllier praised him at the time, saying:

'Grégory's must be one of the best debuts I have seen. He kept his head very focused and he was very cool. He did the job I asked him to. That was enough for me. He's not the finished article, of course. I think he is still maybe a year-and-a-half away, but what he has done so far he has done well.'

Houllier added: 'First of all, Grégory is a very good defender. Also his passing is sharp and slick, and very accurate. Considering he'd never played a league game before, you have to give the boy a credit for what he did against West Ham. He played in front of around 45,000 people and did very well. There's a big difference between playing in the Second, and even the First Division in France, and the Premiership in England – especially at a club like Liverpool. But Grégory has got the ability, and he showed it.'

Praise indeed for the kid from Marseille, whose parents just so happened to be over for a weekend in England when Vignal made his debut. 'It was completely by chance that they were here,' he recalls. 'They had no idea that I'd be playing against West Ham because neither did I. Never in my life would I have thought I'd be in the Liverpool first team after only a few months here, and at 19 years of age. I managed to sleep fine the night before, without any pressure. I didn't even feel tense or nervous before kick-off. I think that's why I had such a good game.'

He adds: 'Things have gone much quicker than I had imagined. My debut could easily have gone wrong for me, but I was delighted. That match changed a lot. The French press wrote good things about me and so did the English. It showed what I was capable of.'

Like his fellow-countryman Mikaël Silvestre of Manchester United, the feeling is that he may not be the most natural of defenders, but Vignal is quick and gives attacking options. 'Being a natural left-footer helps,' he says, 'because it means I am not necessarily coming back inside all the time.'

The good performances were cut short by a cruel foot injury, which eventually kept Vignal out for a large part of the 2001–02 season. After a summer of hard work, though, he is back on form and raring to go again for the 2002–03 campaign. He says that the support he received from his adoptive Liverpool family helped him recover quickly. 'People have been great to me at Liverpool,' Vignal says. 'I get on well with everyone. I don't have a problem. I think the fact that I've played a few games helps, but all my teammates have been very supportive, whether they be the English or the French ones.'

Houllier, too, has played his part in keeping an eye on the youngster, even when the French manager was not in the best condition himself. 'Gérard has always looked out for me,' Vignal says. 'Like my real family, he has always been there to make sure I'm OK. I'm sure that's part of the reason for my success.'

HOULLIER'S WARNING

While the Liverpool manager does not have a bad word to say about his young defender, it is interesting to note that he seconds Wenger's concerns over young players becoming successful too early. Houllier, therefore, praises Vignal, while offering a note of caution. 'Grégory has a big future,' he says, 'and he has shown that he is not afraid to play no matter what the occasion. But he must not be too hasty in his ambitions. He still has a lot to prove.' Vignal agrees: 'I know that my career is just beginning. It's for that reason that I can't get carried away. But I believe I have proved I can play at this level. That's a start.'

Vignal also points out that life in England would not be every young Frenchman's cup of tea. 'I love it,' he says, 'but it depends on the circumstances. I wouldn't say you should just leave France for the sake of it. You should only leave if you are 100 per cent sure. You have to be tough because when you go abroad you can find yourself alone in the world and there are a lot of sharks out there. It's every man for himself. Basically I would say you should only make the move if it feels right and if you are mentally strong. In my case, I had finished my studies and I came over with my fiancée, with whom I had already been living in Montpellier. It would've been much more difficult otherwise.'

Vignal continues: 'In other words, at least I didn't come over here with nothing. It's just that from a football perspective I wanted to take another step forward. In my head I thought it was better to do it now than later. I couldn't let this opportunity pass me by.'

Arrogance? Cockiness? A touch of the Eric Cantona, perhaps? Either way, both Vignal and Aliadière are proof that the French Revolution lives on.

Alex Hayes
(with Xavier Rivoire)

CHAPTER 12

Squad Players: Grimandi, Garde and Co.

He left the same way as he arrived. Discreetly, on the tip of his toes. What a paradox for a player who, on the football pitch, was so animated, in central defence or in midfield, and who inspired so much worry in his opponents. He was always on their backs, looking for the ball, tackling, running. Gilles Grimandi will probably remain the only player able to play 171 games over 5 years at Arsenal and complete a double Double (1998 and 2002), but never to be bothered when walking in the streets of London.

'One of our friends once asked Grimandi for an autograph, and he answered: "Me, but I am no star!" This was so cute!' The anecdote comes from Josie, a very respectable Arsenal fan in her 70s, who earlier in this book professed her love for Patrick Vieira. Her good friend Peggy, another die-hard Arsenal fan, but slightly younger, around 60, will never forget the shy Frenchman: 'I remember one match in particular, the fans were chanting his name and clapping for him. When he heard his name for the first time, he pointed a finger at himself, as if he was saying: "My God, it's for me." I remember that scene. He was just stunned that fans could acclaim him, because he was not as popular as Vieira or Petit. He was doing his job, discreetly and rather efficiently.'

Henry Winter, the chief football writer for the *Daily Telegraph*, tries to summarise the views of his journalist colleagues about Grimandi: 'He is a very intelligent man, but we did not understand what he was doing at Arsenal, playing in that team. So he got a beating from the press, all throughout. However, he is a really interesting character, he talked to me about his love of skiing, because he grew up in Gap, and he said he could not go skiing because of the football. I remember him at the end of the season, before he left Arsenal, he was in the car-park at Colney, there were all these Ferraris and fantastic cars, and there was Gilles Grimandi with his little Mini, the old one, from *The Italian Job*, and I thought: "Good for him."'

Dubbed 'Bouclette' (referring to his curly hairstyle) by his French teammates, Grimandi has always kept a low profile, as if he were trying not to wake up from his living dream. 'When I'm now looking back over my shoulder, I realise that so far I've had an untypical career full of success.' Born in Gap, in the south of the French Alps, Gilles could have been a skier rather than a footballer. But he grew up next to the local tiny stadium: 'From my bedroom window, I could watch the training sessions and the games. I wanted to go to a secondary school in Nîmes, but I got injured during the test and I never made it to the Nîmes college. I can say now that for me it was a real chance not being selected and staying in my home town with my friends. I remained in my little cocoon, enjoying an easy life with my friends.'

This anecdote sums up Gilles's career. A career which started as an amateur with Gap, and almost reluctantly led him to Monaco, after being spotted by regional scouts, and then to Arsenal. When he joined Monaco, he met the man who then always believed in him, probably more than Grimandi believes in himself. 'When I arrived at Monaco, I worked incredibly hard. As a reward, I joined the professional squad trained by Monsieur Wenger. I always refer to Arsène Wenger with the word Monsieur, because he is such a great coach, such a gentleman. When he was sacked, I was a bit lost, so it was a pleasure when he contacted me to come to Arsenal, and to form a new back four as an alternative to Adams, Keown, Winterburn and Dixon. I was pleased to be in a situation where I could join the coach who had faith in me for four years and gave me the directions to follow as a player. The negotiation with Arsenal's vice-chairman, David Dein, didn't last very long, I was immediately attracted by the new challenge and I quickly signed my contract. There was only one problem: the weather. I thought I was going to miss the sunshine I enjoyed in Monaco and Gap, but it didn't bother me too long. I was fascinated by the idea of playing in front of 40,000 fans at Highbury.'

Even though Gilles was excited by the idea of a reunion with Monsieur Wenger, he wanted to ask someone else for advice, someone with a great history in English football: 'The Cantona family has a house in a tiny village not far from Gap. There is absolutely nothing but four or five houses. I went there to speak to Eric but I could not find him. He was probably fishing or hunting. It's a pity, because I really wanted to talk to him about England. I am just like the other French players, we owe him so much, he gave us so much credibility.'

Grimandi joined Arsenal for the 1997–98 season: 'I found myself in the same position as two years before with Arsène Wenger [before he left for Nagoya]. Monsieur Wenger was still the same, very close to his squad, trying to give responsibilities to the players, always dedicated, working harder than ever, with more experience after his stay in Japan. At first, it was not as easy as I thought it would have been, to settle down. I learnt English and I tried hard to be accepted as a member of a squad where a lot of players had been playing for very long. I remember being amazed by Ian Wright and the atmosphere he used to create before a game.'

'UNCLE RÉMI' AND THE CRAZY DANCERS

Rémi Garde moved to Arsenal one year before Grimandi and for all the same good reasons. He also remembers Wright, the natural goalscorer soon to become a TV star, for everything he did to improve the cohesion of the team, between shy Frenchmen and loud Englishmen: 'When I arrived at Arsenal, the training camp was in a hotel [Sopwell House], near the city of St Albans. It was a very British atmosphere, with big leather armchairs and sofas, tea. At the beginning, the English were on their own, speaking so fast that we could not understand one word. And we were on our own. It lasted for six months, maybe one year. Then, suddenly, one day, Ian Wright entered the quiet and posh dining room, screaming and asking the English players: "Why don't you like the French?" And to us, he said: "Why don't you speak to the English?" It broke barriers, Ian was a very important link between us.'

Garde continues: 'When I got the phone call from Arsène, it was a bit of a surprise. Although I had a pretty average career, I was about to retire. When he called, he said to me: "It may be your destiny." Even though it was a trial, I was ready to seize the opportunity. First, I met Patrick [Vieira] in London just before we signed our contracts. When we arrived at Highbury, someone told us that before entering the chairman's office we had to wear a tie. We were about to discover the specificity of English football, tradition, respect.' Three months later, Garde made his first official appearance in an Arsenal jersey: 'I was a substitute and then I came on the pitch, against Leeds United. I still remember the fans being very curious, almost cautious. Then I got a nasty tackle, sort of a "Welcome to the Premier League".'

Before that, Garde had to cope with a transition period, before Wenger actually returned from Japan where he was keen on honouring his contract until the end. So the training sessions were conducted by Stewart Houston: 'We had to be at the training ground at 9.30 a.m. to have tea and biscuits, the training actually started at 10.30 a.m. In the meantime, every player took a football to play on his own, waiting for the start of the session. I was a bit lost. In France everything was so organised. Here, it was so laid back, so cool. I was also struck by the numbers of players showing up at any training session, more than 35.'

Dubbed 'Uncle Rémi' by his younger French teammates, Garde also discovered the atmosphere before a game in the dressing-room: 'Music was loud, some players were dancing. At first, I said to myself: "How the hell are we going to play in front of 40,000 fans, in 15 minutes, when some of my teammates are dancing?" I was surprised, because in France you never hear players laughing in the locker-rooms, it would be the sign of a lack of concentration. Here, it is a good way to evacuate pressure, and a much more relaxed way to get in the mood for entering a football game.' Before Wenger's arrival, Garde even remembers some players eating jellybeans and chocolate bars at half-time, and junk food after a game. 'English teams have won European Cups with that kind of diet,' Garde jokes, emphasising his love for England in general, and English football in particular.

All the way through their spells at Arsenal, Garde and Grimandi felt the pressure to show the fans in the North Stand and at Clock End that they deserved to be in the squad. 'I know I cannot be compared with Patrick [Vieira], Robert Pires or Sylvain Wiltord,' Garde says, 'but I think I've been adopted. I am very proud that I gave the best of my ability. I really have the feeling that I have brought my stone to build the success of Arsenal.' The former Strasbourg player will even remain forever in the Arsenal history books, as the first foreigner ever to bear the captain's armband, in the winter of 1997. Now Uncle Rémi is also a TV star, almost like Ian Wright. He is a quiet but brilliant consultant for Canal Plus, the famous cable and satellite TV channel which owns the rights of the Premiership for France.

Among the seven or eight dozen of French players of all ages who have crossed the Channel in the past ten years, almost two-thirds were regular first-team players who would never make it to the national team. Some had only known the French First Division almost all their lives and eventually decided to see something else before the end of their careers. Eric Roy and Patrick Colleter did not go for the easy trip when they left Olympique Marseille for England, within six months of each other. Incidentally, they both chose a club with red-striped kit. Roy landed in the north, at Sunderland, freshly promoted to the Premiership, and Colleter in the south, at Southampton, trying to avoid relegation to Division One. Then, times were sometimes tough, but neither of these explorers in shorts regrets the journey.

ROY: HAPPY MEMORIES OF THE BLACK CATS

Eric Roy started his career at OGC Nice, and he also played for Toulon, Lyon and then Marseille. The first thing he recalls about England is fashion: 'I love clothes and I found that London, and England, are much more "fashion", more eccentric. A store like Harrods, anyone should see it once in his life. It is exceptional, not only for fashion, but also for food. There is plenty of fruit, you want to buy everything. Every time I was in London for the weekend, I spent four or five hours at Harrods, with my wife. Sometimes, we did not buy anything, we just stayed there, because it's such an exceptional store. We had some surprises with the prices, it's an expensive store. London is expensive.'

However, the southerner didn't come to England for the sake of shopping or fashion. He was ready to leave France, the sun and the good food in order to bring a new direction to his career: 'After playing for various important clubs, and spending three seasons at the top level, in Marseille, I had just turned 30 and I thought it was this year or never to make it abroad. I had better offers in England but had I been able to choose, I would have picked Italy, because I am of Italian origin. When I got the opportunity to play in the Premier League, I went to see the club and its facilities. I did not have to think too much. I went there with my wife, we found a fantastic stadium, one of the best in the country, and an extraordinary atmosphere. The choice was quick to make. They really wanted me at Sunderland, so I thought: "I'll be in the team." I soon realised that my CV would not be of any use. I had to win my place in training, by showing my qualities. It took me one month to find my way around. The team had started the season well. I missed the first five or six games; I had to fight to get in the team. But that's all right, it means that I had to prove myself; it's a different approach, fair enough.'

Roy was amazed by the welcome in the land of the Black Cats. Even though he has been plying his trade for a couple of other clubs around Europe since his departure, he still feels part of Sunderland: 'I was really welcomed by the fans. The context was different from Arsenal, Chelsea or Liverpool, where managers are from abroad and very few English players make it to the first team. Sunderland is pure British tradition, and Anglo-Saxon style all over, whether players are English, Scottish, Swedish or Danish. I was the only Latin player at that time. We tried to play ball, but it was a very direct game, very British, a slightly improved kick-and-rush. I arrived there with my passing skills, my habit of playing the ball on the ground, so the fans quickly adopted me. They would even cheer when I did a 20-yard pass at ground level. I will always remember that.'

The former Marseille player was also amazed at the respect from both people in the streets and fans around the stadium: 'When you wait at the pedestrian crossing, the first car stops and lets you cross the street. In the south of France, we are not used to this. Here, when you are a player, life is easier, they respect you, even if the wages are in the papers. I never felt that jealousy that you can sometimes feel in France. The footballer is a recognised citizen with a legitimacy to earn a lot of money, which is not exactly the case in France. When you get out of the stadium, or the training ground, the fans are all lining up, they are educated. Without being too familiar, people always have a gesture, a nice word.'

Roy loved the atmosphere, but he had more reservations about the food: 'I was lucky, there was a small Italian restaurant next to the training ground and I became friends with the owners. It's not that English food is bad, it's just different. They eat lots of beans, with red sauce, eggs, toast. You get used to it, but it's slightly exotic for a Frenchman. I sometimes ate at the training ground canteen: beans, chicken, fish and chips, it is not exactly light stuff. However, I loved desserts, especially puddings. There was an old lady, Eileen, we got along well. She was very kind, and very good at desserts, she made me discover things.'

The pasta freak also became friends with the salesman who sold him a car, the golf pro at the local club, and a lad who helped him a lot with the paperwork, when he arrived. 'I invited them to the French Riviera, to thank them, we keep in touch. They are not long-time friends, but I know that if I want to return to Sunderland to see a game, the club, or the coaches, there will still be the same guys at the same gates. It is a culture, they love their club. You don't see that in France. Sometimes I come back to OGC Nice, where I started my career and spent five years at the club. They wouldn't let me into the dressing-room, they treat me like shit. It's absurd, and it would be impossible in England, because they have a culture of tradition: if you wore the club jersey, you represent something, even if you only spent a year and a half at the club, and even if your stay will not make it to the history books.'

After a good first season, Roy was looking forward to the next. But it wasn't to be the best time of his football career, by far: 'I played in 30 games and we finished sixth, along with Aston Villa. Then, we went to Marbella, players and staff, we played golf, we partied, and Peter Reid told me I was the best player of the last four months. I was very happy, and expected a lot from the second season. I came back one month later and there were lots of new players. There is a lot of money in the Premier League. My place in the team was not assured, I played but then I got injured and the team started to play well. For three months and 13 games they remained unbeaten, and made it to the top of the Premier League in December. No wonder I could not get back into the team. I was on the bench. I had six months left on my contract, I wanted to play, so I left for Troyes.'

PATRICK COLLETER: 18 MONTHS WITH THE SAINTS

When Patrick Colleter left Olympique Marseille, at the respectable age of 32, with his wife and children, he also wanted to see something else, just like Roy. After playing for Paris St Germain, Montpellier, Bordeaux and Marseille, the tough and reliable full-back joined Southampton: 'I was fed up with the routine of the French league, the same people, the same stadia. They wanted to see me for a one-week trial. I did not speak one word of English when I arrived. I had forgotten, since English at school. They came to the airport with a small sign, and got me into a hotel. The next morning, they picked me up to go to the training ground. Fortunately, Hassan Kachloul, a Moroccan, spoke French, so he explained what was up. I had to prove myself within a week, but as my wife and children were with me, I was not alone, and I did not think too much. I trained every day. They played on Wednesday night against Wimbledon, they won 3–1. I was surprised by the small stadium, 15,000 seats, all wood [The Dell], typically English, but with a crazy atmosphere. It was brilliant, for a guy like me, who enjoys physical commitment. That's why I wanted to play in England, it's a game that fits me, and they don't care about the age on the passport.'

Saints' manager David Jones then decided to sign Colleter: 'The contract was written, I came back to Marseille on Tuesday to give them my letter of dismissal, and Tuesday night I was back in London, to pass the medical. Well, you cannot really say it was a medical. No X-rays, I saw a doctor at 10 p.m., in a room. He looked at my knees, my ankles, just like that, did not bother to take a blood sample, nothing. It's their way of doing things. In France, they would check everything from A to Z, do a heart-check, X-rays of the knees and ankles, etc.' Colleter was not impressed by the medical, but he was happy about the salary: 'I trained on Wednesday, signed my contract on Thursday, my wages doubled, free of tax, not like in France. On Saturday, we played at home against Chelsea, at noon, on TV. Playing on a Saturday, at noon, it had never happened to me before. I got up at 10 a.m., and two hours later I was playing football, it's crazy. We had a good game, but we lost 2–0 and I injured [Gustavo] Poyet, who then spent three months on the sidelines. So my name was in the papers the next day. I also remember my second game, against Charlton at home, I scored a goal. I never score. In France, I must have scored eight goals in my whole career, one every three years. It was only my second match, and it was important because Charlton were fighting relegation, just like us. The score was 1–1. For me, it was fabulous. People were very happy, it was brilliant.'

One year later, in February 2000, Glenn Hoddle took over from David Jones. This was basically the end of Colleter's journey in English football, due to an injury against Aston Villa, followed by a major communication problem with Hoddle (see Chapter 13). 'At the beginning, I really liked it, but at the end, it was too much, as Hoddle took away my desire of playing football. I did not want to train any more. Eventually, they released me, and paid all the money. We found an arrangement, I took my money and left.'

Colleter had to leave, and the Hoddle incident will just remain as a bad memory in an ocean of good memories: 'England was a super experience for me. I still watch the Premier League on TV, the fans cheer when the player kicks the ball in touch; you don't see that in France. I even buy English newspapers, when I find them, to see the results. I will never forget this period of my career, and it was an enriching experience for all my family. My children now speak fluent English, it's fabulous. My 14-year-old son did not want to leave. He was the skipper of his school team, he really loved it. As soon as his hair was too long, they would tell him to cut it. And his shirt was inside his trousers. He learned respect for values. Now that we are back in France, he has kept those values . . . but he cannot go to school with a suit, he does not want to be bullied by his friends. He wants to be a footballer. He will try, he is good at school. It was harder for him to leave than for me. If I tell him to go and study in England, he goes tomorrow. He wants to spend his holidays in England.'

WILLIAM PRUNIER: ONE MONTH WITH THE RED DEVILS

Along the years, there were a few shorter experiences than Colleter's in English football. The shortest one, apart from one-week trials, is still one of the most vivid recollections of William Prunier's long career. Now well over 30, Prunier is the skipper of Toulouse, a team which used to be in the French First Division but went two divisions down, in a day, after being hit by financial problems. He played for Man U twice, once in December 1995 and again in January 1996. Eric Cantona was still at Manchester, but he didn't play any part in Prunier's arrival: 'Eric was a good friend of mine, we played together at Auxerre, but Sir Alex Ferguson already knew me. He called me for a trial. I was experiencing problems with my team, Bordeaux, because I gave the V sign to some guys in the crowd.'

Prunier continues: 'It was a short experience, to say the least. I arrived in Manchester on Monday, and I had a good game with the reserves on

Wednesday. So Sir Alex offered me a one-month contract. I accepted, even though I would have preferred a longer deal. At that time, Man U had a lot of injured players, but the atmosphere was very good during the games and amongst the team.

'Man U were a very organised and professional team. I joined the first team for Saturday's game lost to Queens Park Rangers. The fans even started to sing my name. We lost 2–1. The next game, we also lost, 5–1 to Tottenham [4–1 in fact]. It was my last game with the Red Devils.

'Alex wanted to keep me, but there were financial problems, the contract they offered me was too short, the wages were not that exciting. What would happen to my family if I got injured and wasn't able to play the rest of the season? But still, what an experience, I have only good memories of Man U.'

It was a quick spell, but it gave Prunier the incentive to continue travelling in Europe. He then went to Denmark, Italy, Belgium, and eventually back to France. Just like Grimandi, Garde, Roy, Colleter and most of the others, he will cherish his memories forever: he played in the Premiership, he was part and parcel of the French Revolution across the Channel.

Daniel Ortelli
and Jérôme Rasetti

CHAPTER 13

The French Sceptics: Graham, Gregory and Hoddle

George Graham, John Gregory, Glenn Hoddle: there seems to be a small anti-French coalition of managers operating in England. Is this a hasty generalisation? Are two of them just anti-Ginola? Or is it just a coincidence? In the past ten years, whenever one of these three managers came across a French player in the club that he was taking charge of, there was a problem. And as a matter of fact, the manager did not sign any other French player in his time at the club.

Of course, it is difficult to know what really happened, because nobody will say anything, neither the manager . . . who wants to keep his job, nor the player . . . who wants to find another job. And you cannot count on the chairman, because he needs to keep a secret weapon in his drawer, just in case he has to sack the manager, or on the agent either, because he (or she) is working with the player in order to find another club. Everything is off the record, so all we are able to do is to speculate about what went wrong, brewing a strange mix of tactical, technical and psychological considerations, an interesting cocktail of pride and prejudice, of shame and mystery. It sometimes makes for good reading, but not always.

GINOLA: EIGHT MANAGERS AND FOUR CLUBS IN SEVEN YEARS

The topic of the day is French players in England, so let's start with one of the most sexy and glamorous, the L'Oréal man, who also happened to fall out with two of the three managers quoted at the beginning of this chapter. David Ginola eventually opened his mouth when he left Aston Villa in the spring of 2002, three months before the end of the season, claiming that it was like 'awakening from a nightmare'. The French ace joined Everton on a free transfer, soon after Gregory was replaced by Graham Taylor at Villa. Goodison Park was to be his fourth home in England since 1995, after Newcastle, Tottenham and Villa.

'I woke up this morning and thought that I had just had a nightmare. I'd had three great years at Spurs but at Villa not so much football, which was a shame for me and the fans.' Obviously, 'Gin Tonic' was still hurt by his treatment by former Villa boss John Gregory, who gave him just 19 starts in his 18 months in the Midlands: 'There were times at Villa when I felt humiliated. The way I was treated, that was the worst thing to do for a man with pride.' However, he kept his head high, and his mouth shut. He also tried to help young Darius Vassell with some advice, although he was in competition with the young England striker for a place in the team. 'People will never take away from me my confidence and my ability. I wanted to shout "Let me play" but that didn't happen enough. So the main thing I wanted to do was to help create a positive feeling in the dressing-room. You find out that, as a senior player, even if you are badly treated, you can still help to create a positive attitude. And I must say that the players were always great with me. I tried to be an example for the others. But for a year and a half, it was difficult to keep smiling every day.'

Anyway, this nightmare was over, and, as always with Ginola, a new fairy tale was about to start. He was so excited about playing for the 'Toffees': 'I will be just delighted to be involved in playing football again. All I have ever wanted to do was to play football. I'm not bitter about what has happened, I'm an entertainer and all I wanted to do was to play. But all I have seen today is people talking about me being too old, a luxury who has cost too much. Nobody said it is good to see David Ginola on the pitch again.'

And Ginola went on, on the Everton website, in the papers, everywhere: 'This is a great feeling now because it is a beginning again. And the reality is that I can play in the FA Cup for Everton – I didn't play in the competition for Villa, I hardly played at all! Now I want to be able to express myself again. I have not left Graham Taylor on a bad note. I would have loved to work with him and he said he would be delighted if I was to stay. But he only has 14 matches left to build for the future and I wanted to play in as many matches as possible. When you reach a certain age, all you want to do is to play in every match and that was not going to be possible. I said it would be better for me to leave now and play more for someone else.'

During his time at Villa, there had been interesting controversies about Ginola's fitness, and even Gregory could not resist giving his view on the topic, publicly. Ginola's agent, Chantal Stanley, even threatened to sue Gregory, and hire Cherie Blair to defend David's interests. That would have been interesting to watch.

When Ginola landed at Goodison Park, he was honest and acknowledged that he was not exactly in the best shape of his life: 'I'm fit, but maybe it will take a week or so to get match fit. It was hard at Villa, I didn't play enough games. But I was always positive, I always came in every morning smiling and wanting to be very positive about my game. Every time I went onto the pitch I was positive, and you only want to give the fans wonderful things to see. I always kept my confidence in my own ability, I have had that since I was four, and people will never take that away from me. It has all been very frustrating for me, but I have now signed for a club where I will be able to play.'

Three months later, Ginola had only played in five league games and two cup games. A new young manager, David Moyes, had come in to replace old Walter Smith, and he did not hold out his hand to Ginola. There had been no miracle and anybody could understand why by watching, on the same super Sunday, two FA Cup games in a row: the one with Laurent Robert, his successor at Newcastle, and the one with Ginola wearing an Everton jersey. It was as if something was wrong with the TV, the speed of the images was not right, too quick for the first game, or too slow for the second. The English Premiership may be very good with old pros, but you tend to see more 35-year-olds in defence than up front, and if Ginola still loves to play, as he claims, he might give a serious thought to operating as a sweeper, like Laurent Blanc, rather than a winger, like Laurent Robert, for the next few years of his career.

Flashback. When Ginola arrived at Newcastle in 1995, on Kevin Keegan's insistence, everything was rosy, except the weather in the North East (see Chapter 7). The Magpies even led the Premiership for a while. At one point, they could even count on a comfortable 12-point margin on the Red Devils, at the beginning of 1996, and then everything went pear-shaped. There was the Keegan–Ferguson incident, the fact that Cantona was back on top of his game, and all sorts of other factors. Eventually, Man U won the league and neither Ginola nor Cantona took part in Euro '96, although they both had a pretty good season behind them to back their claims to be in the team. But even then, some spectators had their doubts about Ginola, such as Henry Winter of the *Daily Telegraph*: 'For me, Ginola did not make a mark at Newcastle; he was everything that was wrong with French football. He was about the image, about highlights. He was not about the team, but the individual. He was wonderful to watch, but for a coach he must have been horrible, because he could ruin a game. I always gave Ginola a beating, because I think he has so much talent, but never used it for the team. We voted him Footballer of the Year; I didn't, I thought it was an embarrassment, I keep going round to English journalists and asking them: "Did you vote for him?" I've only met two people so far who admitted voting for him. I thought it was ridiculous.'

In 1999, both the Football Writers and the Football Players decided, in secret ballots, that David was the Footballer of the Year. He had single-footedly won the League Cup by scoring goals and providing assists, whenever necessary, in a very modest Tottenham team. This was quite an achievement, it was the first trophy in ages for Spurs, and it was Ginola's very first in England. No wonder he was happy, and it was also a sweet revenge on all these journos who had ridiculed him since his arrival, for his long hair and his TV ads.

'It went really fine with the English journalists, it was really friendly,' a smiling David told me in the spring of 1999, after receiving his trophy. 'When you win their trophy, the journalists are proud, they come to you, they look at you, and you can see what they imply: "We voted for you." It is their trophy, so I made sure I said, "Thank you very much, thank you, thank you." They were very happy. For me, it was a bit special, but the most important is the players' trophy: to be acknowledged by one's peers is quite something, in any profession. To be recognised by the journalists is a different story, it goes both ways, because my relationship with them is slightly . . . tense. I sometimes read their pieces after the games, although I'm often advised not to read them. However, this year, they wrote a lot of good things.'

David was radiant, we were at the Orange Tree, in Totteridge, his favourite pub, and he kept on gloating about the scope of his win: 'I got

37 per cent of the votes, although in general, northern and southern journalists are chauvinistic, they vote for players in their area. There are a couple of journalists per club, I don't know how they work it out, but one representative of the association told me: "This year, it's really stunning. People from the north voted for you, from Newcastle but also from Manchester, Nottingham or Blackburn." So I have all reasons to be proud.'

Then I could not help asking David about this new landmark in the French Revolution: 'It's not so much that it goes well for the French, but for quality players. You only have to look at the names; you are talking Leboeuf, Vieira, Petit, Cantona, Ginola. I don't want to look like I'm sending roses like that, for free, but we are quality players, any football would fit us. When someone has skills, it just takes some time to settle down, to feel good in life and football. Then, success must come naturally.'

In the general euphoria of the day, Ginola even had some very kind words about George Graham: 'I was never worried about a new coach; I know that I can work a lot. There was always the same question with his predecessor, Christian Gross. People would tell me: "The German-Swiss rigour, it's going to be tough for you," but everything went well. With George Graham, it is just the same, and it also shows that I am able to work hard. Graham is very rigorous, he has strong tactical views, and he really knows where he wants to go. At the training ground, we do lots of tactical drills. He is fed up with silly goals, we are a bit too naive sometimes. With Keegan at Newcastle, we hardly ever did this, but we played a lot, and it was almost the same with Dalglish [Kenny, who succeeded Keegan and then let Ginola go]. Graham really is the first English coach with whom I feel a tactical will to improve, and to be tactically strong. He has the mentality of a Continental coach.'

The honeymoon was not meant to last, especially with no presents on a regular basis. One year later, David and George broke up, after two very disappointing decisions for David: he was on the bench for the second leg of a UEFA Cup game against Kaiserslautern, and the Spurs went out. He was also on the bench for the last Premiership game of the season, against Manchester United. At that time, once again, Ginola was gutted, he did not want to leave Tottenham, he loved the fans and the fans loved him, but Graham was slowly pushing him to the door. Chantal Stanley, his agent, could only provide one explanation: 'George is jealous of David.' Who knows?

At that time, Martin Lipton wrote for the *Daily Mail* and followed Tottenham closely. He does not mind playing the devil's advocate for Graham: 'George wants players to perform to his model, and David is a maverick, a free spirit, he does not want to be shackled. It's great, and George loved it when he was on the ball and doing things, but there were too many games, particularly away from home, when he went missing. George did not have a particularly good team, so when that defensive discipline was lacking, it used to drive him mad. Ginola always played his best football when he was on the left-hand side of the pitch, attacking the left-hand goal, because George could shout in his ear. It is a discipline thing as well, because he could not ignore this, and he would keep the team shape. George believes in team shape, discipline and organisation. He likes to control, there is no right or wrong way, it is his way. To be fair, Ginola has also fallen out with other managers in the past. Ginola is very good at falling out with managers, and it was easy for him to fall out with George.' Quick, precise, a bit harsh maybe, but right to the point. Thanks Martin.

HODDLE COMES, COLLETER GOES . . .

Now to another example, at the other end of the scale, with a rather less glamorous footballer: Patrick Colleter, a rough and tough French full-back with 12 long years of experience in the French League, normal hair, no international cap. Signed by David Jones at Southampton, he was quite confident when Glenn Hoddle arrived 15 months later to take over. 'I thought: "Very good, he played for Monaco, he spent three years in France. He must speak a little French, it will be easier for me to have a dialogue, to tell him what I think, how I feel like playing, and to understand what he wants me to do." I will always remember our first meeting. He spoke English right away. He told me: "I know you, I like your style of play." I thought: "This is great," so I told him: "I would love it if you spoke French to me, it would be easier for me." "No, no," he answered dryly, "I forgot everything, I don't speak French any more."'

What followed was even more disappointing. Colleter played against Sheffield Wednesday (1–1), then he got injured against Aston Villa, 'a bad tackle on a thigh', but he agreed to play, under Hoddle's insistence, against Arsenal. At half-time, Arsenal led 2–0 and Hoddle subbed him. 'I was OK, but it was Arsenal. I don't blame him for subbing me.' It was Colleter's

24th Premiership game with the Saints, but it was also the last, and he did not know it. 'After that day, I never played again, with no explanation. I played with the reserves, it was absolute madness. One day, he was watching the reserves, I played in midfield, but I got sent off . . . after an opponent elbowed my back. The next day, he summoned me to his office, it was three months after his arrival, and he told me: "In *my* club, I cannot tolerate this, you have no right to do this." Two days later, I got a letter telling me that the club, via Hoddle, had fined me. They took two weeks of my salary. I learnt that it was legal, I was really upset. This was the end of it. I never said hello to him any more.'

Colleter is still very angry at Hoddle: 'Several players had a problem with him. Strangely enough, we were all foreigners: me, but also some Norwegians, and Boa Morte [Luis, a Portuguese] who decided to leave. With David Jones, there was a rotation, of course, with 30 players. But with Hoddle, it was specifically directed at foreigners, and that's what I did not like. I had one year left on my contract. I wanted to sort it out, so I returned to his office. He told me: "You cannot stay here, you have to go." I answered: "I'm not going anywhere, unless you give me my money. Talk to your chairman. I'm ready to play with the reserves for one year." At the end, I was not even allowed to play with the reserves, I was with the youth team, the only pro. The other players could not believe it, they thought: "What the hell has he done?" The coach of the reserves could not help me, because he could not decide. The other [Hoddle] would come and tell him: "You take him, play him here." There was nothing he could do about it. He would have liked to let me play, because it would have been good for his team, but he was stuck.'

There was also a controversy in the papers: 'The English journalists loved it: he said something, I answered, the snowball effect, etc.' Plus a bit of administrative misunderstanding about a letter. Eventually, after six more months of arm-wrangling, Southampton released Colleter and he signed for Cannes in November 2000, in the French Division Three. But he cannot stop talking about how Hoddle ruined the end of his English journey. 'When he arrived at Southampton, it was not exactly what he wanted as a coach. He brought something, for sure, they came close to Europe, but his goal was to be in charge of a London club, Tottenham or Chelsea. As soon as the job was available, he jumped at the opportunity. For me, this summarises the man: he left them in the shit.'

Colleter, now a retired footballer, does not have enough harsh words in stock for Hoddle: 'It's true that Tottenham is something else compared to Southampton, but there are ways to do it. From one day to the other, he left, and they were left with the assistant coach. He could have made it easier for Southampton, but I'm not surprised. He had managed England, coached the best English players, his foreign influences had enriched him. He was a very good player, he played in France, it brought him a lot of experience. Still, he was a bit particular as a coach. When everything went well, he wanted the honours. When things were going wrong, he blamed it on the players. As a player, it's always difficult to accept.'

Same old story of a strong difference of views between a player and a coach, but who knows if this had to do with the fact that Hoddle is very English and Colleter very French? If this was not a culture shock, it looked a lot like it. Again, Martin Lipton is willing to play the devil's advocate, this time for Hoddle, who succeeded George Graham at Tottenham: 'Glenn has not had that many French players, has he? Glenn likes to get a player that he does not know, and to prove how good he is. He is a better passer of the ball than anybody in the whole Tottenham squad. If he had younger legs, he could do it now. He has bought Serbs and Slovenians, but no French players. But if a real quality French player was available, I don't think he would have a problem with that at all, because he cites Wenger as the most important influence in his career after their time together at Monaco. And if you ask Wenger about Hoddle, and Hoddle about Wenger, it's an illuminating conversation. Wenger recognises the tactical vein in Hoddle. Hoddle could be like his thoughts on the pitch, and do things that Wenger never could do as a player. And Hoddle admits that Wenger made him believe that he could become a coach, he opened his eyes. He had never thought about it.' If this were rugby, not football, one could say that Martin kicked into touch.

That's all folks, it was just a couple of stories of players falling out with managers; it's just as universal as football. You won't learn anything more about 'the anti-French coalition'. It's a good topic, but that's all we know, or at least that's all we can write in a book. But feel free to dig for yourself . . .

Daniel Ortelli

CHAPTER 14

A View from the Stands: Fans and Journos

In a football book about passion, the fans deserve a chapter of their own, as a tribute to their dedication, their commitment, their addiction to the beautiful game, whatever the weather, the scandals, the price of the season tickets, official kits and programmes. Across the years, from Cantona to Pires, all the French players who crossed the Channel have enjoyed an incredible amount of love pouring from the stands, everywhere in England, and they have given their best to please the crowd. It's only fair that we start with them, because they are just as passionate as the fans.

Robert Pires' love for English football is already well documented, but it cannot hurt to hear some extra explanations from only the third Frenchman to be distinguished as Footballer of the Year, after King Eric (Cantona) and Gin(ola) Tonic: 'We try to give the best possible image of the French player in England, because we know that this League is watched almost everywhere. With this label of World and European champions [Pires was speaking before the 2002 World Cup], you cannot disappoint the people. All of us playing here are a little bit like ambassadors, because we represent France. We are lucky that we are in a position to allow lots of young people to dream. People tend to identify with us, so that's why we always have to give the best possible image. One day, during my first season, I had a big argument with Dennis Wise [then at Chelsea]. I got excited, and then I quickly came back to reality. I'm not a rebel, I'm a rather quiet guy. When there is an argument between players, I'm always trying to help out, so that everybody calms down; when we play Leeds for example . . .'

Pires is always ready to elaborate on important matters, especially if you talk to him in French, but his English is improving by the day: 'The real spirit of English football is this passion they can put on the pitch. Respect, it's as simple as that. The English have created this sport and they have always tried to preserve its rules. It has not changed, even with money. I've always respected others, it's obvious, but living here has reinforced this attitude of mine. Referees are more respected here than in other leagues. Players complain, but not as much as elsewhere. There is always this element of English culture reappearing at the surface. Before I came here, my idea of English football was Liverpool, because the club left a mark on Europe during its euphorical years. And also the physical combat, the lads who never give up anything, and who give it all during 90 minutes. This is terrific, and I can still see it these days. It is something that I was missing before coming here: agression, but in a good positive sense.'

Do you like that? Do you want a little bit more? No problem, Pires is a good talker: 'I did not realise that when watching from abroad, from France, but now that I'm here, I know that the communion between fans and players, fans and the team, only exists in England. They go to the stadium, they have their shirt, wife and children. Some even put their name and favourite number on the back of their shirt. In France, Italy or Spain, the fact that there are fences in the stadia says a lot. Here, you can see the face of the fans before you kick a corner. They are only five yards from you, maximum. To know that they are here, ready to help you, to support you, means a lot. Systematically, whatever you do, an attacking move, a tackle, anything technical, people are very happy, and they clap, even if it's not an extraordinary gesture. They are right, because it is a show. They go to the stadium to see a good show, it's the way they were born and educated. We get ready just like actors going on stage. When you know that you are going to do something that they will appreciate, and that they will clap, it makes you even stronger. It's the main difference between England and the other leagues. I had lost that in France, the communion between players and fans is missing, but France deserves better. It's important for me, and also for the others. Without that, Patrick Vieira and Arsène Wenger would not have stayed that long in England.'

On a good day, Emmanuel Petit also explained the reason why he returned to England (besides the money, of course): 'There is one thing that English clubs have and that other players will never have elsewhere, this brotherhood in football, it is extraordinary. Merchandising in England is one of the best in the world, but it is also because most of the bosses are passionate. They have been fans since they were little boys, and this is formidable. I say that because I had formidable times at Arsenal, and it could have been different elsewhere, but when I watch an English team playing, I never get bored. I know there will always be something happening, pace, commitment. Sometimes it may still appear like kick-and-rush, you don't have the impression that the guy is going to lift his head, but it is still a game, and everybody has understood that. Everybody knows it's a sport, and unlike in the movies you are not allowed two takes for every action. That's why everyone is a fanatic, the players just like the supporters. When we are on the pitch, we get so much love from the crowd that we want to give it back a hundred times. I don't know if it's the same elsewhere . . .'

FANS FOR LIFE

Now to fans like 70-year-old Josie of the Arsenal Fish Bar, who has only missed one game since 1967, 'because of a bad flu', but 'woke up at three o'clock in the morning' in order to travel to see the Gunners crash badly at Old Trafford in February 2001 (6–1). She has some reservations about the two Anelka brothers, but, on the whole, Josie is very positive about French players: 'French football is fantastic. The French players protect each other, and they are well behaved, contrary to these English thugs. I may not be neutral, but there is nothing bad to say about our Frenchies, they are fantastic. I can see why all the other clubs are doing the same. One day, one of my friends was kissed by Robert Pires. She came back to me and said: "I'm not going to wash my face any more." Now, that is passion for football!'

One of Josie's friends is Peggy, the 60-year-old in charge of the Arsenal fan club: 'I have to admit that when we started buying these French players, I was not in favour of that. A lot of our players come from the youth ranks, they have this passion in them, they want to win at all cost. I had never heard of these French players, they were like Bambis: the other players only had to look at them, and they were down. They did not enjoy the physical contact. The exception was Vieira. I always said that he is an Englishman born in France. The French Connection, on a number of aspects, was good for Arsenal. I am just disappointed that we don't have more English players. I also regret that we have not seen the players at the annual dance for a long time, since Petit and Vieira showed up three years ago. But I like the fact that Wenger is an educated man, and that he does not wear a training kit on the touchline.'

In the French Revolution, there are also French fans who cross the Channel on a regular basis, to follow their favourite English team. The living proof of this is Benjamin Lambert, a 26-year-old cook for a French government agency, a season-ticket holder at Paris St Germain and an Arsenal supporter since 1994: 'My first time at Highbury was in 1994, for a Cup-Winners' Cup semi-final between Arsenal and Paris St Germain. It was like a click, I was lovestruck. The atmosphere was *magnifique*, nothing to compare with other stadia in Europe, thanks to the touchline three metres from the crowd. More than a stadium or a club, I discovered a whole area of London, and a mentality. I remember an outstanding stadium stuck in the middle of a residential area. I had the feeling that I was entering a house, not a stadium. Arsenal has lost some warmth these past few years, and sometimes it is considered some sort of cathedral, but the crowd is still behind the team for 90 minutes, pushing, pushing.'

Benjamin is hooked, and he told us why: 'English football is like an Eldorado for me, more than a huge passion, almost a *raison de vivre*, like a virus maybe, but a good virus, allowing you to get on with your life. Once you've got it, it's very difficult to get rid of it. For me, as a fan, it's a wonderful way to express myself, cheering all the time for 90 minutes, going to the away games with 3,000 or 4,000 people. I had never seen anything like that, and it leaves me with unforgettable memories. One Sunday, I had not planned anything, there was an Arsenal v. Newcastle game. I suddenly decided to rush to the Gare du Nord, got myself a ticket, then a seat at Highbury, watched the game and came back. I was in Paris by midnight, worn out but happy, because Arsenal had won. I went to bed and woke up at 5.30 a.m. the next day, to go to work.'

Young Lambert also remembers 'an FA Cup third-round game at Carlisle, waking up at 4.30 a.m., a 13-hour return trip in the coach, and the coldest I've felt in all my life. As any supporter, I have to follow the team through the good and the bad times, home and away. Sometimes my family and friends don't understand this. But by going to Arsenal, I discovered the Anglo-Saxon way of life, a mentality which really fits me, and I met people who are now a big part of my life, because they brought a lot to me, on the human side. I spend three months of my salary every year to follow Arsenal. I have this club flowing in my veins. Arsenal is part of my life. This shirt is my second skin.'

Last but not least, Steve, a 40-year-old Arsenal supporter, provides a broader, more analytical view of the whole phenomenon: 'Cantona, you can compare him to Maradona. He was unique. There was no Cantona before him, there will be no other Cantona after him. He was not created in a mould that others could duplicate. The present ones, Vieira, Henry, Wiltord, they have their own game, but they have the same ethics of football. You cannot compare Desailly with Henry or Leboeuf with Grimandi or Silvestre, but they share the same values in the way they play the game. They are very keen to play a passing football, their control and their first touch are solid, their movement is good, they work hard. This comes from the academies, the coaches, and all the thinking behind the French game. This includes dietetics and the refusal to drink, all these things that England never took into account for years, because we are so arrogant that we think we know it all!'

Steve is a social worker, so he knows a thing or two about racism: 'There is a form of partiality with regards to the French players. It's not open racism, but there is a stream of thought where the French are not liked, as a whole, by the English. We people are from an island. There is no xenophobia, but there is something like: "We don't speak to you from the other side of the Channel." I think the French are the new Dutch. Just look at the mid-1970s, when there was a wave of Dutch players. They had a definite style of play. There are similarities with that era. My vision of French football dates back to Euro 84: Platini, Tigana, Giresse, Fernandez, Rocheteau . . . what a great team! And the people behind that team were then behind the academies *à la française* which produced the footballers of today.'

JOURNOS BARE ALL

Steve could have been a journalist, just like Martin Lipton (*The Mirror*), Richard Williams (*The Guardian*) and Henry Winter (the *Daily Telegraph*) are still fans, but not many people know which team they support. I interviewed them during the World Cup, at Osaka, Kobe and Niigata. I asked them the same three questions, and they were kind enough to forget about their professional neutrality. After all, they are just football fans who don't have to pay for their ticket. Some even get paid to watch the games.

Will the English press respect the French players less after the World Cup failure?

ML (in Osaka Stadium press restaurant on 11 June, not long after watching the French early exit on TV): 'I would be surprised, because we still have enormous respect for the players, Henry, Pires, etc. I think certain players, if they appear to be playing on their reputation, will be put aside a bit more. It's hard to conceive that players of this quality are out of the tournament. They are not bad players, they did not become bad players overnight. If we could get a team as good as France these past four years, we would be absolutely over the moon. Clairefontaine is the role model for every European team, and England wants to copy every aspect of the French organisation of football. There is a little bit of pleasure at the exit, but there is no questioning of the quality of the players. Initially, there was more scepticism: what are these foreigners doing in English football, we don't need them. This may have lasted a season and a half, and then you realise: they are here because they are sensational players.

'Pires got the vote of the press because he was just brilliant, and also because he had been criticised the season before, when he did not play very well: he was a coward, he looked scared of it. Henry always looked like a wonderful player. We want players who care, in England, and as long as they care, like Henry and Pires, they will never get criticised for having a bad game. We are aware that the Premier League is as great as it is because of the quality of the overseas players that came in. If it was a purely homogeneous league, with only English players, it would not be a particularly good league. You can't tell me that Beckham and Scholes did not develop by playing alongside Cantona, that Owen is not a better player because he had Houllier to tell him how to become a better player, that Campbell has not improved with Wenger's tutelage, and getting confidence from having Vieira in front of him.'

RW (outside the England base camp in Tsuna, near Kobe, on 13 June): 'The World Cup won't change anything, as long as they perform for their club. I don't think people will be looking at Vieira and Henry any differently. I think the English people recognise that the success France had in the World Cup and the European Championship was very well deserved, and because there was a very good foundation, not just a great generation of players. It was not just a bit of luck. It could only happen with a lot of hard work. We also know what Wenger and Houllier brought to our clubs, so I don't think this World Cup will change anything at all. English fans will not be affected either. They see the French players as talented individuals, and it does not affect them, at that stage, what happens to their team.'

Who are your favourite French players?
RW: 'Eric is the most interesting, of course. Cantona introduced the idea that French players could be taken seriously, and there is no question that he was the catalyst of Manchester United. It would not have happened in the same way, and so quickly, if he had not come to Old Trafford. At that time, nobody had ever heard of Kopa, Fontaine. Eric made all the difference, and in terms of being a star, he is the most compelling figure. When Cantona came, Manchester United players copied his training habits, he was very influential, but I don't think they copied the way he plays. There is not a French way of playing, and it's not very different from an English way of playing. You would not say that a French defence is very different from a good English defence. It happened that in the last few years France had more talented players, that's the only difference.

'You would never be able to do exactly the same thing, but I think Henry has been a very impressive character since he arrived in England. I don't think he spoke any English at all, but now he has a very good command of the detail of English, the nuance. He is more eloquent than most English footballers. Desailly does not speak a lot of English, but people respect him, for what he is as a player. Vieira is an emblematic player, the most symbolic player. If he plays well, it reflects quite well on the group of French players as a whole. I felt the same way as everybody when Pires came, I thought he was a very skilful, lightweight player, but no real heart for the game, and then last season he showed us what he really is, so now we have an enormous respect for the man. But I don't think he would have made a huge difference to France's performance in this World Cup.'

HW (at Niigata Stadium, on 15 June, before England–Denmark): 'Thierry Henry is such a charming person, he is really interesting to talk to. I remember talking to him after the sending off against Newcastle, it was Graeme Poll at the end. Arsenal set up the interview but they were a little bit worried, because it was at the time of the disciplinary panel. The point I made is that the reason he got upset with the referee is because he cared, and a lot of foreigners who come over here are just accused of being mercenaries, but I think Henry actually cares, he just feels for Arsenal. Pires is very popular as well, Vieira to a lesser extent, but the problem is that he is very cautious with the English press because we just ask him about Real Madrid.'

What are your best memories as an English journalist covering the French Revolution 1992-2002?
RW: 'A better memory than the World Cup in France? Seven or eight years ago, I went to visit Houllier, in France, mostly to talk about Cantona, but he told me about the French structure, the formation of young players, what had been done, how it all worked, and what the philosophy of football, for these young players, was. And that was so impressive. I wish I had been someone from the Football Association, because at that point I would have gone back to London and said: this is what we must do. That sounds boring, but for me that was the most interesting. And then it took a few more years, but Howard Wilkinson knew already, he had been in contact with Houllier for a long time. It took the World Cup for the people in blazers to agree to it.'

HW: 'I quite liked Cantona. Cantona was fine, he would say "*bonjoouur*", but nobody interviewed him. Cantona is not from

France, he is from another planet. I think he is a very simple person, not complicated at all. All the bit about the seagulls who follow the trawler, it's just a joke with Cantona. I think he is having fun at our expense. Cantona had his problems on the pitch, but off the pitch he was the hardest trainer at Manchester United, always looked after his body, the lowest body fat, so all the other Man U players said: "This is the way we have to be to be professional." So I think Cantona coming over actually taught English players how to be professional, not to drink so much, which was the problem of all. Talk to Beckham. Beckham is amazing. He says: "Cantona, practice, practice, practice." Beckham has worked so hard because of Cantona's example. I interviewed Anelka once, and he was very strange. He was very unpopular with the English, and I just found him very shy. One game against Dynamo Kiev, he travelled with the team, even though he was injured, and I was sitting down in the Olympic Stadium in Kiev, writing my piece. It was about four or five years ago, and there was an empty seat next to me. Anelka appeared and sat down, we had a chat and he was fine. But he has strange brothers.'

ML: 'I always find the French players very very polite. Thierry Henry is an interview waiting to happen. Obviously, he gets it out by talking after the game. But the strongest memory must be when I went to speak to Desailly in 1998, in Casablanca. There was a lead to Chelsea and he said: "Why should I go to England? I'm only 28, I could wait till I'm 32. All you need is the fighting spirit." That was his view of English football, and I'm sure his vision of football has changed now. But he knew he could play anywhere, because he's a wonderful footballer. I don't think the French footballers of now would be as dismissive as Desailly, because English football has helped make them the players that they are as well, it's a mutually beneficial thing. English football is better, thanks to the French players who came here, and it's got to be good for everybody.'

Daniel Ortelli
(with Xavier Rivoire)

CHAPTER 15

Extra Time: Is England the New France?

After ten years of French Revolution in English football, World Cup 2002 was a stepping stone in the construction of the new England team, on the same sort of foundations as France ten years ago. There are numerous parallels between the evolution of both teams, and the way England stalled in the quarter-final, hitting the Brazilian monument at full speed, with no gas left in the tank, is comparable to the way France hit the Czech wall in a semi-final of Euro '96, with no strikers to go round the wall. In both cases, everything was very promising, until there was something missing at the crucial moment. It was to come later.

Looking forward to Euro 2004 and Germany 2006, England supporters have all the good reasons to be cheerful: they already have a great manager on the bench, Sven Goran Eriksson; a star leader on the pitch, David Beckham; and a great team spirit forged by the difficulties of the last two years before World Cup 2002, from the qualifying inferno to the cascade of injuries. Of course, they also have the support of a whole nation, and there will be many more fans in Portugal and Germany than the 30,000 cheerful and exemplary ones who made it to Japan, and back, with smiles on their faces.

'The football was the cherry on the cake, because the country and the people were absolutely brilliant,' I heard an English fan say, on his mobile phone, as he was leaving Tokyo Narita Airport on the day after the amazing win over Denmark (3–0) in the second round of the World Cup. He knew that there was more to come, later, so he enjoyed the trip to the full, and opened his eyes wide, until the end. Just like thousands of others, he had probably spent the whole Saturday night singing in Niigata Stadium, during and after the game. This second half was extraordinary to watch, not the English players on the pitch, but the English fans laughing their heads off in the stands, because England were so dominant against Denmark, the defeaters of the French world champions a few days before. There was a spot in the quarter-finals of the World Cup at stake, against Brazil, but there was no pressure. Captain Becks could not run any more, but he was in full control of 'Mission Asia'.

Beckham, just like Zinédine Zidane, is one of the top five players in the world and his influence on his team is immense, not only for his goals but for the rest of his game: assists, crosses, free-kicks, penalties. He contributes a lot to the team effort, especially in defence, and he is also the skipper, whereas Zidane has always concentrated on his game, leaving the general team responsibilities to Didier Deschamps and Laurent Blanc, and then to Desailly. Just like Zidane, Beckham's mix of energy and calm irradiates his teammates. It is also part of the legacy of Eric Cantona, because that's how King Eric gave confidence to his younger teammates, by staying as calm as possible. It was obvious at this World Cup, especially when England were working or relaxing at their base camp in Tsuna. They were like the fans, enjoying the moment, recording everything they could from that experience abroad, not for their family, but for their own future.

Second common feature: Sven Goran Eriksson is just as good as Aimé Jacquet was, at installing some strong belief in a group of very different players, of all ages and clubs, and sorting them out from Day 1 to create some balance in the team. The system may evolve, if necessary, but if it works well, he tries to stick to it, and he just changes the players sometimes, to get them used to the system. 'Eriksson is the nearest thing the FA could find to Arsène Wenger,' journalist Martin Lipton stresses, 'but they would have liked Wenger.'

Lipton is able to elaborate on the reason why Wenger's success in 1998, one of the landmarks of the French Revolution, 'helped English football to realise that it had to change, just like France in 1994'. England saved time in its building process, thanks to Monsieur Wenger: 'With all of his thinking, Wenger won the Double in sensational style, playing great football, with a team which had English characteristics but also a lot of French quality, as well as Marc Overmars. And the FA realised this was the way it had to be done. There were talks with Gérard Houllier before [when Houllier was still the national technical director of French football], about setting up a structure. The two models they took from early on were the French and the Dutch, and they tried to fuse the two. And it was also easier to sell the idea to the wider public, to say: look, this is why we are doing it.'

Wenger and Houllier know that success in modern football starts at the back. This is the third common feature. The strength of France '98 started at the back with a steady and reliable defence, around Blanc and Desailly. It was almost the same for England 2002, until the double contribution by Ronaldinho, who provided Rivaldo and then scored by stunning Seaman. Before that, in over six hours of open play, classy Ferdinand and powerful Campbell had only let one goal in, against serious customers such as Sweden, Argentina, Nigeria and Denmark. With Rio Ferdinand and Ashley Cole, two leaders of the new generation, Danny Mills and Sol Campbell, two no-nonsense defenders, England had a very decent back four in Japan, and there is more cover coming.

Houllier has often repeated recently that England has one of the best crops of young players between 18 and 24 in the world. It is because the new academy system is helping England to catch up with France fast. According to Professor John Williams, it is due to 'the new ways of preparing players here, the decline of the old forms of masculinity and bonding which were the features of the English game, the emergence of the skill bases that the academies are teaching'. At the same time as England is producing more talented midfielders, such as Joe Cole, and strikers, such as Darius Vassell, French football academies are being flooded with skilful African youngsters. The difference with the individuals who made up France '98 is that, once they are well trained, most of the young pros will wear the colours of Senegal, Cameroon or Nigeria. No wonder England did not try to win their game against Nigeria in the first round of the World Cup: they wanted to avoid Senegal in the next round; they probably felt they were not ready for that experience yet. It may have been a mistake, but it was part of the learning process.

Times are changing, and English football is better equipped for the change, in the years to come: more money in the game, and already more players to pick from, just like France in the 1980s and 1990s, when all the public money invested in the 1970s started to bear fruit. In the 1970s, training centres had been created in every French professional club, it was compulsory. Young people could learn football skills, but they also had to go to school, pass the *baccalauréat*. Other clubs at lower levels organised strategies to find players, a big network of people looked at the new talent. Eventually, France won, three times in a row, thanks to a lot of work and a bit of luck. Then, France was satisfied with the achievement and went back to rest.

Journalist Richard Williams reflects one last time on the past World Cup: 'The French thought that the way they played was good enough, with the same individuals, and there was a tactical complacency. England certainly does not have that at the moment: the English players want to learn, the English coaches want to learn, and they all want to know how to be better. France's influence has been very important, but it's not particularly tactical, it's more in physical and mental preparation, how to conduct yourself, the attitude you bring on to the pitch, and speed as well. We've learnt a little about speed by watching Henry and Pires.'

It is this desire to learn which separates most of the Fabulous Beckham Boys from some of the Desailly Men in Blue. In Japan, any reporter could feel that England were in the middle of a learning process, and that most players were eager to learn the maximum amount of things in the minimum amount of time, trying to benefit from any minute on the pitch, on such a big occasion, but also on the training ground or in the press conference room. At the same time, in Korea, the French internationals were bored to death, hanging around in the corridors of the Sheraton, having drinks with captive journalists, accumulating clichés in their interviews. They knew it all already, so they lost interest, and so did everybody around them.

Players like Henry and Pires are of the first 'Cantona generation', the generation of French players who moved to England in order to improve their skills, their physical commitment, their versatility, following the example of King Eric. This allowed France to win three competitions in a row; it was the French legacy of Cantona, to a country which literally kicked him out. But this may well be history now, as 'Cantona generation II' is coming. It is a generation of players born in England, who watched the same games on TV as the French aspiring pros, except that it was on Sky Sport instead of Canal Plus. They have the same culture of the game, the only difference is that it took more time for them to mature.

To cut a long story short, the young French pros, the 'Cantona I' class, had trouble improving in France, because it is not a football country. However, the set-up was good, thanks to political will and public money, so they were well trained. They added the finishing touch when they moved abroad, just like Cantona, and forgot about the comfort of their early years. It was tougher, there was competition from older players, especially in Italy, but it was the experience they needed in order to face the challenges of the future. Eventually, some came to England, and were taken care of by Arsène Wenger at Arsenal. In the meantime, the 'Cantona II' class, the young English pros, stayed at home, for obvious reasons (money and language for example), but had to fight as well, against foreigners flooding the English leagues. The progress of some of them was monitored by Gérard Houllier at Liverpool. They had no other solution than to improve, so they started practising more and more, just like Cantona, to become better footballers. Now they are ready.

France were ahead, and now England are ahead, because the squad is younger and playing in a World Cup is a very important experience for a player, so it will benefit the whole England team in 2004 and 2006. France is also at risk, if half a generation gets lost, just because Roger Lemerre refused to take players like Olivier Dacourt, Laurent Robert and Eric Carrière to Asia, where they should have been. And if the next coach, Jacques Santini, skips directly to the Under-21s of 2002, in order to build for the future, it is even better for England, because playing catch-up is not easy in modern football. So yes, England may well be the New France. And if some time in the next few years, at Euro 2004 or World Cup 2006, an England v. France game is scheduled, I know that Arsène and Gérard will be in the stadium, because they always get the good seats, close to the pitch. And someone who played football with his collar up will be in front of his TV, somewhere in Marseille or in the Alps: King Eric himself. The three of them are supposed to be French, but they will all be cheering for England. Now you know why.

Daniel Ortelli

All Statistics provided by
(and Reproduced from) the Opta Index

All data compiled by Justin Villelongue and Pierre Hiault

CHAPTER 16

Silverware and Statistics

1. ENGLISH TROPHIES WITH A FRENCH ATTITUDE (1992-2002)

YEAR	PREMIER LEAGUE	FA CUP	LEAGUE CUP	CHARITY SHIELD
1992	Leeds United			Leeds Utd
1993	Manchester United			Manchester Utd
1994	Manchester United (Double)			
1995		(Cantona was suspended for 8 months)		
1996	Manchester United (Double)			
1997	Manchester United	Chelsea		
1998	Arsenal (Double)		Chelsea	Arsenal
1999			Tottenham	Arsenal
2000	Manchester United	Chelsea	Leicester	Chelsea
2001	Manchester United	Liverpool	Liverpool	Liverpool
2002	Arsenal (Double)			Arsenal
2003		To be continued . . .		

The cast of French actors (in order of appearance):
Leeds Utd '92: Cantona
Manchester Utd '93 to '97: Cantona
Chelsea '97 and '98: Leboeuf
Arsenal '98: Wenger (manager), Anelka, Garde, Grimandi, Petit, Vieira
Tottenham '99: Ginola
Arsenal '99: Wenger, Anelka, Grimandi, Petit, Vieira
Manchester Utd '00: Silvestre

Chelsea '00: Leboeuf, Deschamps, Desailly, Lambourde
Leicester '00: Arphexad
Manchester Utd '01: Silvestre, Barthez
Liverpool '01: Houllier (manager), Arphexad, Diomède, Traoré, Vignal
Arsenal '02: Wenger, Aliadière, Grimandi, Henry, Pires, Vieira, Wiltord

The trophy cabinet of the French directors:
Arsène Wenger (Arsenal):
Home: 2 Doubles (2 Premierships and 2 FA Cups), 3 Charity Shields
Away: none

Gérard Houllier (Liverpool):
Home: 1 FA Cup, 1 League Cup, 1 Charity Shield
Away: 1 UEFA Cup, 1 European Super Cup (2001)

The silverware addicts
1. Eric Cantona: (7 major trophies), 5 League titles, 2 FA Cups (2 Doubles)
2. Frank Leboeuf: (4 major trophies), 1 European Cup-Winners' Cup, 2 FA Cups, 1 League Cup
3. Patrick Vieira and Gilles Grimandi: (4 major trophies), 2 Doubles (League title and FA Cup)

THE TOP 7 FRENCH SCORERS:
1. Eric Cantona: 102 goals in 226 games
2. Thierry Henry: 80 goals in 149 games
3. David Ginola: 34 goals in 251 games
4. Nicolas Anelka: 33 goals in 113 games
5. Sylvain Wiltord: 32 goals in 101 games
6. Frédéric Kanouté: 28 goals in 75 games
7. Frank Leboeuf: 24 goals in 203 games

2. MANAGERIAL PERFORMANCE

A. The 'Carré d'As' (Premier League record since 12 November '98 when Houllier took sole charge at Liverpool)

B. Some of the others, as a matter of comparison (Total Premier League record since taking charge of respective club)

	GAMES	WIN%	AVG. GOALS CONCEDED PER GAME	AVG. GOALS SCORED PER GAME	POINTS PER GAME
A. Ferguson	141	65%	1.1	2.3	2.2
Wenger	140	60%	0.9	1.9	2.0
Houllier	140	53%	1.0	1.7	1.8
O'Leary	140	54%	1.1	1.6	1.8
B. Ranieri (Chelsea)	70	47%	1.1	1.8	1.7
Robson (Newcastle)	108	45%	1.3	1.6	1.6
Gregory (Aston Villa)	148	41%	1.1	1.3	1.5
Hoddle (Tottenham)	82	37%	1.4	1.3	1.3
Reid (Sunderland)	152	34%	1.3	1.1	1.3
Souness (Blackburn)	38	32%	1.3	1.4	1.2
Tigana (Fulham)	38	26%	1.2	0.9	1

Three French Managers

LEAGUE GAMES ONLY

	PLAYED	WON	LOST	DRAWN	DRAWN %	WIN %
'Wenger	220	127	37	56	25%	58%
Houllier	140	74	34	32	23%	53%
Tigana Premiership	38	10	14	14	37%	26%
Tigana Division One	46	30	5	11	24%	65%

Arsenal and Liverpool in the League

	PLAYED	WON	LOST	DRAWN	DRAWN %	WIN %
Wenger	220	127	37	56	25%	58%
Houllier	140	74	34	32	23%	53%

Arsenal and Liverpool in Europe

	PLAYED	WON	LOST	DRAWN	DRAWN %	WIN %
Wenger	49	21	17	11*	22%	43%
Houllier	36	15**	5	16	44%	42%

*Includes UEFA Cup final that ended in a draw with Arsenal eventually losing the game on penalties

**Includes UEFA Cup final that was won in extra time. Also includes Super Cup play off game against Bayern Munich.

Liverpool under Houllier and other managers

	PLAYED	WON	LOST	DRAWN	WIN%
Houllier	207	111	47	49	54%
Evans	244	123	58	63	50%
Souness	157	65	45	47	41%

Arsenal under Wenger and other managers

	PLAYED	WON	LOST	DRAWN	WIN%
Wenger	332	184	63	85	55%
Rioch	47	22	10	15	46%
Graham	460	225	102	133	49%

LIVERPOOL

SEASON	MANAGER	FINAL LEAGUE POSITION
2001–02	Gérard Houllier	2
2000–01	Gérard Houllier	3
1999–00	Gérard Houllier	4
1998–99	Gérard Houllier/Roy Evans	7
1997–98	Roy Evans	3
1996–97	Roy Evans	4
1995–96	Roy Evans	3
1994–95	Roy Evans	4
1993–94	Graeme Souness/Roy Evans	8
1992–93	Graeme Souness	6
1991–92	Graeme Souness	6

ARSENAL

SEASON	MANAGER	FINAL LEAGUE POSITION
2001–02	Arsène Wenger	1
2000–01	Arsène Wenger	2
1999–00	Arsène Wenger	2
1998–99	Arsène Wenger	2
1997–98	Arsène Wenger	1
1996–97	Stewart Houston/Arsène Wenger	3
1995–96	Bruce Rioch	5
1994–95	George Graham	12
1993–94	George Graham	4
1992–93	George Graham	10
1991–92	George Graham	4

3. ALL THE FRENCHIES IN ENGLAND (1991-92 TO 2001-02)

All the French players who played in at least one top English league game, from 1991–92 (Division One) to 2001–02:

A-LIST: The Crème de la Crème (Top 30)

A selection of the Top 30 French players over 10 years, according to the number of games played and the number of goals scored in the League and all cups: Champions League, Cup-Winners' Cup, UEFA Cup, FA Cup, League Cup (capped players appear in capitals).

	GAMES	GOALS
1. Patrick VIEIRA (Arsenal '96–'02)	277	20
2. David GINOLA (Newcastle '95–'97, Tottenham '97–'00, Aston Villa '00–'02, Everton '02)	251	34
3. Eric CANTONA (Leeds '92, Manchester United '92–'97)	226	102
4. Franck LEBOEUF (Chelsea '96–'01)	203	24
5. Gilles Grimandi (Arsenal '97–'02)	171	8
6. Marcel DESAILLY (Chelsea '98–'02)	164	5
7. Emmanuel PETIT (Arsenal '97–'00, Chelsea '01–'02)	157	12
8. Thierry HENRY (Arsenal '99–'02)	149	80
9. Mikaël SILVESTRE (Manchester United '99–'02)	126	2
10. Nicolas ANELKA (Arsenal '96–'99, Liverpool '01–'02)	113	33
11. Olivier DACOURT (Everton '98–'99, Leeds '00–'02)	109	6
12. Sylvain WILTORD (Arsenal '00–'02)	101	32
13. Robert PIRES (Arsenal '00–'02)	96	21
14. Fabien BARTHEZ (Manchester United '00–'02)	93	—
15. Laurent Charvet (Chelsea '97–'98, Newcastle '98–'00, Manchester City '00–'01)	93	3
16. Alain GOMA (Newcastle '99–'01, Fulham '01–'02)	85	1
17. Frédéric Kanouté (West Ham '00–'02)	75	28
18. Didier Domi (Newcastle '99–'01)	70	4
19. Louis Saha (Newcastle '98–'99, Fulham '01–'02)	61	16
20. Marc KELLER (West Ham '98–'01)	57	6
21. Sébastien Schemmel (West Ham '00–'02)	54	1
22. Didier DESCHAMPS (Chelsea '99–'00)	47	—
23. Steed Malbranque (Fulham '01–'02)	46	10
24. Laurent BLANC (Manchester United '01–'02)	46	3
25. Rémi GARDE (Arsenal '96–'99)	45	—
26. Laurent ROBERT (Newcastle '01–'02)	42	10
27. William Gallas (Chelsea '01–'02)	41	2
28. Christian KAREMBEU (Middlesbrough '00–'01)	36	4
29. Steve MARLET (Fulham '01–'02)	32	9
30. Youri DJORKAEFF (Bolton Wanderers '01–'02)	12	4

B-Side: Best of the Rest

All the other players who played ten games or more in the Premiership (capped players appear in capitals)

	GAMES
Bernard Lambourde (Chelsea '97–'01)	40
Sylvain Legwinski (Fulham '01–'02)	33
Thierry Bonalair (Nottingham Forest '97–'98)	31
Lionel Perez (Sunderland '96–'97)	29
Franck Queudrue (Middlesbrough '01–'02)	28
Sylvain Distin (Newcastle '01–'02)	28
Eric Roy (Sunderland '99–'01)	27
Bruno NGOTTY (Bolton '01–'02)	26
Patrick Colleter (Southampton '98–'00)	24
Youl Mawéné (Derby County '00–'02)	24
Kaba Diawara (Arsenal '98–'99, West Ham '00–'01)	23
Mickael MADAR (Everton '98–'99)	19
Pierre Ducrocq (Derby County '01–'02)	19
Frank Rolling (Leicester '95–'97)	18
Pegguy Arphexad (Leicester '98–'00, Liverpool '00–'02)	17
Olivier Bernard (Newcastle '00–'02)	16
Jean-Claude Darcheville (Nottingham Forest '98–'99)	16
Louis-Jean Matthieu (Nottingham Forest '98–'99)	16
François Grenet (Derby County '01–'02)	15
Patrick Valéry (Blackburn Rovers '97–'98)	15
Valérien Ismaël (Crystal Palace '97–'98)	13
Lilian LASLANDES (Sunderland '01–'02)	12
Bernard LAMA (West Ham '97–'98)	12
Alexandre Bonnot (Watford '99–'00)	12
Fabrice Fernandes (Southampton '01–'02)	11
Grégory Vignal (Liverpool '00–'02)	10

C Minor: the under-achievers (who played less than ten Premiership games):

9 games   David Bellion (Sunderland '01–'02), Djibril Diawara (Bolton '01–'02), Lilian Martin (Derby County '00–'01)

8   Patrice Carteron (Sunderland '00–'01), Djimi Traoré (Liverpool '99–'01)

7   Xavier GRAVELAINE (Watford '99–'00), Laurent Courtois (West Ham '01–'02)

6   Patrick BLONDEAU (Sheffield Wednesday '97–'98), Franck Dumas (Newcastle '99–'00), Jean-Guy Wallemme (Coventry '98–'99)

5   Sébastien Perez (Blackburn Rovers '98–'99)

4   Stéphane GUIVARC'H (Newcastle '98–'99), Mickael Debève (Middlesbrough '01–'02), Pierre Laurent (Leeds '96–'98)

3   Mario Espartero (Bolton '01–'02), Christian Bassila (West Ham '00–'01), Samassi Abou (West Ham '98–'99)

2   Bruno Rodriguez (Bradford '99–'00), Bernard Allou (Nottingham Forest '98–'99), Bernard DIOMÈDE (Liverpool '00–'02), Jean-Michel FERRI (Liverpool '98–'99), William PRUNIER (Manchester United '95–'96)

1   David Grondin (Arsenal '99–'00), David Terrier (West Ham '97–'98), Ulrich Le Pen (Ipswich '01–'02), Jérémie Aliadière (Arsenal '01–'02)

Grand total: 82 French players at 26 English clubs

The hit-parade of the 26 francophile clubs

1. Arsenal and Newcastle: 11 Frenchies in 11 seasons
3. West Ham: 9
4. Chelsea: 7
5. Liverpool: 6
6. Manchester United, Fulham, Sunderland: 5
9. Nottingham Forest, Derby County, Bolton: 4
12. Middlesbrough, Leeds, Everton: 3
15. Southampton, Blackburn, Leicester, Watford: 2
19. Ipswich, Bradford, Coventry, Sheffield Wednesday, Crystal Palace, Manchester City, Tottenham, Aston Villa: 1

4. PLAYERS' PERFORMANCE

A. Thierry Henry the Best Striker in the Premiership

GOALS SCORED 2001–02

Rank	Player	Club	Goals
1	**Thierry Henry**	Arsenal	24
=2	Jimmy Floyd Hasselbaink	Chelsea	23
=2	Ruud van Nistelrooy	Man Utd	23
=2	Alan Shearer	Newcastle	23
5	Michael Owen	Liverpool	19

SHOTS ON TARGET 2001–02

Rank	Player	Club	Shots on Target
1	**Thierry Henry**	Arsenal	68
2	Kevin Phillips	Sunderland	66
3	Jimmy Floyd Hasselbaink	Chelsea	62
4	Ruud van Nistelrooy	Man Utd	45
5	Alan Shearer	Newcastle	44

HOW ARSÈNE WENGER HAS IMPROVED THIERRY HENRY

	1999–2000 Season		2000–01 Season		2001–02 Season	
	1st Half	2nd Half	1st Half	2nd Half	1st Half	2nd Half
Chance Conversion	11%	23%	14%	14%	20%	15%
Shooting Accuracy	47%	61%	51%	51%	58%	41%
Shots	36	56	74	49	80	54
Goals	4	13	10	7	16	8
Assists	1	7	3	6	2	3
Dribbles per Game	5.9	6.1	6.2	7.5	7.2	8.2
Fouls Won	11	21	26	13	23	14

B. Sylvain Wiltord's Impact in the Premiership (2001-02)

Player	Minutes on Pitch	Goals	Average Minutes Per Goal
Thierry Henry	2775	24	116
Sylvain Wiltord	2043	10	204
Dennis Bergkamp	1954	9	217
Nwankwo Kanu	923	3	308

Player	Goals	Shots on Target	Shots Attempted	Chance Conversion	Shooting Accuracy
Sylvain Wiltord	10	32	51	20%	63%
Dennis Bergkamp	9	32	61	15%	52%
Thierry Henry	24	68	134	18%	51%
Nwankwo Kanu	3	8	31	10%	26%

	2000–01	2001–02
Appearances	20 (7)	23 (10)
Chance Conversion	15%	20%
Shooting Accuracy	57%	63%
Shots	53	51
Goals	8	10
Assists	5	7
Dribbles per Game	6.5	5.3
Fouls Won	25	34

C. Robert Pires, Player of the Year 2001-02

ROBERT PIRES'S IMPROVEMENT

	2000–01 SEASON		2001–02 SEASON	
	1st Half	2nd Half	1st Half	2nd Half
Goals	1	3	5	4
Assists	2	5	10	5
Passing Accuracy %	78%	81%	85%	79%
Dribbles and Runs	84	140	169	83
Crosses	74	135	119	26
Crossing Accuracy %	23%	26%	27%	27%

ASSISTS 2001–02 PREMIERSHIP SEASON

RANK	PLAYER	ASSISTS
1	**Robert Pires**	15
=2	Dennis Bergkamp	12
=2	Ryan Giggs	12
4	**Laurent Robert**	11
=5	Nolberto Solano	9
=5	Ole Gunnar Solskjaer	9
=7	Steven Gerrard	8
=7	David Beckham	8

PREMIERSHIP ASSISTS – 1996–2002

RANK	PLAYER	ASSISTS
=1	**Robert Pires 2001–02**	15
=1	David Beckham 1997–98	15
=1	David Beckham 1999–2000	15
=1	Nolberto Solano 1999–2000	15
=5	David Beckham 1998–99	14
=5	**Eric Cantona 1996–97**	14

D. Laurent Robert, the most exciting player in England ?

SHOTS, CROSSES AND DRIBBLES

RANK	MIDFIELDER	CLUB	SHOTS
1	**Laurent Robert**	Newcastle	85
2	Gustavo Poyet	Tottenham	76
3	Paul Scholes	Man Utd	71
4	David Beckham	Man Utd	70
5	David Dunn	Blackburn	57

RANK	PLAYER	CLUB	CROSSES
1	Nolberto Solano	Newcastle	345
2	**Laurent Robert**	Newcastle	340
3	Ian Harte	Leeds	295
4	**Steed Malbranque**	Fulham	280
5	Darren Anderton	Tottenham	277

RANK	PLAYER	CLUB	DRIBBLES & RUNS
1	Damien Duff	Blackburn	287
2	**Laurent Robert**	Newcastle	257
3	**Robert Pires**	Arsenal	252
4	Harry Kewell	Leeds	250
5	Thierry Henry	Arsenal	236

RANK	PLAYER	CLUB	PENALTIES WON
1	**Laurent Robert**	Newcastle	4
=2	Kevin Campbell	Everton	3
=2	Freddie Ljungberg	Arsenal	3
=4	Paul Scholes	Man Utd	2
=4	**Thierry Henry**	Arsenal	2

5. ALL THE FRENCHIES IN SCOTLAND

The 44 players who played for at least one Scottish Premier League club in the past ten years, by total number of games played and showing goals scored in the league (capped players appear in capitals)

A-LIST (the Top 11)

	GAMES	GOALS
Gilles ROUSSET (Hearts '95–'01)	133	–
Stéphane Adam (Hearts '97–'02)	111	28
Stéphane Mahe (Celtic '97–'01, Hearts '01–'02)	111	6
Jérôme Vareille (Kilmarnock '97–'02, Airdrie '02)	103	15
Ludovic Roy (St Mirren '98–'02, St Johnstone '02)	103	–
Frédéric Dindeleux (Kilmarnock '99–'02)	91	4
Didier Agathe (Raith Rovers '99–'00, Hibernian '00)	82	15
Franck SAUZEE (Hibernian '99–'02)	77	13
Antoine Kombouare (Aberdeen '96–'99)	71	6
Christophe COCARD (Kilmarnock '99–'02)	68	13
David Zitelli (Hibernian '00–'02)	51	10

B-SIDE

Bernard Pascual (Dundee United '98–'00)	48	–
Frank Rolling (Ayr United '94–'95)	35	2
Michel Pageaud (Dundee '93–'97)	35	–
Basile BOLI (Rangers '96–'97)	28	–
Jean-Marc Adjovi-Bocco (Hibernian '98–'99)	28	–
Frédéric Arpinon (Hibernian '01–'02)	27	2
Eric Delomeaux (Motherwell '01–'02)	23	–
Bobo Balde (Celtic '01–'02)	22	–
Vincent GUERIN (Hearts '98–'99)	19	1
Stéphane PAILLE (Hearts '96–'97)	18	2
Lionel CHARBONNIER (Rangers '98–'01)	18	–
Stéphane GUIVARC'H (Rangers '98–'99)	13	5
Yann Soloy (Motherwell '01–'02)	12	1
Eric Garcin (Motherwell '97–'98, Dundee '98)	14	1
Marc Libbra (Hibernian '01)	10	5
David Ferrere (Motherwell '02)	10	3
Alex di Rocco (Aberdeen '00–'01)	10	3
Fabien Leclercq (Hearts '99–'00)	10	–
Samassi Abou (Kilmarnock '00)	10	–

C MINOR (LESS THAN 10 GAMES PLAYED IN THE SCOTTISH PREMIERSHIP BETWEEN 1998 AND 2002)

Fabrice Henry, Hakim Sur-Temsoury (Hibernian), John Licina, Stéphane Leoni, Joachim Fernandez, Antoine Preget, Roger Boli, Jean-Pierre Delaunay (Dundee United), Moussa Dagnogo (St Mirren), Fabrice Fernandes (Rangers), François Dubourdeau, Franck Bernhard, Hervé Bacque (Motherwell), Stéphane Pounewatchy (Dundee)

Grand total: 44 players at 14 Scottish clubs

The Top 6 Francophile Scottish clubs (37 players in 6 clubs)

1. Hibernian: 8 players
2. Hearts: 7 players
3. Motherwell and Dundee United: 7 players each (mostly short term)
5. Rangers and Kilmarnock: 4 each

THE TOP 3 FRENCH SCORERS

1. Stéphane Adam, 28 goals in 111 games
2. Didier Agathe, 15 goals in 83 games
3. Jérôme Vareille, 15 goals in 103 games

Sources of Inspiration (Bibliography)

THE 7 BEST BOOKS ON BOTH SIDES OF THE CHANNEL

Into the Red: Liverpool FC and the Changing Face of English Football, by John Williams (Edinburgh, Mainstream Publishing, 2001)

Eric Cantona by Rob Wightman (London, Virgin Books, 2002)

David Ginola, le Magnifique by David Ginola and Neil Silver (London, Collins Willow, 2000)

Kevin Keegan, My Autobiography by Kevin Keegan (London, Warner Books, 1998)

Robert Pires, Profession Footballeur: Conversations with Xavier Rivoire (Paris, Hachette Littératures, 2002) – English version entitled *Footballeur*, to be published in February 2003 by Random House/ Yellow Jersey

L'histoire Secrète des Bleus, 1993–2002, de la Gloire à la Désillusion, by Eric Maitrot and Karim Nedjari (Paris, Flammarion, 2002)

Nicolas Anelka, Une Enigme by Alain Azhar (Paris, Solar, 2002)

SUPER MAGAZINES

FourFourTwo

When Saturday Comes

France Football

L'Equipe Magazine

The Observer Sport Monthly (OSM) – issue number 4 (August 2000) and issue number 21 (January 2002)

GREAT NEWSPAPERS

The Independent on Sunday – October 2000, February 2001, April 2001,
    September 2001, March 2002
The Independent – May 2002
The Times Football Handbook, every month!
The Guardian Season Guide, every year!

BEAUTIFUL WEBSITES (AMONG OTHERS)

www.442rivals.net (*FourFourTwo*)
38-42 Hampton Road, Teddington, Middlesex TW11 0JE
For back issues and subscriptions:
PO Box 280, Sittingbourne, Kent ME9 8FB
Tel: 01795 414811

www.wsc.co.uk (*When Saturday Comes*).
17A Perseverance Works, 38 Kingsland Road, London E2 8DD
For back issues and subscriptions: tel: 020 7729 9461

www.opta.co.uk for the statistics of the Premiership and all the players
www.liverpoolfc.tv, www.manutd.com, www.arsenal.com, the official websites
of the three best clubs in England, and all their fans in the world
www.nufc.com – the website of the Geordie fans
www.william-gallas.com – the website of the Chelsea player
www.noblesauvage.com – Xavier's website, where book readers and sport
viewers meet on a regular basis

INCREDIBLE FANZINES (A SELECTION)

United We Stand
The Gooner
Up the Arse

Actors and Thinkers (Index)